THE HARROWSMITH ILLUSTRATED BOOK OF HERBS

THE HARROWSMITH ILLUSTRATED BOOK OF
HERBS

BY PATRICK LIMA   ILLUSTRATED BY TURID FORSYTH

CAMDEN HOUSE

Designed by
Ian S.R. Grainge

Colour separations by
Herzig Somerville Limited
Toronto, Ontario

Printed and bound in Canada by
D.W. Friesen & Sons Ltd.
Altona, Manitoba

Printed on 70 lb. Friesen Matte

Reprinted 1987
Reprinted 1988

Canadian Cataloguing in Publication Data

Lima, Patrick
  The Harrowsmith illustrated book of
herbs

Includes index.
ISBN 0-920656-45-5
1. Herb gardening.   2. Title.

SB351.H5L55 1986   635'.7   C86-
094426-3

Trade distribution by
Firefly Books
3520 Pharmacy Avenue, Unit 1-C
Scarborough, Ontario
Canada M1W 2T8

Printed in Canada for
Camden House Publishing
7 Queen Victoria Road
Camden East, Ontario
K0K 1J0

Cover concept and production: Ian
Grainge, Treen Incorporated, Sparks and
Associates, Linda J. Menyes.

ACKNOWLEDGEMENTS

The author wishes to acknowledge the contributions to this book of Margot Barnard, Rachel McLeod, Christine Devai, Margaret Dinsdale and Adrian Forsyth. Finally, without the dedicated efforts of my partner, John Scanlan, there would be no Larkwhistle, and without the garden, no book.

CREDITS

For Margaret Adelman, who
germinated the seed-thought for
this work

CONTENTS

INTRODUCTION

In a sense, every gardener is a pioneer; there are always new plots to be cultivated, new plants to grow, new skills to learn. But some gardeners have more than the usual amount of ground to break. Such was Catharine Parr Traill, a 19th-century Canadian pioneer who settled in virgin wilderness, where she discovered, as she wrote in a handbook for English women migrating to North America, that "a good bed of pot-herbs is essential. I would bring out seeds of balm, thyme and sweet basil, for these are rarely met with here—sage, savory, mint and peppermint are easily got. Sweet marjoram is not commonly met with. I would also bring out some nice flower seeds."

Patrick Lima is a pioneer of a later, but no less remarkable, sort. At Larkwhistle, an extraordinary garden near Miller Lake, Ontario, he and photographer John Scanlan enjoy the truly unusual pleasure of living entirely from their plants—selling herbs, giving tours and photographing and describing what they grow. For them, it is all adventure. Almost every new herb—more than 150 kinds have now been gathered there—must survive a winter with temperatures that may dip below minus 20 degrees F. (A few plants known to be tender are treated to a winter indoors.) Gathered in this unlikely spot, these herbs, together with a large collection of perennial flowers, present pictures that bring visitors back to Larkwhistle year after year. "A herb is as a herb does," writes Lima, and one of the immediately obvious things his herbs do is provide a place of varied delights where beauty is as important as utility; indeed, the two functions intertwine when every herb is in its place.

Like Lima, Turid Forsyth uses herbs daily in the kitchen and is as familiar with their growth and culture as many people are with their friends. Turid is a talented gardener, but with a difference. Many of the plants in her garden are artistic subjects; she is a botanical illustrator with credits in European and American books, magazines and art galleries. She prefers to paint her models in situ and will often work outdoors all day capturing the graceful curve of a poppy petal, the fleeting visit of a hummingbird or wandering bee.

As the chapters of this book arrived, we knew it was something special; not only was it comprehensive, but it was also a really useful book, with everything having been tried, then carefully reported. (Patrick was somewhat dismayed by the supposedly reputable books that parroted old information, some of it inaccurate. "There just isn't a really good herb book written by a gardener for gardeners," he said.) Turid's paintings decorate Patrick's text in the manner of the woodcuts of the antiquarian herbals, but in colourful 20th-century style.

What we have, finally, is a book for today's garden pioneers, those with a spirit of adventure but with their feet planted firmly on northern soil. Now, these gardeners can expand the herb plot beyond parsley and sage and, even at the edge of the wilderness, experiment with plants grown as much for appearance as usefulness. These new pioneers will find, as Catharine Parr Traill did more than a century ago, that "a good garden" will "beautify the home wonderfully and kindle emotions which never die out of the heart."

—Jennifer Bennett

At Larkwhistle, RIGHT, *old-fashioned roses share space with more than 150 kinds of herbs, including tarragon,* LEFT, *drawn in the garden of artist Turid Forsyth.*

CHAPTER ONE

HERBAL BEGINNINGS

Selecting and situating garden herbs

Most visitors finish a tour of Larkwhistle, the Ontario garden I share with John Scanlan, with a hand or pocket full of aromatic leaves, scented souvenirs of an excursion into some special horticultural territory. Many of these visitors have been surprised to discover, growing among the flowers and vegetables, plants that seem to have a root in both camps, that are as decorative as any ornamental flower and as useful as any edible vegetable. These are herbs, plants that seem to invite one to smell, touch, pinch and taste. Often, they comprise the leafy bounty the visitors have gathered.

But defining more clearly what I mean by the word herb is difficult. I can quote a dry three-liner from the dictionary: "Plant of which the stem is not woody or persistent and which dies down to the the ground after flowering; plant of which leaves, etc., are used for food, medicine, scent, flavour, etc.," says the *Concise Oxford*. Or I can conduct a tour of the garden. Among the

A herb is as a herb does. Included in the definition of the word herb are such vastly different plants as the lacy valerian, RIGHT, *a decorative old-fashioned medicinal, and basil,* LEFT, *a culinary herb in good standing.*

Lovage, LEFT, *a valued ingredient in vegetable soups, is a 5-foot perennial suited to the back of a garden bed, while* Iris florentina, BELOW, *whose root is used in potpourris, partners well with tulips, which bloom concurrently and achieve the same height.*

rainbow-hued irises, blue delphiniums and scarlet poppies of the flower border and tucked among the cabbages and green beans in the vegetable plot are plants of a different character. More than simply ornamentals or edibles – although what I consider a herb may indeed be another's flower or vegetable or even weed – the herbs as a group vary considerably from one another in scent, shape, taste, texture and the colour of their foliage and flowers. Some are simply green, some splashed with gold and others quietly silver; some are boldly colourful, many more have small flowers, white, lavender or a curious yellow-green, and a few are flowerless. The finest and the tallest plants I know are herbs. Such plants do not fit neatly into distinct categories. But because my aim is to encourage gardeners to consider herbs for both household use and garden decoration, my definition will be as broadly inclusive as possible. Although not as terse as the dictionary's, it will nonetheless be true to life. And so, into the garden.

Tumbling over a warm stone that edges a flowerbed at Larkwhistle is a low, wiry bush with small, deep green leaves and a sprinkling of pale lilac flowers. It is hardly noticeable at first, but pick a sprig, crush it and inhale. The scent is warm and sweet, a mingling of spice and fruit – lemons. In the bed behind, pressed against a top-heavy peony, is a sturdy plant with pebbled, heart-shaped foliage. A whiff reveals another hint of citrus, milder than the first, a gentle scent – lemon tea, perhaps. Yet a third leafy lemon grows in a pot by the garden gate; its narrow, pale green leaves smell the most citrus-sweet of all, like a lemon drop.

Down the path is an impressive plant, looking like a cross between a giant fern and Queen Anne's lace. Its leaves, too, are sweet; its green seeds taste of licorice, suggesting they might be good baked into cookies or a carrot cake. At the end of the raspberry bed is another green giant resembling

6-foot celery. Its leaves smell and taste of celery as well, but the flavour is deeper and more complex, perfect for soup.

We have just begun to pick and nibble and crush and sniff our way around the garden, but already we have been given a hint of what may be hidden in a leaf – and the start of a personal definition of the word herb. The scents and flavours of those I have just described – lemon thyme, lemon balm, lemon verbena, sweet cicely and lovage – seem suited to culinary uses, perhaps in a special salad or main dish, a pot of soup, a cup of fragrant tea or a dessert. Having taken these few steps into the garden, we can say that a herb is any plant whose constituent parts are used for flavouring.

GOOD SCENTS

The seasoning, or culinary, herbs are the most familiar and therefore usually the first that gardeners investigate, often soon after they begin to grow vegetables. Homegrown beans are just that much better with a sprinkling of summer savory; tomatoes and basil seem made for each other, as do potatoes and chives, cucumbers and dill, vegetable soup and lovage, green salads and tarragon.

But the world of herbs is wide, and our garden tour has just begun. A turn of the path reveals a fragrant corner where an arching shrub heavy with pink flowers hangs over a blur of purple blooms – familiar lavender thriving next to old-fashioned roses, garden favourites from the past, scented as roses should be – potpourri on the bush. Just to breathe here is delicious. And remedial too, say the old herbals: "Sweet perfumes," wrote Ralph Austen in his 1653 *A Treatise of Fruit Trees*, "work immediately upon the spirit for their refreshing; sweet and healthfull ayres are special preservatives to health and therefore much to be prised." So the definition of a

herb widens to include any plant appreciated primarily for its scent, a plant whose aromatic leaves or perfumed petals figure in any of those articles made "for use or for delight" – sachets, potpourris, pomanders, fragrant bath mixtures and scent oils.

Farther along the flower border, the definition expands again. Among the irises are two silver-leaved plants. The finely cut foliage of one is almost white with downy hairs, and it has a strange smell – strong, acrid, bitter. The elegant blue-green leaves of the other seem to shine with metallic lights, but its scent is no more appealing. Nearby is a knee-high shrub with narrow dark leaves and small ink-blue flowers. Crush a leaf and catch a hint of mint, an underscent of pine, almost turpentine. And is that a whiff of fox or skunk? Not for cooking and certainly not for fragrance are these last three – wormwood, rue and hyssop. And yet all are considered garden herbs because they have been valued as medicines. Thomas Tusser, teacher, musician, poet and farmer, rhymed in his *July's Husbandry* of 1577, "What saver be better, if physick be true, For places infected than wormwood and rue." And one Old Testament prophet requested, "Purge me with hyssop." But not even a spoonful of sugar would tempt a recent garden writer to take her herbal medicine. "How terrible," she said, "must have been that cough syrup, once much in vogue, of rue and hyssop boiled in honey."

All these so-called virtuous plants once employed, or currently in use, as medicines must also be included as herbs. Woods, mountainsides, meadows and one's own backyard teem with plants reputed, and in many cases proved, to be remedial. Although some simple medicinal applications are included in the discussion of individual herbs, the healing herbs, per se, are not the focus of this book. But for centuries, certain medicinals have been grown by keen and curious gardeners simply because they are elegant plants, as decorative as any ornamentals.

For example, a gardener need know nothing about herbal medicine to appreciate the beauty of foxgloves' spires hung with freckled pink bells, or the showy, orange-centred daisies of the purple coneflower. But if one is aware that foxgloves are the botanical source of digitalis, a powerful heart stimulant, and that the roots of coneflowers (or *Echinacea*) yield echinacin, an antibiotic, one is apt to see these ornamentals in a new light and identify them as herbs in good standing. Even if a herb is in the garden primarily for its appearance, some gardeners may be drawn (after a bit of study) to try their hand at a simple calendula ointment, a hyssop poultice for wounds or bites, a pot of stomach-soothing bergamot tea or a rosemary hair rinse.

A herb is as a herb does – utility is of the essence. A neighbour and gardening friend of mine is as involved with herbs as anyone I know. Each year, she brews a batch of rose-hip sherry, blends the leaves and flowers of 20 garden-grown and wild herbs into a one-of-a-kind tea (see page 104) and braids her harvest of lavender with ribbon; that is, when she is not developing quilter's thumb from pushing sharp-edged cloves into oranges for drawer-freshening pomanders, or twisting stems of artemisia, thyme and oregano with yellow yarrow and crackling bronze strawflowers into pretty wreaths a cook can snip for winter seasoning.

FAMILY TIES

Having defined what, in general, makes a herb a herb, one must still recognize individual characteristics. If a particular herb is going to grow in my garden, I want to know not only its uses but a few other things as well: its names, for one (or rather two, since both the Latin and common names are useful), and its plant family connections for another – "who its people are," as a neighbour says.

"What's this?" I always ask if I spy an unfamiliar plant in another garden.

"I haven't a clue," is often the response. "A neighbour brought over a slip, and I just put it there because there was a bit of room."

This is the "random collection" (not to say "hodgepodge") approach to garden design, the whatever-comes-along-goes-where-there's-space sort of garden. Tall things hide short, shade plants shrivel in the noonday sun, sun-lovers pine in shadows, and goutweed, which came as a "pretty green and white thing – they say it's a herb," has a stranglehold on whatever space is left. Besides being unsatisfying as a garden picture, an unplanned garden (for all the appealing casualness of the approach) can ultimately be a lot of extra work, frustrating and finally a bore to tend. A bits-and-pieces, here-and-there plot is never as engaging, for either the gardener or its visitors, as a thought-out, focused garden. To paraphrase one writer, "The collector's impulse must be subordinated to the eye of the artist."

While I confess to bouts of collector's fever, I have learned to set aside a little catchall corner of a vegetable garden bed where unfamiliar (but labelled) plants show their stuff for a season. Over the summer, I take note of height, colour, form, foliage and fussiness and watch for signs of weediness or greed. In the meantime, I try to get the "lowdown" on that plant from other gardeners or books. By fall, I have a fair idea where the newcomer belongs in the scheme of things – if anywhere. This trial season and preliminary research means I am not forever moving plants from place to place and can catch any invasive sorts before they get a foothold in the beds.

Knowing a plant's origin is also useful, whether from mountains or lowlands, northern plains or the mild Mediterranean. More specifically, I want to know its local habitat – sun or shade, dry soil or stream-side – so that I can situate it properly in the garden. I want to know its habits too –

will it be tall or short, a stay-at-home or a wanderer, hold itself upright or need a prop if it is not to flop on neighbours? When flowers appear, how long will they endure, and what colour will they be?

Most important, I want to know whether a plant is hardy or tender, an annual, biennial or perennial, so I know where it will go in the garden, what after-care will be required and whether I will have to start over with it each spring. Hardiness and tenderness refer to a plant's ability to withstand degrees of cold ranging from light frosts to a hard freeze to a full-blown five-month northern winter. Those that shrivel at a breath of frost are, understandably, termed tender. Tender annuals such as basil or summer savory are grown only during the frost-free months. Like some people I know, tender perennials –

rosemary, ginger, lemon verbena, pineapple sage, scented geraniums and bay are the most familiar – may spend the summer outside but winter indoors. These perennials are perfect for large (but portable) pots that can be shifted indoors or out as the seasons turn.

I find gardening much easier if I concentrate on plants suited to my climate and site. While I would not be without a few tender culinary herbs, I most appreciate plants that can get through the winter on their own, without elaborate and time-consuming protection. Accordingly, most of the herbs grown at Larkwhistle, and discussed in the chapters to come, are hardy, and most are perennials.

Hardy perennials stay in place for a number of years, the self-same plants growing each spring to repeat the pattern of leafing

Larkwhistle grows a wide variety of hardy perennials outdoors year-round, LEFT, *while tender perennials such as fruit sage, tended by the author,* ABOVE, *do best in portable pots.*

their own stay in a garden by sowing their hardy seeds and reappearing with the robins. At Larkwhistle, self-sowers include some of the best culinary herbs—dill, chervil, coriander, chamomile and caraway (actually a biennial). A handful of colourful herbs also annually volunteers to decorate corners of the vegetable garden: borage, calendula, red-top or painted sage and the pretty blue annual woodruff. Some perennials also self-sow, creating either pleasant surprises for a gardener—more mats of creeping thyme between the paving stones, more foxgloves among the roses—or extra work, weeding out the forest of lovage seedlings or well anchored young lemon balms.

If I know my plants, I can situate perennials so that they need not be disturbed and can give them (within the limitations of my site) the soil and sun they prefer. For annual herbs, I can leave spaces among the permanent fixtures to be refilled each spring or grow the likes of basil, dill and summer savory with the vegetables or in containers. Perennials, be they woody or herbaceous, practical or ornamental, are often grouped together in hardy borders around the perimeter of a yard or in island beds set in a stretch of lawn.

Concentrating the effect of foliage and flowers in one area creates a livelier garden picture than a spotty planting. Grouped perennials are also more convenient to work. If I am trimming back their winter-killed stalks, laying down a fall mulch, applying a spring top-dressing or doing the hand weeding and cultivating that perennials need, and I have them all together, I can complete the work more quickly. And if perennials are grouped, I can take note of their height, habit, colour and bloom-time in relation to one another and then indulge in the more creative side of gardening: dreaming of the elusive, picture-perfect border, I can plan and then plant hardy varieties to create a unique and beautiful garden, by any definition.

out, flowering and seeding. Hardy herbaceous perennials grow a renewable crop of leafy, flowering tops that die back to ground over winter but have more or less permanent winter-proof rootstocks—rhizomes, bulbs or tubers below ground from which new growth sprouts in spring. In contrast, woody perennials (shrubs and trees, leaf-shedding or evergreen) maintain an aboveground framework of trunks, branches and twigs from year to year. Winter-hardy perennials form the backbone of any northern garden more ambitious than a vegetable patch and a bed of petunias, geraniums or marigolds.

In nature, perennial plants predominate. Gardens, I think, are more satisfying, more friendly, somehow, if they mirror the patterns of meadows, fields and forests by including trees, shrubs and perennial herbs. For this gardener, perennials become a little like old friends welcomed back each spring for a seasonal visit.

While perennials go on and on, annuals never see more than one summer. All they need to do—sprout, grow, flower and set seed—is accomplished in a single season. But like perennials, annual herbs may be hardy, half-hardy (another relative term indicating the ability to weather light frosts) or tender. Sweet basil, which withers at a hint of frost and sits still even during cool spells, is the best-known tender annual herb. At the other end of the frost spectrum, hardy chervil thaws out from a hard freeze and grows on despite the cold.

Each spring, a gardener must start most annual herbs anew, from either seeds or nursery plants. But some annuals assure

CHAPTER TWO

GARDEN PICTURES

Soils, structures and designs

My own first interest is in garden-making, and the aesthetics of creating a garden setting that comes together as a "living picture," in the words of Gertrude Jekyll, an influential garden artist of the last century. I like to grow herbs in combination with other plants, rather than in the splendid isolation of a herb garden. For any and all garden settings, there are suitable herbs: thymes, savory and dwarf catnip in the rock garden; lemon balm and anise-hyssop (two for tea) in a mixed bed of hardy plants; sweet woodruff skirting shrubs; borage and calendula in a corner of the vegetable garden; aromatic bush basil edging a border of annual flowers. Many are as decorative as any ornamental, and most are far easier to please. Their gift of fragrance, too, is a large part of their appeal, and the fact that some can turn a meal into a little journey of discovery for the taste buds wins space in the garden composition for even unassuming herbs such as weedy sorrel or dowdy but delicious tarragon.

But the most satisfying plant pictures do not just happen, as much as we might like them to. Good gardens are made; they are built, in fact, like any room in the house, with thought given to the outdoor equivalents of walls and floors—soil, fences, pathways, perhaps paved patio space—before any plant furnishings are moved in. Outdoors, as indoors, design is defined and tempered by practicality. Gardens grow from the ground up. This may seem as obvious as stating that a good house needs a solid foundation or that an artist needs a quality canvas, but haphazard or incomplete soil care at the start is an all-too-common shortcut that almost always means a disappointing garden and unnecessary after-care in seasons to come. Nothing is more frustrating than trying to extract choking bindweed or tortuous sow thistle from the crowns of one's beautiful garden perennials, which can be expected to stay in place for at least three seasons and as many as 10 or more. I have seen too many garden pictures lost to invasive grasses and tenacious weeds. Any work done to properly prepare the ground initially will be rewarded with healthier, more robust growth and reduced maintenance thereafter. Patience is the byword in preparing or renovating a single bed or an entire garden; thoroughness is the goal.

Like all herbs, dill, LEFT, has decorative attributes. At Larkwhistle, RIGHT, such culinary herbs are grown in company with plants that are more often considered ornamental, including irises and lupins.

There is a theory that herbs will grow anywhere, in any ground. Some will, some won't. Not all herbs are small-leaved, drought-resistant aromatics native to sunny, stony lands. Those that do carry on under the sun's glare even after the ground has become dust-dry include all of the thymes, winter savory, the dwarf decorative catnips and many silver-leaved plants, such as woolly lamb's ears, mulleins, some artemisias and yarrows. The bulkier a plant, however, the greater its need for nourishment, so the tall yellow yarrow (*Achillea filipendulina*) and the magnificent ghostly wormwood cultivar 'Lambrook Silver' do better for some richness and moisture at the root.

But given that herbs may be woodland and wetland plants as well, the generalization of sun, sand and stone does not apply to all. Many grow stunted and yellowish if starved or dry. Among those that are at their best only in rich moist ground are the aconites, anise-hyssop, bergamot, parsley, foxgloves, mints, old roses, primroses, shady-side herbs in general and most native woodlanders, ferns and wildflowers.

GROUND WORK

"Skim off the turf," one book blithely recommends as the first step in making a new garden bed. Skimming may be the way to start with tame lawn, but Larkwhistle began as a tangle of twitch grass, bindweed, nightshade and well-anchored campions, all wound together with assorted relics and debris – parts of an old cream separator, rusty skate blades, chunks of harnesses, melted bottles and wide-eyed dolls – left when the former farmhouse burned to the ground years ago. Cut, lift, yank, shake and haul out the turf is more to the point.

Why not just turn the sod over, or take a tiller through it to churn it up? Much easier at the beginning, but every scrap of root, every perennial weed, will resprout to spoil a newly tilled bed. A recipe for converting a lawn or field into garden goes something like this:
¶Measure the area and define it with stakes and string.
¶With a spade (a flat, square-

20

While sun-loving herbs such as lamb's ears and poppies, LEFT, tolerate dry, even poor soil, others, including parsley, ABOVE, and violets, RIGHT, are at their best only in rich, moist ground.

edged digger rather than a rounded shovel), cut the sod into a grid of chunks, each no bigger than a foot square; allow 6 inches extra around all the sides of a bed to make edging easier later.

¶With a spading fork, lift individual chunks of sod and shake them vigorously to remove whatever topsoil falls away. Lay sod on the ground, roots up, and whack it with the fork tines to loosen soil from the roots further; lift and shake again.

¶Pile grass roots, weeds, rocks and rubbish in a wheelbarrow as you go. Civilized lawn sods may be piled upside down in a heap to compost, but twitch roots and perennial weeds soon infest a compost pile and must be dumped elsewhere or burned.

¶Over several days, proceed to remove the sods. This is heavy work at the best of times, but the worst of gardening jobs is coping with sticky clay – try to time sod breaking so that the ground is at its most friable or crumbly; that is, when it is not sodden in early spring or just after a rain.

¶When the sods are gone, dig lightly over the bed, then rake to catch stray roots, rocks and weeds, levelling as you go.

¶If possible, allow a newly dug bed to lie fallow for a month, and watch what sprouts; a little spot digging should clear the ground of the last troublemakers.

To prepare the ground for most herbs, it is not necessary to go to the work of double-digging or trenching. This process involves removing soil from a rectangular area, mixing it with additives and replacing it, working gradually, trench by trench, across the garden. The prospect of double-digging a stretch of ground is enough to deter even the most ardent garden-maker from proceeding. But for deeply rooted very permanent things, such as old roses and peonies, or for very hungry herbs that will be planted in lean ground, it is worthwhile preparing a special hole. Dig out and place to one side all of the topsoil from an area 18 inches in diameter. Loosen and remove the subsoil (which will not be used to refill the hole) to a total depth of 16 to 20 inches. Pile in a mixture of topsoil and humus with two cups of bone meal, filling the hole to the top. Some extra topsoil may be needed. Stir and blend everything together, then tread lightly to consolidate the soil and leave a shallow concave saucer of earth on the surface. Trowel or spade out enough earth to plant the perennial or

Compost, ABOVE, *is the heart of the garden. It can be made by mixing organic garden materials and household scraps in any of a number of homemade containers and added to the soil as needed to produce lush growth,* BELOW.

rosebush without cramping its roots; backfill with earth, poking and tamping with fingers or trowel handle for good earth-root contact. Water well. Then, as a neighbour said after watching us go through this work before setting in a skinny peony root, "it's not your fault if it doesn't grow." But, of course, things do grow; they can't help growing. Generosity and thoroughness at the start are the keys to a better garden. And gardeners must know their plants and what they need to thrive – which is one of the themes of this book.

Clearing a piece of ground is a good way to become acquainted with the tilth and texture of one's soil. The spectrum of soils ranges from pure beach sand, light and infertile in the extreme, to potter's clay, which is heavy, gummy and unworkable. Most garden soils are somewhere in between: often a blend of sand and clay with an admixture of silt and stones, mellowed and made fertile (if a gardener is wise) by a year-in-year-out replenishment of organic matter. Few new gardens are blessed with that magical growing medium, loam – earth light enough with sand to be well drained and early-warming without drying to dust in a period of drought, yet heavy enough with clay to retain adequate reserves of moisture and fertility without shedding water like a duck's back or baking into a web of cracks in the heat; dark and nourishing with organic matter as crumbly and moist as, says one writer, "the richest chocolate cake."

The original soil at Larkwhistle was thin and pale, an anaemic sandy loam that drained far too well. I have seen two feet of water from a sudden spring thaw flow into this low garden and disappear overnight, leaving the ground firm and dry enough to work that day. But fast drainage takes plant foods deep into the subsoil, out of reach of plant roots (a process called leaching), and a week-long dry spell can turn a too sandy garden into a little dust bowl. Every application of organic matter, also called humus, shows in darker colour, better moisture retention and healthier plants. A "grateful soil," the old garden books call this sort of sandy loam; "responsive," I would say. But humus also renders clay soil more manageable and less dense and crusty.

There was a time when my partner and I climbed the fence of an abandoned zoo and hauled burlap sacks full of water buffalo and yak manure home on the streetcar to a cindery city garden. But our sources of organic matter are now fairly traditional:

¶Farmyard manure chosen, if possible, from the dark hill that has stood the longest behind a neighbour's barn. Very old manure, earth-dark and crumbly, is less fertile than fresher stuff but mixes more easily with garden soil. Flecked with bone meal, it can be dumped by the double handful into a hole for transplants or spread as (an admittedly weedy) mulch around the primroses and over a herb or perennial bed.

¶Maple leaves (or other thin-skinned leaves that disintegrate quickly) raked from the woods, lawns and roadsides. Freshly fallen leaves should not be used as mulch; they harbour slugs and, as tests at the University of Connecticut have shown, exude chemicals that can actually inhibit plant growth. But the effect does not continue into the second year of leaf decomposition; maple leaves left in a heap for a season or two turn into a finely textured fertilizer called leaf mould. If it will grow trees, it will grow anything. City gardeners, especially, have access to leaves that considerate neighbours may have already raked and bagged.

¶Grass clippings, hay or straw (straw is better than hay because it is seed-free) can be used as mulch, then either turned under in the fall or left to rot.

¶Black swamp muck dredged out of culverts and left in a convenient pile beside the road is almost pure humus and free for the taking in this area.

¶Store-bought humus is especially useful where there are few natural sources; peat moss contains almost no plant foods but helps to bind sandy soils and holds 20 times its weight in water. Peat moss should be thoroughly dampened before it is applied, and then well mixed with the soil; dry lumps steal water from the surrounding ground and are difficult for roots to penetrate. Gardeners with no access to farmyard manure or piles of leaves take note: damp peat moss mixed half-and-half with bagged composted manure and some bone meal – two trowelfuls to a pail or a shovelful to a wheelbarrow of mix – is rich humus, ideal for digging into the soil for hungry herbs or for stirring deeply into a hole for transplants. Sifted compost may substitute for either ingredient or may augment the mix.

Compost, of course, is the heart of any good garden. Recipes abound for making perfect compost in no time but usually call for shredding ingredients and repeated turnings. Lacking both a shredder – although a machete makes short work of cornstalks, cabbage stumps and the like – and the inclination to turn and re-turn the mountain of compost that this garden generates, we build a long heap, approximately the dimensions of a full cord of wood, of layered garden remnants (avoiding woody ingredients such as raspberry canes and tree prunings) and let it be for at least a year. Usually, winter squash is planted directly on top of the heap to make use of all that richness; the lush squash leaves also effectively suppress weeds. By the second spring, the compost is ready to use as is – dug into the soil, spread as mulch or sifted and mixed with soil, peat moss and perlite for seedling flats and potting.

There are two ways to get organic matter into the ground for hungry herbs. If plenty of humus is on hand, a 4-to-6-inch layer is spread over the cleared surface of a bed that has been well dusted with bone meal, and the works turned under and further mixed with a spading fork or tiller. But if supplies of organic matter are limited or expensive, they must not be frittered away by being spread so thinly that no plants benefit. Rather, decide which herbs require the most nutrients, stir up a bucket or wheelbarrow full of a nourishing mix as described above, and spot-enrich. For instance, for a drift of bergamot, a planting of sweet cicely or foxgloves or a shady-side corner, pile humus deeply over the necessary area, dig it in, stir and rake smooth. For smaller herbs with big appetites, such as primroses, sweet woodruff, chives and parsley, trowel out an oversized hole, trowel in a generous helping of humus, and stir it into the surrounding soil. Tamp and firm the ground with a blunt stick, trowel handle or fist, and you are ready to plant.

A rich mix has other uses. Plants that are "just sitting there" often jump if a quantity of good humus is spread all around them and stirred in lightly with a hand fork; no matter if a few roots are severed in the process, for new roots will soon sprout to take up the additional nutrients. In a new – and planned – herb bed, spot enrichment is the best way to fatten the soil for some herbs while leaving it leaner or even lightening it for others.

Another way of adding organic matter to the soil is mulching with materials ranging from newspapers to cacao bean shells; about $8 buys a huge sack of lightweight husks that, after the first rain, scent the air with chocolate. This ornamental mulch is especially good for corners of the garden that are always in view. Mulching is one of those garden tasks that sounds so good in theory: cover the ground around the plants thickly enough, and you will never have to weed, water or fertilize again. In practice, however, other things enter the picture – slugs and earwigs, to name two. Both of these creatures love the damp shady spots created by an organic mulch. Still, the idea is sound, and if mulch is laid down selectively and with certain considerations, a garden can only benefit.

In a herb bed, the plants that profit most from mulch include the tea plants bee-balm, lemon balm and anise-hyssop; the colourful crew of aconites, old-fashioned roses, hollyhocks and foxgloves; the stronger-growing shade lovers such as Solomon's seal, snakeroot, purple loosestrife, sweet cicely, angelica and others. All of these can be mulched heavily with leaf mould, straw or rough compost – peat moss is a poor mulch because it dries to an unyielding crust – either in the fall, when a layer of mulch is good winter protection, or in early summer, when the ground has warmed and plants have grown out of reach of slugs. Primroses, violets, wildflowers and other dwarf shady-side herbs benefit from a mulch of very old manure or screened compost, but a gardener must be prepared to catch the crop of weeds and grasses that is almost certain to sprout. While they do not absolutely need it, the taller yarrows and artemisias do better for mulch in dry sandy gardens.

As a rule of thumb, mulch the largest, latest-flowering herbs, but hold back on smaller, early-flowering plants. In fall, when leaves are abundant, I like to lay a heavy layer of leaf mulch around tall herbaceous plants and shrubs in the back rows of perennial beds. This saves much of the work of watering and cultivating these hard-to-reach herbs the next summer.

As decorative as cacao bean shells, and longer lasting, is a mulch of small pebbles, stone chips or gravel. These materials provide a warm, dry surface for thymes, creeping savory and oregano to sprawl over. A little sunny sunken garden or patio can be completely covered with 3 or 4 inches of gravel (with or without the addition of a few flat stones to define paths), and a selection of herbs that like sun, stones and warmth can then be planted through the gravel. Any of the grey-leaved herbs would do – mulleins, artemisias, yarrows – and these might be chosen exclusively to create a restful silvery corner. Such a spot could also be home to a large collection of thymes, several sages, savories and oregano, as well as colourful lowdianthus, feverfew and golden marguerites.

The Larkwhistle garden design, TOP, *includes dirt pathways and an old rail fence, while a new path,* RIGHT, *is laid with flagstones on a sand fill. For gardeners lacking access to compost or livestock, a rich mixture of peat moss, purchased manure and bone meal,* ABOVE, *is ideal for most planting needs.*

GARDEN STRUCTURES

In 1916, in her friendly and informative first book, *My Garden*, Louise Beebe Wilder reminded "all gardeners, present or prospective," that the words "garden", "yard" and "orchard" all spring from the same root word meaning an enclosure, a protected or guarded place, "a spot converted from the common land and made intimate and personal, sacred to beauty and sweetness, to delightful work and quiet meditation." I share Wilder's "rare enjoyment of passing through [a garden gate] and closing it behind," the pleasure of stepping into an enclosed garden.

There are many ways of encompassing a garden. Granted that "walls of old brick or stone create an especially agreeable atmosphere," as Wilder wrote, and a clipped evergreen hedge "creates a charming foil for the luxuriant unrestraint within," but walls and formal hedges are clearly impractical for gardens smaller than estates. I have plenty of demands upon my gardening time without manicuring a hedge to perfection. And few of us have the dedication that prompted Helen and Scott Nearing to spend 14 years building a stone wall around their garden.

A wooden fence gives protection from cold winds, wandering animals and short-cutters of all sorts; wood is also friendlier for enclosing a city or suburban yard than cagelike chain link or chicken wire. Split cedar rails spiked to well-anchored cedar posts make a fence of great charm and character. In the field behind our garden, we discovered a long zig-zagging line of moss-covered but still good-hearted cedar rails, remnants of an ancient snake fence long tumbled and now woven through with the accumulated grass thatch of many summers. Purchased or recycled boards and posts of all

sizes, provided they are pressure-treated, treated with wood preservative, conscientiously painted or made of cedar or redwood, will also create a long-lasting wooden fence. For gardeners who would rather grow things than cut them down, a green and flowering living fence of shrubs is an alternative to boards. In either case, just be sure the garden wall is not so tall that it will shade plants that need sunlight.

Fences need not enclose one's entire property, of course. Many country gardens or even larger city yards present the owners with an opportunity to create within the overall landscape a special "garden room," an enclosed area, however small. Planted with perennial culinary and ornamental herbs, such a space can be beautifully practical; a few tubs or pots of annual aromatics complete a classic garden scene. At Larkwhistle, a small herb garden built on the rubble-strewn site of a burnt-down farmhouse just outside the kitchen door is surrounded by a lattice fence of 1-by-2-inch spruce lumber nailed to a 1-by-3-inch frame. Sections of

Lattice fencing, ABOVE, *is easily constructed and particularly successful in the herb garden. It allows the plants themselves to create a "living fence," as was the custom in early knot gardens,* LEFT.

mountain of snow. It leafs out early, withstands drought, thrives in sun or shade and opens clear yellow, white or rusty orange edible flowers, like small single roses, the summer through. A little pruning keeps cinquefoil shapely. For a more strictly herbal hedge, southern-wood (*Artemisia abrotanum*), clipped in spring and in summer, creates a shimmering grey-green background. Lavender planted around the perimeter of a small herb garden of any design produces a neat, fragrant, foot-high hedge, silver year-round, bristling with bloom for weeks in summer.

Lavender is equally useful for hedging or, less conspicuously, for edging. Where a fence or hedge is obtrusive yet a gardener wants to define a garden space, edgings, whether inert or living, create clear boundaries between cultivated ground and "common land." At Larkwhistle, we edge beds or borders in four ways:

¶At close intervals along the length of some raised beds, blocky limestone rocks have been sunk by at least half, the earth firmly tamped around them with a blunt stick, leaving a level top and vertical face, like a cliff in miniature. Between and just behind the rocks grow creeping and trailing herbs, including a variety of thymes, mounds of dianthus and dwarf catnip, sheets of creeping savory and billowing Lady's mantle. The plant roots seek out moisture beneath the stones, while tops spill over the warm rock surfaces.

¶Other raised beds are edged and defined by 1-by-8-inch unpainted rough cedar boards nailed to 2-by-4-inch stakes hammered into the ground. Such beds, a practical solution where topsoil is thin or where bedrock is close to the surface, can be filled with a mixture of topsoil, peat moss, aged manure and/or compost. Railroad ties are familiar edgings, ideal for creating multilevelled or terraced gardens on sloping sites; bricks sunk into the earth or set into concrete are also fine.

¶In our lattice-fenced garden, a 6-inch-wide concrete curb

lattice 4 feet high by 6 feet long were nailed to cement-anchored cedar posts. The simple criss-cross design was improvised and built with the most basic hand tools—a small square, tape measure, hammer and nails. Although at first I was all for staining or painting the lattice-work forest-green or sky-blue, in one season it had weathered to an unobtrusive and no-

maintenance silver-grey. "Don't do it unless you're prepared to redo it every spring" was wise advice about painting.

A living fence of some small shrubs or taller, bushy herbs is also suitable for defining a herb garden. The 4-foot shrubby cinquefoil (*Potentilla fruticosa*), or any of its cultivars, is hardy well into the north and springs back even if crushed under a

outlines the beds; hand-mixed concrete was poured into a two-board form to a depth of 8 inches and then well tamped. Tumbling greenery soon softened the sharp edge.

¶Elsewhere, a border between shrubs and lawn has no constructed edge at all. Low plants – primroses, violas, English daisies – come right to the front of the border, and once or twice a year, the turf is cleanly edged by slicing away a little band of sod and pulling back any invading grass roots. A sharp spade, not a shovel, is better for this than one of the flimsy, awkward things sold as special edging tools.

Beyond the edgings are garden "halls," the pathways, and "floors" such as lawns. Some areas of a garden invite strolling and touring, and the gardener must consider what will be underfoot there. Most paths need extremely tough ground covers, as they will certainly be travelled. Grass is fine in paths wide enough to be mowed (or sheared, if the gardener is energetic) but will be troublesome along narrow, well-travelled routes, as it requires frequent clipping and can spread into neighbouring beds. Where the garden soil is sandy and well drained, level, bare earth is the simplest of paths; even persistent bindweed calls it quits as the path is firmed by a season or two of foot traffic and wheelbarrowing. Sandy ground is never muddy, even in early spring or after a summer deluge.

Heavier loam or clay do not make an acceptable path unless topped with a layer of mixed sand and gravel at least 3 inches thick. Laying a sheet of plastic under the sand/gravel mix to suppress weeds ensures only that the path will become a little canal after a rainstorm. Better to have a dry walkway and wield the hoe as necessary.

For paths, also consider flat, relatively smooth stone slabs, at least 1 inch thick for stability, laid as level as possible in a 6-inch bed of sand. The interstices between the stones may be packed with sand, small stone chips or pebbles, or the

spaces may be planted with creeping thymes, Corsican mint, silver pussytoes (*Antennaria dioica*), even tiny spring bulbs. But remember that a path is for walking, and if the planting is overdone, a stroll through the garden becomes a game of hop, skip and jump or an anxious tiptoeing to avoid crushing the small greenery. Thymes will take some treading on, and grass is the most resilient of ground covers, but no plant will live with constant traffic.

Alternatives to stone slabs are bricks, old or new, laid down in any of a variety of patterns; commercial interlocking paving or concrete-path patio slabs; large rounds of wood (but I do not like the idea of an ancient tree being felled for a pathway) interwoven with rounded stones; shredded bark or wood chips. The latter two can be difficult to maintain, however, in a garden overshadowed by deciduous trees, whose leaves will need to be raked every fall. In that case,

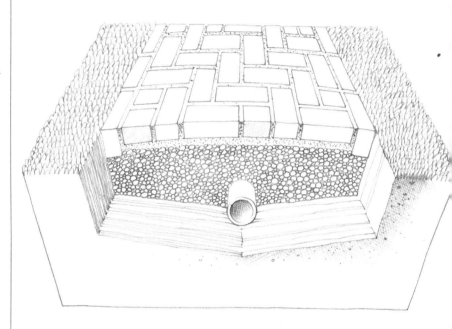

Pathway and patio construction, ABOVE, *involves laying the paving material over a bed of at least 6 inches of sand or other fill. A drainage pipe ensures that a pathway will not become a little canal. Plants can grow between paved areas,* RIGHT, *or in barrels and raised beds that border or top the paving,* BELOW.

bare earth, grass or any material suited for a patio will be most suitable for paths.

GARDEN DESIGN

There is something exciting about a new garden bed, carefully cleaned, well enriched, raked fine and smooth—a blank canvas awaiting the gardener's art. But like any painting, a garden bed is better for a preliminary sketch or at least a little daydreaming and imagining beforehand. Often, planting proceeds intuitively: a gardener may be interested in herbs for tea or seasoning or may want to create a quiet enclosure of silver herbs or a bright border sparkling with bergamot, foxgloves, old roses, ornamental onions and similar colourful herbs. Such a space then has a theme or focus.

But how to begin? A collection of plants—herbs or otherwise—is a garden in roughly the same way that a palette of colours is a painting. Two things are required to turn the ingredients into a work of art: imagination and information. A healthy dose of patience is also an asset. Every gardener who has ever sown a seed or set out a tiny twig has a measure of imagination. Information can be obtained about each plant as it is acquired or discovered; I find keeping a garden notebook essential.

The notion of what works or not in garden design and planting is different for each of us. Gardeners of the random-collection school may never stop to consider if their beds and borders are pleasing to look at, but most of us give some thought to the end result before we plant the first seed or dig the first transplanting hole. Any garden, even a vegetable or herb garden, is partly an exercise in aesthetics.

Height, habit, form, colour of leaf and flower and season of bloom all influence where a plant will best fit in a bed or border. For culinary herbs, easy accessibility is also important. At Larkwhistle, herbs in daily demand for spring-to-fall seasoning—including lovage, thymes, oregano, savory and others—grow just outside the kitchen door in narrow raised beds surrounding a stone-paved patio. Over the years, little colonies of fragrant seedlings—thymes in particular—have sprung up between the chinks of the warm rocks. Two half-barrels planted with annual herbs sit in corners of the patio. What was introduced for convenience has become one of the garden's most appealing landscape features.

"Beauty deprived of its proper foil," a sage once said, "ceases to be appreciated as such." It is not lack of good plant material that keeps gardeners from turning out attractive beds; almost everything that grows has some beauty of leaf, flower or seed pod. But any plant is enhanced or diminished by the company it keeps. It is instructive to set

aside a bed or section of the garden—a newly cleared, well-enriched spot, if possible—and approach it as a blank canvas in the spirit of picture-making. "Take thy spade, it is thy pencil; take thy seeds, thy plants, they are thy colours," I once read.

Rules of garden composition may spoil some of the spontaneity, but a few principles can only help. Start by making a list of plants suitable for your site, including any you have admired in books or other gardens and any you already have somewhere in the garden but think would be useful in your picture-making. Some you can raise from seeds, others must be found in nurseries; it is useful to determine which are which. Stay with perennials at the outset; annuals can always be tucked in here and there or given a place in the vegetable garden or in containers. At the pencil-and-paper stage it is better to have too many plants than too few—

you can always edit the list.

While some of the work of planning and composing a bed or border goes on indoors with pencil, paper and books, sooner or later, I feel the urge to get down to ground level and do a little on-site sketching. With notes, lists and diagrams near at hand, I take a long stick and divide the smoothly raked bed into front, middle and back sections. I do not say "rows," because a section may be two or three rows deep, depending on the width of the bed. Then, I draw circles on the soil for specimen plants, as well as some overlapping ovals, "drifting" shapes and kidney shapes and, within them, little holes 8 to 18 inches apart to mark the placement of individual herbs. Of course, I erase parts of the sketch now and then and begin again. Labels are handy to reserve a place for a particular plant, such as thyme, yarrow, chives or tarragon.

Now is the time to think of the distances between plants. Once, I used to crowd plants mercilessly because I was eager to get as much into a bed as possible. But if each herb is given adequate room, growth is better and the whole picture is less cluttered. It may seem foolish to set tiny transplants 18 inches or even 2 feet apart, but it is wise gardening in the long run.

In general, robust edging herbs, like Lady's mantle, lamb's ear, 'Silver Mound' artemisia, dianthus and dwarf catnip, will easily fill a square foot of space in a season. These, then, go 12 inches apart. More restrained dwarf herbs—I have in mind thymes, creeping savory and the pretty, low woolly yarrow (*Achillea tomentosa aurea*)—are set a hand-span or 8 inches apart; in time, they run into each other to make an uninterrupted band of foliage and flowers along an edge or down a rock-garden slope.

Medium-tall herbs (12 to 18 inches tall) go two hand-spans or 16 to 18 inches apart, while tall aconites, bergamot, anise-hyssop and yarrows (or any plants taller than 4 feet) are better as much as 2 feet apart.

Divide your plant list into dwarf, medium and tall specimens, and beside each name, jot down a bit of pertinent information. For example, in the dwarf column, you might have "Ornamental catnip (*Nepeta × faassenii*), 8 inches, lavender-blue flower spikes in May and June." Under tall, "Scarlet bergamot (*Monarda didyma*), 4 feet, bright red flowers, July, rich ground, attracts hummingbirds." Then proceed to mix and match plants that you think would be suitable companions, grouping two or at most three different plants which you feel would complement each other in height and habit and, preferably, share a season of bloom. I suggest you consider

height and habit first, so tall things do not hide dwarfs, and sprawlers do not smother others. Tall things, of course, go toward the back of the bed, shorter herbs in front. But by swinging a 6-foot aconite toward the middle of a bed or a 3-foot hyssop or hardy sage toward the front, one avoids a look of strict regimentation and creates little bays or pockets for a picturesque grouping. A border planted in this drifting, weaving fashion produces a series of small surprises and enticing glimpses. Finally, for May through to August, consider the refinements of colour and form. Spring takes care of itself, and if the garden is good all summer, you can rest on your laurels after Labour Day.

Consider form and growth habit too. Some herbs naturally grow and flower in stiffly upright spires — anise-hyssop, aconites and hollyhocks come to mind. Others, like tall yarrows,

southernwood and 'Lambrook Silver' artemisia, feather out gently. Lemon balm is roundly bushy, while dianthus and 'Silver Mound' artemisia are low and mounding. A garden bed is more effective if its plant forms are contrasted: herbs with feathery foliage are juxtaposed with those with broad, solid leaves; those with slender, upright flower spikes grow next to others with more rounded shapes.

Certain bold or broadly spreading plants are fine as specimens — that is, alone. These include wormwood, tall yarrows, hyssop, southernwood, lovage, anise-hyssop, angelica and bronze fennel. But most herbs are more effective in groups of at least three and as many as five or seven. The hardy sage *Salvia superba*, for instance, looks a trifle weedy as a single plant, but its violet-purple flower spikes glow dark and brilliant when five or six are massed together. If you have several plants of any

In designing the garden, LEFT, situate taller plants behind shorter ones. Hollyhocks are the tallest flowers in a bed at Larkwhistle where yellow yarrow constitutes the central element behind edging plants, and nicotiana (at right) stands alone as a specimen.

Properly constructed stairs, ABOVE, are built with materials that harmonize with pathways and patios.

type of herb, it is usually a mistake (in terms of a picture) to dot one here and one there in hopes of making them "go farther" – you're more apt to lose them.

Finally, consider colour. In general, colour harmony is easier to live with than a confusion of brilliance. Seed catalogues encourage gardeners to aim for a "riot of colour," but who wants a riot in the garden? In any case, a herb bed is almost never riotous. Most herbs are rather subdued, decorative in a quiet way. A herb gardener would have a hard time duplicating the garish effect of a bed of red and yellow tulips, for instance, or the gaudy glare of scarlet salvia and yellow marigolds. If you must have red and yellow in the herb bed, try setting a few plants of golden marguerites (*Anthemis tinctoria*) in front of scarlet bergamot (*Monarda didyma*) – and don't say I suggested it.

Many gardeners are so keen on colour and flowers that they forget entirely the value of foliage in the garden picture. But nothing does more to keep a garden looking fresh and full than fine, lasting foliage. In a hot, dry season, when flowering plants are rushed into bloom and then out again just as quickly, others with persistently good foliage set in prominent places along the edges and through the middle of beds keep the garden lively despite a lull in the fireworks. Fortunately, herbs are useful foliage plants in almost all gardens, since most keep their looks from spring until long after iris leaves have gone spotty, poppy foliage has disappeared into the ground and delphiniums, tattered and mildewed, have been cut back. Chapter 5, on thymes, and those about silver-leaved and shady-side herbs (Chapters 9 and 10) describe many excellent foliage plants.

Edging plants should be chosen for lasting foliage rather than colourful flowers; indeed, several of the best herbal edgers have the tiniest of pale flowers, and one has none at all. From spring through fall, these plants hold a bed together and set it apart from the surrounding lawn or

paths. If a bed is neatly (but not necessarily evenly) bordered, it always has its "best foot forward." At Larkwhistle, the edge of a long iris border, dry and sandy in the extreme, is home to 10 species of thyme – mats and mounds of green, grey and gold – alternating with various nonherbal sedums.

Other edging ideas will suit other beds:
¶For a sunny bed, alternate three plants of hardy, sweet-scented dianthus with one of dwarf catnip, and then repeat the pattern for the length of the bed to make as good an edging as any I know.
¶Fragrant, slightly fuzzy fruit thyme can alternate with 'Silver Mound' artemisia around a bed of roses or herbs.
¶Silver thyme alternated with winter (or creeping) savory creates a light-and-dark effect.
¶In areas where they are hardy, both the silver and green forms of lavender cotton (*Santolina chamaecyparissus*) work well along dry, sunny edges. Looking like strange vegetable corals, these two are often seen in public parks lined up to spell or artistically represent something.
¶In shade, nothing could be finer than mingled primroses, cowslips and sweet woodruff.

To show their true form, edging plants must not be pressed or crowded by taller plants behind. Space to spread is important for all of the meek thymes and savories, among the best of border herbs, and the flowerless but no less lovely 'Silver Mound' artemisia. Most edging plants stay nicely compact and winter better if they are given a shearing back by at least one-half sometime in midsummer. I always wait until a plant has finished flowering, just because it seems a considerate thing to do.

CONTAINER HERBS

Garden designing becomes more flexible and more portable if one is able to make use of

Even in the herb garden, colour is an important design consideration. A stand of red hollyhocks, ABOVE, *is complemented by red bergamot. If herbs are in containers,* RIGHT, *they can be moved from place to place within the larger garden picture as desired.*

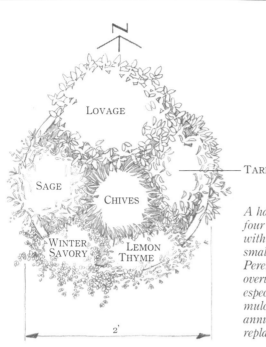

LOVAGE

TARRAGON

SAGE

CHIVES

WINTER SAVORY

LEMON THYME

2'

A half-barrel planted with four or five species in scale with each other can become a small, perfect herb garden. Perennials, LEFT, should overwinter successfully, especially if pruned and mulched, while barrels of annuals, BELOW, are replanted each spring.

containers. In the case of herbs, each container becomes a little garden in itself, requiring its own design, and then assumes its proper place in the overall scheme of things. Since many herbs, especially annuals, take to containers, a porch, patio or balcony can be arranged with large clay pots, wooden boxes or half-barrels for a lovely decorative effect. Needless to say, meals will be livelier if a barrelful of basil, summer savory and sweet marjoram is situated within reach of the cook.

If a sunny balcony, rooftop or deck were my only growing space, I would concentrate my gardening efforts on cultivating culinary herbs in containers. Simultaneously decorative and useful, herbs qualify on many counts as near-perfect container subjects. First, they are at their aromatic best if snipped fresh just before they are needed to season a salad, sauce or soup; but, excepting parsley and perhaps dill, fresh herbs are not commonly available in markets. A well-stocked container herb garden is virtually an outdoor spice rack supplying a daily harvest of flavour and fragrance from May until October; then, with some timely snipping and drying, one can easily capture summer scents for winter seasoning. Herbs are seldom bothered by insect pests or plant diseases, and since many herbs can stand dry ground with impunity, they are among the best choices for containers that are apt to dry out in a single day of sun and wind.

Container herbs are not only for high-rise or otherwise landless gardeners. Even though we have garden space to spare, we chose to get some herbs off the ground, a decision made after several seasons of setting basil and summer savory seedlings in the open garden only to watch them disappear into the maws of night-stalking slugs and earwigs. Our containers of choice were several wooden half-barrels designed originally for ageing wine or whisky and selling for about $10 apiece. As planters, half-barrels have the edge over clay pots. Comparable terra cotta containers or large strawberry pots (generally Italian imports and admittedly lovely) cost well over $100 at last check, and if left out over winter, earth-filled clay containers are sure to dissolve into shards, while sturdy half-barrels come through the cycle of freezes and thaws unscathed. As important for busy gardeners, half-barrels need only a fraction of the watering that porous clay requires; a good soaking once a week is usually enough, so a gardener can have his herbs and a holiday too.

In a recent herbal reference book, there is a photograph of a decorative low clay pot, "small enough to be carried from one part of the garden to another," planted prettily with sage, rue, tarragon, two kinds of thyme and (unbelievably) angelica. Frankly, the photo is misleading, as no gardener should be encouraged to expect this to be a workable arrangement. Angelica, for one, is a 6-foot herb, while a single tarragon, sage or rue plant would soon spill over the pot sides, smothering the meek thymes on the way. Such a planting is good for three weeks at best.

That said, a half-barrel, 2 feet across and 18 inches deep, planted with four or five species in scale with each other, can become a small, perfect herb garden, knee-high and easy to tend. Here's how: decide on the herbs you want to grow, consulting Chapters 3 to 6 for a discussion of seasoning herbs. If there are annuals and perennials among your favourites, two half-barrels are better; one is used to grow permanent things, the other is renewed each spring from seeds and/or transplants. Position the containers where they will catch the most sun. Check for drainage holes, and if necessary, bore a 2-inch hole in the bottom of each. While the drill is out, consider boring two or three more 2-inch holes on the sunny side of the half-barrels just below the topmost iron hoop; parsley or small trailers such as thymes, creeping savory or sweet marjoram can be tucked into these holes to take advantage of the depth of soil.

The soil is our next consideration. After covering the drainage hole with crockery shards or stones, fill the barrels (or other containers) with a growing medium composed of roughly two parts light loam or bagged potting or topsoil, one part each of perlite, dampened peat moss and very old, crumbly manure (purchased is fine) or sifted compost. To each half-barrel, add four trowelfuls (or two double handfuls) of bone meal and mix thoroughly. This blend provides enough nourishment for most herbs for a full season, probably more. In summers to come, water the barrels with a balanced liquid fertilizer, fish emulsion or manure tea once a month *only* if herbs show signs of weak growth or yellowing. In the process of filling the containers, firm and consolidate the earth with your hands or the end of a board; bring soil to within an inch of the top, and level it. Do not water now, or you will be planting in mud.

Perennial cooking herbs suitable for a half-barrel include: lovage, the tallest contender (suitable if a gardener is prepared to prune away branches that will certainly crowd the other herbs); medium-sized chives, sage, tarragon and sorrel; and the shorter hardy savories and lemon thyme (hardier and more delicious than regular cooking thyme). A few planting tips: lovage goes right against the north side of the half-barrel (the back), so it does not cast a long shadow over the rest; if the dwarf herbs are not planted in holes in the barrel side, they are tucked along the south rim, 8 inches apart, to tumble over; three medium-tall herbs are set a foot apart through the centre of the half-barrel. Judicious pruning over summer, which counts as harvesting if you dry or freeze the cuttings for winter, keeps stronger herbs from pushing the little guys around.

As November comes to a close, give some thought to bringing a barrel of perennials through the winter. The danger is not freezing but, rather, alternate freezing and thawing as well as waterlogging. After trimming back the herbs, perhaps the simplest way to protect a container is to bank numerous bags of leaves (a common commodity street-side in cities and suburbs in fall) all around and over it, leaving a few small gaps among the top bags for air circulation so that the herbs do not rot.

Fans of herb teas (see Chapter 7) could grow several mints, bergamot and lemon balm in one half-barrel, but the dense mats of these root-running herbs must be lifted entirely each spring and replaced by small divisions. Three to five shoots of mints and small wedges of the other two will suffice. Let go for more than a year, these tea herbs soon weave themselves into a confused tangle of weak stems.

Virtually any annual culinary herb can fill a half-barrel. As the container can be placed within easy reach of the kitchen, consider filling it with the herbs you use most. Basil is a favourite, along with summer savory, dill, chervil, sweet marjoram and indispensable parsley. Set store-bought or homegrown transplants 6 inches apart around the barrel just after the last spring frost date; a month earlier, sow the hardy seeds of dill and chervil in small groups of five to eight seeds 6 inches apart, thinning later to the strongest single seedling in each spot. A few dwarf calendulas or nasturtiums can add colour, but the likes of big blue borage would take over.

If half-barrels make the most satisfactory container for a herb garden outdoors, large pots are perfect for tender perennial herbs that must winter indoors: rosemary, bay, ginger, fruit and pineapple sage, all scented geraniums, myrtle and the Costa Rican mint bush. A 12-inch pot will grow any of these comfortably for three or four years, after which plants that have grown overlarge and woody are renewed from cuttings (see page 163). The soil mix for potted tender perennials is the same as that for a half-barrel herb garden, described previously.

HANGING BASKETS

Although I admire flower- or herb-filled baskets in nurseries or other gardens, I have never grown plants in this way. With a large ground-level plot to tend, I would no doubt neglect to give an airborne garden its daily drink, with disastrous results. Still, there is no denying that a swaying basket cascading with colour or greenery is a lovely way to make the most of available porch or balcony space. In her *Culinary and Salad Herbs* of 1940, Eleanour Sinclair Rohde wrote, "In my childhood, cottagers used to make parsley baskets, and very pretty they were." She described how a dozen "parsley roots" – seedlings, I assume she means – were planted in the top, sides and bottom of a wire basket lined with moss and filled with rich soil. Hung on a porch or in a sunny window, well-tended specimens (that means watered faithfully and fertilized monthly) looked like "balls of foliage; the more leaves were picked, the more thickly plants grew." Nasturtiums make a brilliant hanging basket, while any annual herbs or small trailing perennials are also suitable, for a single season only.

Window boxes, too, can be space-saving small herb gardens. If you are constructing your own, choose rot-resistant 1-by-8-inch cedar boards, and build the boxes to last. Fill them with the moisture-holding soil mix described on page 35. If a window catches enough sun to grow herbs during summer, it will be fairly bright in the winter as well; a box, herbs and all, can be shifted indoors to the safe side of the glass in September. A window box 8 inches wide by 2 feet long will grow a dozen assorted annual herbs (perhaps the better choices for such a small container) spaced a crowded 4 inches apart in two staggered rows. Consider small- or medium-sized herbs that will

not block the view from the window, such as marjoram, summer savory and various shapes and colours of basil, mixed with calendulas, nasturtiums and other small flowering annuals. Or grow six to eight perennials including trailing rosemary, a small division of tarragon, a few dwarf trailers, a well-pruned sage bush or chives – but leave out lovage.

As long as herbs can sink their roots into nourishing, evenly damp (but not waterlogged) earth, they will grow along merrily in all sorts of containers. I have seen plants tumbling out of battered old paint cans hung on pegs hammered into a crumbling stone wall, and sprawling over the top of leaky

In order to maintain aesthetic control over the garden, plan frequent visits and take notes. In spring, narcissus, orange cowslips and purple rockcress, LEFT, harmonize at Larkwhistle. One gardener grows an assortment of herbs, including rosemary, mint, thyme, sage and tarragon, in clay chimney-flue tiles, ABOVE.

path or by the garden gate — a fragrant welcome within easy reach. Just remember to check for dryness at least once and preferably twice daily, especially in small containers sheltered from rainfall and dew. Frequent garden inspections are as necessary as they are pleasant.

In order to keep in touch with the comings and goings of all our plants, to make on-the-spot appraisals of what is happening in the garden and to determine what we want to do, my partner and I go out into the garden once a week from May through September and just survey the scene for a while. In years past, we used to list by colour all of the plants in flower that week. Each page of a "what's-in-bloom" book was divided into 7 columns, each column headed by a colour or colours: white and cream, yellow and orange, violet and purple, blue, pink, scarlet, crimson. This is an excellent method for three reasons: reviewing the plants in the garden and learning their names; keeping track of what blooms when, and for how long; and keeping in touch with the ebb and flow of the garden — seeing what does particularly well with little attention, what responds to extra attention and is worth the effort and what is just plain miserable.

As the number of plants grew too large to list each week, we changed our approach. Now we keep a "picture book." Every couple of weeks, we take a look at each section of the garden and simply jot down how that stretch of bed or border might be improved. For example, "Extend lavender (from cuttings) in front of old roses" or "Interplant pink bergamot with new deep violet aconite (enrich heavily) in top border."

During September and October and again in April and May, we consult the book to see what needs doing to make the garden lovelier. After 12 challenging seasons, we can echo Epicurus when he said, "I am not only well content but highly pleased with the plants and fruits growing in these my own gardens."

sap buckets. At Kiln Farm in Puslinch, Ontario, dedicated herb grower Rachel MacLeod has arranged tall and short sections of clay chimney-flue tiles to make a terraced garden that is an unusually decorative focal point for her extensive barn-side herb plot. The tiles contain several mints and other herbs.

Container-grown culinary herbs are an obvious choice for cramped quarters. In any garden, however, portable potted aromatics can be placed to best advantage in the landscape, perhaps where they catch the most sun in a shady yard, or handy to the kitchen door. Potted herbs make eye-catching accents on either side of a garden

A Shaded Garden

This garden creates a cool, leafy space by combining herbs with ferns, evergreens, wildflowers and hardy bulbs. The emphasis is on season-long foliage of different textures, colours and shapes. Spring bulbs and primroses provide early colour; bergamot, lamium, aconite and others give sparks of colour during summer. Refer to Chapter 10 for a full description of these herbs and a list of bulbs.

While this garden is designed for a city yard, variations may be adapted to any shady site. For example, a section of border containing plants 1 through 16 could be planted on the shady side of shrubs or near a north wall. The shape and width of the beds may be altered for a less symmetrical design. But consider that after a season or two of growth, the formality of the design will be softened by the varying habits of the plants, whether creeping, bushy, upright or tumbling. This combination of a formal design with informal planting is a time-honoured garden principle, seen at its best in the Sissinghurst gardens of Vita Sackville-West.

This garden could take several seasons to complete. Since large numbers of many plants are required, a few of each species can be set out and left to spread the first year; clumps can then be divided in fall or early spring to cover more ground. This method reduces the cost of the garden enormously. Paths are best made with a sand/gravel mix set with a few stepping-stones or completely paved with flat stones, bricks or interlocking garden paving.

The first season (spring or fall), set out the cedars, evergreens and shrubs. From seed, start foxgloves, primroses, lemon balm, lovage, sweet cicely and violets. The second and third season, divide and spread out ground covers as needed. Plant bulbs in fall.

Plant List

PLANT (Number of plants in brackets)	Distance apart	Propagate by: Seeds (S) Plants (P) Division (D)
1. Lovage (1)	–	S, P, D
2. Lady's bedstraw (3)	16 in.	P, D
3. Variegated apple mint (1, initially)	clump	P, D
4. Meadowsweet/Ferns (6-10)	18 in.	P
5. Parsley (10)	10 in.	S, P
6. Foxgloves (6)	18 in.	S, P
7. Ajuga (8)	15 in.	P, D
8. Elderberry (1)	–	P
9. Hosta or Lady's mantle (1)	–	P
10. Primroses (12)	12 in.	S, P, D
11. Tall ferns (10)	18 in.	P
12. Lady's bedstraw (1)	–	P, D
13. Lamium, white-flowered	16 in.	P, D
14. Cedar or other evergreen	–	P
15. Tall ferns or small shrubs	18 in.	P
16. Primroses	12 in.	S, P, D
17. Lamium 'Beacon Silver'	16 in.	P, D
18. Cedar or other evergreen	–	P
19. Tall ferns	18 in.	P
20. Lady's bedstraw (1)	–	P, D
21. Primroses (12)	12 in.	S, P, D
22. Serviceberry (1)	–	P
23. Hosta or Lady's mantle (1)	–	P
24. Ajuga (8)	15 in.	P, D
25. Aconite (3)	24 in.	P, D
26. Variegated apple mint (1, initially)	clump	P, D
27. Bergamot (5)	18 in.	S, P, D
28. Lemon balm (1, initially)	clump	S, P, D
29. Lady's bedstraw (3)	16 in.	P, D
30. Sweet cicely (3)	24 in.	S, P
31. Sweet violets (7)	10 in.	S, P, D
32. Trilliums (10)	12 in.	P
33. Sweet woodruff (20)	12 in.	P, D
34. Solomon's seal (15)	16 in.	P, D
35. Hosta or Lady's mantle (5)	18 in.	P
36. Small ferns or primroses (5)	12 in.	P, D
37. Primroses or violets (7)	10-12 in.	S, P, D
38. Calamus (1) in pool	–	P

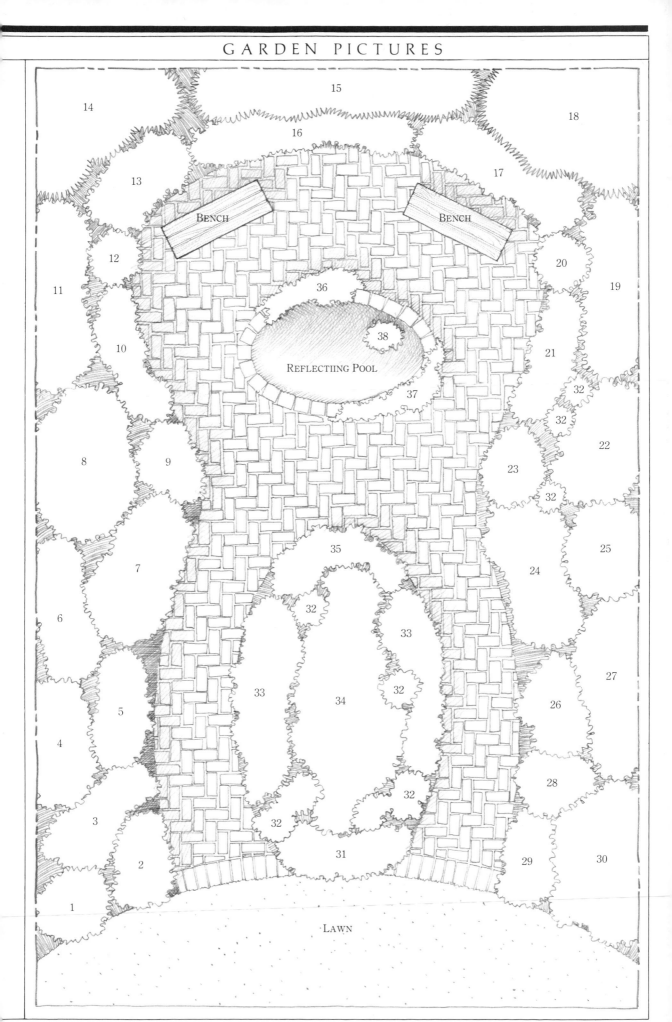

A TEA GARDEN

A year-long supply of herbs, fresh and dried, for teas comes from a garden designed to be both attractive and colourful, but easy to maintain as well. It is a simple 7-by-12-foot rectangle that can be set in a stretch of lawn, incorporated into an existing vegetable garden or connected with other garden areas, provided the bed receives at least six hours of sunlight daily.

It may be level with the surrounding land or raised behind an edging of railroad ties, rough 2-by-8-inch cedar boards, or a low wall of stones, bricks or cement blocks; a simple concrete curb poured into forms could also define the bed. A semi-circular stone or brick step provides an entrance, and a paved area above creates a place for tender tea herbs in pots, while a Y-shaped path of earth, flat stones or bricks leads through the bed on both sides and provides working space. The path should be 18 inches wide initially but will shrink as plants fill out.

As the year progresses, allow the calendulas to self-sow, thinning them to six to eight inches apart. Remember to water the tender, potted herbs as necessary – possibly every day in dry weather – and feed them once or twice during summer with dilute fish emulsion (or equivalent). Bring them indoors for the winter.

For drying, harvest the tea herbs just before the first flowers open. Harvest calendulas when the blossoms are fully open but still fresh, and rose hips as they ripen.

PLANT LIST

PLANT (Number of plants, and part used for tea—Leaves (L), Flowers (F), Roots (R), Seeds (S), Hips (H), Decorative only (D)	Distance apart	Propagate by: Seeds (S) Plants (P) Division (D)
1. Sage (1, L)	–	S, P
2. Woolly lamb's ear (3, D)	12 in.	S, P, D
3. Peppermint (1, initially, L)	clump	P, D
4. Rosa rugosa 'Scabrosa' (1, H)	–	P
5. Horehound (2, L)	10 in.	S, P
6. Calendula (6-8, F)	6 in.	S
7. Lemon balm (1, initially, L)	clump	S, P, D
8. Lemon or other thyme (3-5, L)	8-10 in.	P
9. Mullein (1-3, L, F)	10 in.	S
10. Anise-hyssop (1, L)	–	S, P
11. Valerian patch (1, initially, R)	clump	S, P, D
12. Hyssop (1-3, L) and/or Achillea 'Moonshine' (1-3, L, F)	12 in. / 12 in.	S, P / P, D
13. Scarlet bergamot (3, L)	16 in.	P, D
14. Silver thyme (6, L)	8-10 in.	P
15. Lavender (2-3, F)	12 in.	S, P, cuttings
16. Hyssop (1, L)	–	S, P
17. Anise-hyssop (1, L)	–	S, P
18. Lavender (2-3, F)	12 in.	S, P, cuttings
19. Variegated apple mint (1, initially, L)	clump	P, D
20. Lavender (1, F)	–	S, P, cuttings
21. Sweet cicely (1, L, S)	–	S, P
22. Golden lemon balm (1, initially, L)	clump	S, P, D
23. Calendula (6-8, F)	6 in.	S
24. Rue (1, L)	–	S, P
25. Rosa rugosa 'Scabrosa' (1, H)	–	P
26. Curly mint (1, initially, L)	clump	P, D
27. Dwarf catnip (3, L)	12 in.	P
28. Sage (1, L)	–	S, P
29. Lemon verbena (1, L)	potted	P
30. Fruit sage (1, L)	potted	P
31. Pineapple sage (1, L)	potted	P

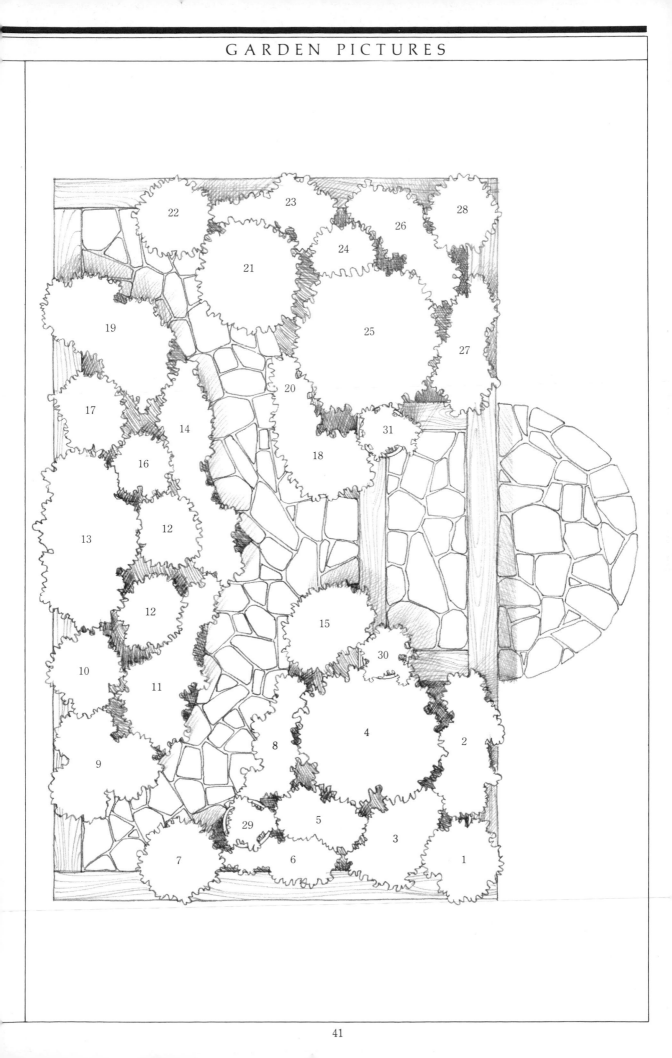

A CULINARY GARDEN

This garden, which is designed for beauty and low maintenance, provides a wide range of culinary (and some tea) herbs easily accessible from the house. It is designed on and around a patio or deck that receives full sunlight for at least six hours a day or all-day flickering sun/shade. The shape can be altered to suit other landscape features, and the bed may be below or level with the patio or deck; it could also be raised, if it were framed with cedar boards or a low wall of stone or brick.

Included in the design are six wooden half-barrels planted anew each spring with seeds; two 12-inch pots grow tender perennial herbs that are moved indoors over winter. See the information on growing in containers on pages 150-153.

Remember to:

¶Plant cloves of garlic and shallots from August to October, as early as they are available.

¶Reduce the size of the lemon balm clump if it is taking over.

¶Trim thymes, winter savory and sage if they are winter-damaged.

¶Trim thymes back by half after the flowers are past.

¶Cut chives to 4 inches after the flowers are past.

¶Mulch Greek oregano and French sorrel with evergreen boughs in late fall and remove the mulch in spring.

PLANT LIST

PLANT *(Number of plants in brackets)*	Distance apart	Propagate by: Seeds (S) Plants (P) Division (D)
1. Lovage (1)	–	S, P, D
2. Lemon balm (1, initially)	clump	S, P, D
3. Sage (2)	12 in.	S, P
4. Top onions (6)	6 in.	S, P, D
5. Garlic (15-20)	4 in.	Cloves
6. Parsley (6)	6 in.	S, P
7. Greek oregano (1)	–	P
8. Silver thyme (5-7)	6 in.	P, D
9. Lemon thyme (5-7)	6 in.	S, P, D
10. Shallots (10-15)	4 in.	Bulbs
11. Winter savory (2)	12 in.	S, P, D
12. French sorrel (1)	–	S, P
13. Chives (3)	clumps	S, P, D
14. Tarragon (1, initially)	clump	P, D
15. Red bergamot	–	S, P, D
16. Sweet cicely (1)	–	S, P
17. Borage (1)	barrel	S, P
18. Nasturtium (4-6)	barrel	S, P
19. Purple basil (12)	barrel	S, P
20. Dwarf calendula (8)	barrel	S, P
21. Sweet marjoram (1)	barrel	S, P
22. Rosemary (1)	12 in. pot	P
23. Lemon verbena (1) or	12 in. pot	P
Pineapple sage (1)	12 in. pot	P
24. Sweet basil (12)	barrel	S, P
25. Nasturtium (4-5)	barrel	S, P
26. Dill (6)	barrel	S, P
27. Summer savory (6-8)	barrel	S, P
28. Chervil (6-8)	barrel	S, P

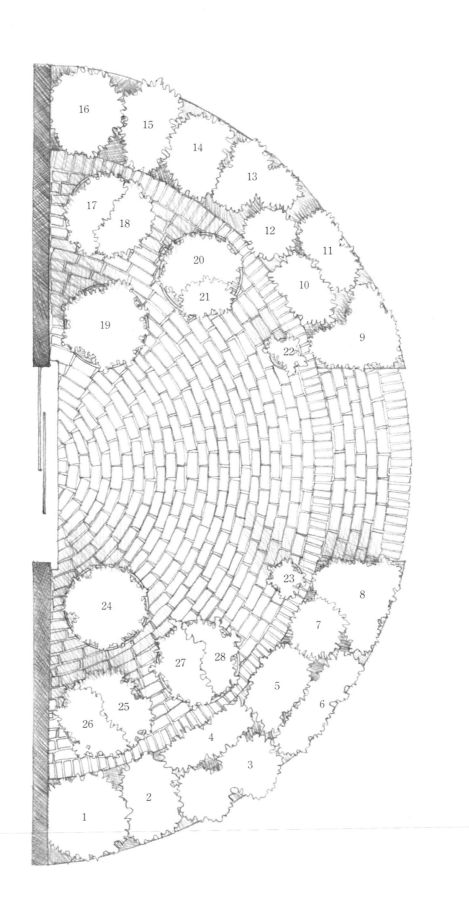

CHAPTER THREE

THE GARDEN PANTRY

Perennial kitchen herbs

Soon after the snow disappears from our garden, I begin to harvest fresh herbs for the kitchen. Chives and other perennial onions have been busy sprouting under the cover of winter; thymes, sage and winter savory are in fairly good condition if they have been protected by snow or evergreen boughs and may be usable, if not exactly convenient, all winter long. Lovage is one of the first herbs to stir in spring, with sorrel and then tarragon not far behind. Sweet cicely, too, is an early riser. Hardy perennial and biennial herbs, these are the stalwarts capable of surviving most northern winters and of returning each spring. At the fall end of the growing season, they persist until the going gets very rough indeed.

High summer, of course, brings a lavish bouquet of annual herbs – dill and coriander, sweet basil and summer savory – to enhance the seasonal abundance of tomatoes, green beans, lettuce and summer squash. Fresh seasonings of one sort or another are available from our garden for a good eight months, from April through November, and many can be harvested year-round on the balmy West Coast. Favourites are easily dried for winter use.

When it comes to choosing which culinary herbs to grow, I encourage cooks who garden to check their spice racks and see which herbs they use most. That jar of Italian seasoning so useful to spike spaghetti sauce and chili or to sprinkle over pizza is likely a blend of oregano, thyme, rosemary and certainly basil. The list is started. The cook may notice, too, that garlic powder, cayenne, parsley flakes, dried dill or chives and perhaps caraway seeds are depleted quickly and are expensive to boot. You taste something unfamiliar but good in a Middle Eastern or Mexican restaurant – fresh coriander leaves, the chef says. The list grows. A corner of the garden – in many cases, containers will do – can grow all of these in abundance.

What would I grow if pressed to choose just a half-dozen herbs? Not an easy decision. Of the annuals, I would not like to do without basil, summer savory or dill; among perennials, I use lovage at least once a day, as long as it is green and growing. Nor could I cook without garlic. Just one more? Let it be parsley (but I would miss tarragon and chives). A silly game – but not a bad way of discovering the essentials.

Where should one grow culinary herbs? In theory, the answer is easy: grow herbs as close as possible to the door nearest the kitchen – nothing encourages use as much as accessibility. In a country garden, it is a mistake to hide the herbs at the bottom of the vegetable garden. Although a special bed or even a garden of herbs is a pleasant feature, herbs do not need that sort of splendid isolation. There are many nooks in the landscape where they are at home: annuals at the edges of vegetable garden beds, chervil under shrubs, dwarfs in a rock

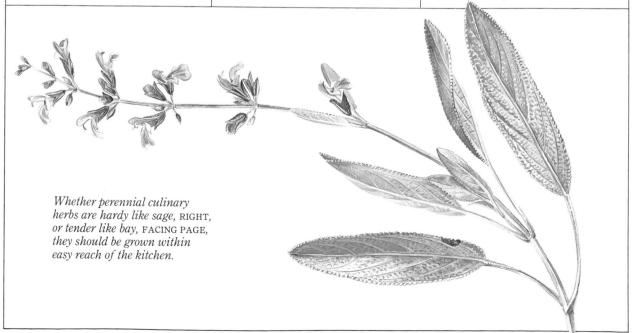

Whether perennial culinary herbs are hardy like sage, RIGHT, *or tender like bay,* FACING PAGE, *they should be grown within easy reach of the kitchen.*

garden, others among the flowers. At Larkwhistle, perennial flowerbeds are edged with various thymes and savories, and the likes of lemon balm and lovage rub shoulders with poppies and delphiniums.

In a city garden, any place is close at hand, so choose a spot for culinary herbs that meets their need for sun or, in a few cases, shade. Grow tall lovage against a fence (in shade if need be); creeping savory or any of the thymes on a sunny slope of a rock garden; annual basil in a bed of flowers; parsley in a hanging basket with nasturtiums; dill wherever its feathery seedlings find a foothold, and so on. A couple of wooden half-barrels – one for annuals, one for perennials – on a sunny deck or patio will grow a surprising quantity of seasoning herbs.

BAY

Laurus nobilis

Two perennial herbs for pots are bay and ginger, frost-tender delicacies that thrive outdoors year-round only in the warmest northern gardens. Both, however, are virtually carefree indoors. Bay produces shiny evergreen foliage on a neat-looking shrub that can, given enough root space, sunshine and fertilizer, become several feet tall. But it will stay at a convenient foot-tall height if confined to a 6-inch pot and pruned if it becomes ambitious. Even a northern exposure will keep it producing leaves suitable for seasoning soups, sauces and stews.

Buy bay plants from a herb nursery, if possible. New plants can be propagated from cuttings, but not as easily as some other plants, like rosemary. If you do want to try multiplying a plant, dip cuttings of new growth, all but the top two or three leaves removed, in rooting hormone, and plant them in damp vermiculite. Cover both pot and plant in a plastic bag, and keep it in a warm, shady spot until the cutting roots. After it is planted,

Horseradish roots are as pungent as they are tenacious and hardy. Never till a patch, since every severed piece of root grows into a new plant.

HORSERADISH DELIGHTS

Mix 2 tablespoons of grated fresh horseradish root in 1 cup of mayonnaise, homemade or otherwise, for roast beef sandwiches. A perky salad is made by adding grated horseradish (to taste) to any or all of grated carrots, apple (tossed immediately with lemon juice to keep its colour), raw or cooked beetroot, thinly sliced celery or Florence fennel and cubed boiled potatoes. Dress with oil, lemon juice and yogurt or sour cream, chopped dill, parsley and tarragon. For a special lunch, dress the salad ingredients separately and arrange them in mounds of orange, crimson, pale green and creamy white on red or green lettuce leaves; some hard-boiled eggs, smoked fish and/or cold meats turn a salad into an easy summer meal. A little grated horseradish also adds a bit of bite to most dips.

Northern Europeans have a variant on horseradish sauce. Peel and grate a quantity of fresh root, and leave the slivers on a paper towel for a half-day to dry a little – some of the hotness disappears in the process. Make a simple white sauce of butter, flour and milk, and stir in the grated horseradish. Serve with beef.

keep the soil somewhat dry, never waterlogged, and fertilize only during the spring and early summer.

Bay can spend the summer outdoors in its pot, but it is very susceptible to sunburn; it must be allowed to adapt gradually to outdoor light by being exposed initially to only short periods of deep shade. Plants that spend the winter indoors should not be exposed to greater light than dappled or brief sunlight in summer.

CHIVES, GARLIC AND GARLIC CHIVES – See pages 83-86

GINGER

Zingiber officinale

A flavouring that is almost indispensable in Chinese stir-fried dishes, not to mention desserts and ginger beers, ginger is easily grown from pieces of living root. Unfortunately, they may not always be available; even whole supermarket roots may be shrivelled and dry by the time they are purchased. If in doubt about the vitality of a root, buy several and plant them all; and have patience – ginger may not produce its first green spikes for more than a month.

Plant the roots horizontally, one per pot just under the soil surface in a foot-wide container filled with a nourishing soil mix – one part compost or well-rotted manure, one part potting soil and one part peat moss will do nicely. Keep the soil damp. Eventually, a fat grasslike spear should appear. It will become about 3 feet tall with glossy, dark green alternate leaves. In about six months, dig down into the pot with a sharp spade and sever a piece of the root to use in the kitchen. Or dig up the entire root annually, cut off some for the kitchen, and replant the remainder.

Like bay, ginger can spend the summers outdoors, provided it can first adapt to brighter light with a period of rest in the shade. However, it will grow perfectly well without ever seeing the outdoors; even an eastern or western window will keep it green and growing. Fertilize it throughout spring and summer.

HORSE-RADISH

Armoracia rusticana

When my partner and I first began to clear a corner of an old farmstead for a new garden, we uncovered some unfamiliar leaves in the grass under the lilacs. They were large, glossy, oval and sharply serrated along the edges. A bit of digging and a few neighbourly enquiries identified the plant as horseradish, a wickedly hot herb, stalwart enough to survive the tide of twitch grass and clovers that soon swamps an untended garden.

Horseradish grows itself – no need to coax this herb along. It is sufficient to plant, in any out-of-the-way corner, pieces of crown or chunks of the thong-like roots that grow laterally from a clump; roots from a grocer will do as starter stock. But the most succulent roots grow in ground deeply prepared with good compost, manure or other humus. If you have a permanent compost bin, consider planting horseradish beside it; the lush, decorative foliage will help hide the compost while the roots feed on the extra nutrients. Never till a patch, because every severed piece of root grows into a new plant; horseradish can be a nuisance in a small garden. A permanent mulch means next to no maintenance in the horseradish patch.

During the earliest centuries of horticulture, horseradish had medicinal applications only. Taken internally, it was thought to stimulate the appetite, aid digestion and improve the functioning of the liver; a source of vitamin C, horseradish was also long used to prevent or cure scurvy. Since some of the chemicals in this hot herb are identical to those in mustard seed, a poultice of grated

A tender perennial that is easily grown in a large pot is ginger, BELOW, whose pale roots season desserts, Oriental stir-fries and other dishes. The plant sports dark green alternate leaves and grows to about 3 feet tall.

horseradish applied externally heats the skin like a mustard plaster. Said Nicholas Culpeper, "If bruised and laid to a part grieved with sciatica, gout or joint-ache, it doth wonderfully help them all."

At some point, however, some European decided that horseradish, for all its remedial uses, was good enough to eat for its taste alone. Calling it *Raphnus rusticus*, the rustic radish, John Gerard recorded that horseradish "stamped with a little vinegar is commonly used among Germans to sauce fish and such like meates as we do mustarde." In the early 1600s, the habit began to catch on in Britain. But considering that horseradish sauce is as necessary as Yorkshire pudding to that quintessentially English dish of roast beef, it is curious that in 1640, John Parkinson of England still considered "coarse-radish too strong for tender and gentle stomachs" although quite fit for "country people and strong labouring men."

LOVAGE

Levisticum officinale

Best of the essential culinary herbs, at least to my taste, is lovage. Many other gardener cooks agree, but I know one who has taken lovage out of her herb bed entirely. "Too strong," she says, "and takes up too much space." Growing over 5 feet tall and widening eventually to several feet around, lovage is the green giant among herbs. But it is handsome enough to be planted at the back of a flower-bed or to stand sentry by the kitchen door and is also well placed in a bed of strong-growing perennial vegetables and herbs—horseradish, rhubarb, Jerusalem artichokes and asparagus. One of our plants competes with raspberries and does just fine. Locate this heavyweight carefully; it is not easy to move once established.

Lovage is the preeminent soup herb, just the thing to simmer in chicken broth with the usual onions and carrots. But I like to flavour almost any savoury dish with its dark green leaves, which taste sharply of celery and parsley with a spicy depth. Use lovage—sparingly at first—to season all hot dishes including bean, pea and lentil soups, slow-cooking chili and beef stews, chicken pies or tuna casseroles. The taste of lovage does not dissipate with cooking. A snippet spices an omelette, and I like the tenderest leaves raw in a sandwich or finely chopped into green, grain or potato salads, alone or with dill, basil, spearmint and other milder herbs. With garlic and ginger, lovage deliciously flavours stir-fried vegetables, especially bland summer squash.

In Europe, the plant, called *Maggikraut*, gives the liquid or dry-cubed herbal flavouring extract Maggi much of its tang. Fresh leaves are traditionally used with potatoes in all forms— mixed with sour cream to spoon onto baked potatoes, added with marjoram to potato soup, flecking buttery mashed potatoes or in a white sauce (parsley and dill are also good here) for boiled potatoes.

Lovage grows easily from fresh seeds sown in late summer or fall; freeze and thaw the spring-bought seed to break dormancy. The plant takes a full season to fatten up but returns faithfully every year thereafter. Divisions may be cut from the outside of an established plant, without lifting the well-anchored clump, and set out in nourishing soil. Lovage flourishes in, but does not demand, damp ground. A single plant supplies an eight-month harvest of leaves, and a few branches hung in an airy, shaded place become crisp in a few days and stay nicely aromatic for winter.

An interesting biological note: lovage flowers are "typical wasp flowers," attracting hosts of the tiny, beneficial social and parasitic wasps that prey on garden pests such as cutworms, spruce budworms and tent caterpillars. Organic gardeners often send for trichogramma wasp eggs without realizing that unless the emerging young wasps have access to certain

kinds of nectar in the garden, they will either starve or head for the fields in search of Queen Anne's lace. So let the 6-foot flowering stalks stand. But just before the seed ripens, cut them back to avoid having to root out the small forest of lovage that springs up all around the mother plant. If hung to dry, these dill-like seed heads add interesting cartwheel shapes to dried flower bouquets. Dry seed may be harvested as a celery seed substitute.

MINTS – See pages 90-95

OREGANO

Origanum spp

There is no such thing as oregano, pure and simple. One catalogue lists Greek, wild Greek, Italian, golden showy, beautiful, woolly and white oregano. Another assures the reader that theirs is the "true oregano collected wild in the mountains of Greece." Few plants, herbs or otherwise, suffer such a confusion of Latin and common names. Let me spare you the tangled taxonomic details and say, first, that oregano grown from seed labelled *Origanum vulgare*, wild oregano, is likely to be a sprawling, scentless disappointment despite its clusters of small, reddish flowers humming with bees and butterflies in September. Better to pick up plants in person. Here is a herb, like lemon thyme, that ought to be pinched, sniffed and nibbled if possible, so that you can be sure of its potency.

Currently, in our garden, we have – or rather, had, because one is now gone – four plants labelled oregano. 'Showy oregano' looks more like thyme than oregano and has pretty magenta tubes for flowers and no scent. The late 'golden oregano' looked sickly, as do many yellow-leaved plants, and sat absolutely still one season and the next until it was finally shown the garden gate – well, in truth, dumped without ceremony or regret onto the compost heap.

Although herbs are surprisingly versatile and worthy of culinary experimentation, they tend to be associated with certain foods: sage, LEFT, with turkey; lovage, RIGHT, with potatoes; and oregano, BELOW, with Italian dishes.

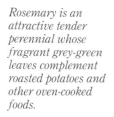

Rosemary is an attractive tender perennial whose fragrant grey-green leaves complement roasted potatoes and other oven-cooked foods.

In summer, a northern herb garden, BELOW, features clumps of sage, woolly lamb's ears, chives and calendulas between paths mulched with bark chips.

(But another gardener tells me that this herb romps freely and is very decorative for her.) The Italian oregano resembles the Greek, but the former has a scent and flavour that are mild to the vanishing point. Laurels go, finally, to the herb labelled mysteriously, first name only, *Origanum* spp, Greek oregano. It is properly pungent-smelling and peppery on the tongue.

Greek oregano is said to be only half-hardy, needing pampering in a flower pot indoors over winter, but ours has lived outdoors over four seasons in a gravelly pocket of a stone patio. The secret may be to situate this sun- and stone-loving herb in the hottest, driest corner (conditions appropriate to its Mediterranean origins), mulch it with gravel or small pebbles, and if lacking snow cover, protect it with evergreen boughs during winter.

So much for rules and botanical confusions. Oregano supplies fresh leaves for tomato sauce, salad dressings of olive oil and lemon juice, sautéed summer squash (with tarragon and lovage), chili and hamburgers through the summer, and it dries in a twinkle for winter pizza, meat loaf or thick soup. This is one herb I use more of dried than fresh, the robust flavour being more appropriate to fall and winter dishes. The dried branches with their grey-white flowers are woven into herbal wreaths by a neighbour, who also uses silvery artemisias, branches of thyme and a few crackling pink strawflowers to create decorations that are as useful as they are beautiful over the winter.

ROSEMARY

Rosmarinus officinalis

Neither a hardy perennial nor a tender annual but, rather, a tender perennial shrub that can overwinter nowhere in the north but on the West Coast, rosemary fortunately adapts well to pot culture. I know several gardeners who go to great trouble to transplant this herb from an indoor pot to an outdoor garden bed each spring, then back again in fall. But it is far easier to set a small starter plant directly into an oversized pot—12-inch diameter is good, but no less—of nourishing soil and leave it there. Winter the potted rosemary in a sunny but not overly warm place indoors; in deference to its seaside origins, give it a biweekly misting—and set it outside in good sun from mid-May to October. It withstands light frosts but must not be frozen hard. If you find that a potted rosemary on the patio or porch dries out too quickly, sink plant, pot and all, into the ground up to the pot rim. An annual pruning, just before rosemary goes out for the summer, keeps the shrub shapely and densely leafy; shorten the winter-spindly stems by at least one-half. I like to wait until flowering is over before pruning any plant, just because it seems a considerate thing to do.

After three or four seasons, it is sometimes necessary to start again with a new small plant as the "mother" rosemary may have grown lanky, woody and often leafless along the lower part of the stems. Cuttings are a sure and simple means of renewal. Snip a 3-inch piece from the tops of several branches, remove the lower few leaves, and dip the ends of the cuttings in the grade of rooting hormone powder sold for softwood cuttings. Plant three to six cuttings firmly in a 4-inch pot of very light soil, then slip a clear plastic bag, punctured with a few tiny holes, over the pot, fastening it with an elastic band. Keep the pot in a bright place out of direct sun; roots should form within three weeks, after which the new plants are potted singly.

The scent of narrow grey-green rosemary foliage is cool and resinous, a little piny or camphoric—I find it invigorating just to tousle a bush and breathe deeply. My favourite way to use rosemary in the kitchen, however, is to sprinkle halved or quartered potatoes generously with rosemary leaves, either dried or fresh, drizzle potatoes with olive (or other) oil and roast until done. Rosemary is a natural for other oven-cooked foods as well, such as chicken and roasts.

SAGE

Salvia officinalis

All herbal literature holds sage in highest esteem as a medicinal plant. The name salvia comes from the Latin verb *salvere*, to heal, root of our words salve, salutary, salvation, sage (wise) and the French toast *salut*, "to your health." The sagacious Chinese once valued the herb so highly that they willingly exchanged three pounds of black tea for a pound of sage from Dutch traders. The reputed link with long life and glowing health is illustrated in *The Virtues of British Herbs* of 1776 by English herbalist Sir John Hill, who recounted the story of "a woman so old that for that reason alone she was called a witch. About five yards square of ground before the door of her little habitation was planted with sage, and 'twas not only her account but that of all the village that she lived on it. Her exact age was not known, for she was older than the church register, but people remember their fathers calling her the 'old woman.' "

Nowadays, sage is better known for its starring role in the festive turkey—this herb seems a necessary complement to fatty poultry and other meats. Unlike mild-mannered basil or dill, sage is too potent to be used with a lavish hand. I like to tear a leaf into bean soup or minestrone; a little goes a long way in cream cheese. The taste of fresh sage is balsamic and slightly bitter (but much less so than the dried, powdered herb), making a pleasant spring tea when blended with milder lemon balm and spearmint.

At one time, English peasants ate fresh sage with their bread, butter and cheese. This is, in fact, a simple way to get to know the flavour of many culinary herbs: spread some good bread with sweet butter and lay on a few whole leaves or a sprinkling of minced herbs. Or melt cheese over bread under the broiler and press fresh herbs into the top. Another way to become acquainted with a variety of herbal flavours is to include small labelled bowls of chopped or whole leaves at a wine-and-cheese party. One garden writer passed along a suggestion that sage leaves be dipped in a flour-and-egg batter and deep-fried. "These are gobbled up," she said, "when served with drinks, and people rarely guess what the crusty tidbits are." Parsley, too, can be batter-dipped and frizzled in oil, and if these two, why not lovage leaves, the tender tips of oregano, marjoram or rosemary, dill flowers or sprigs of coriander?

Sun and well-drained soil are all sage needs for good growth, but it responds best to the shelter and warmth of a house wall, to the north if possible. With its grey-green pebbled foliage and spikes of lavender bloom, it can decorate a sunny corner of a flowerbed or rockery. At the top of a dry wall, "where it can indulge in a tendency to lounge," wrote an old-time gardener, "the slurred softness of grey-green leaves and violet flowers makes sage a herb of real beauty."

An easy herb to grow from spring-sown seed – an indoor start is best – sage can also be propagated from cuttings, and local nurseries usually have sage plants (if few other herbs) in spring. But the half-shrubby bushes do not divide well. Occasionally, a "lounging" branch will root where it touches the ground. This natural layering can be encouraged by anchoring branches to the ground with stones or hairpins and tossing a few handfuls of earth over them. Allow at least a month for roots to form.

In early spring, we clip the straggling winter-worn branches back by about half (but not to the woody portions); new growth soon sprouts, and the plants stay compact. Even given this treatment, sage may need replacing after three or four seasons. In our garden, the bushes seem to become overly woody and then succumb to a hard winter. Other gardeners tell me that sage goes on and on for them. They must be living right; legend says that sage follows the fortunes of the house, dwindling during evil days and reviving miraculously when things are bright again.

SALAD BURNET

Sanguisorba minor or *Poterium sanguisorba*

A perennial pretty enough to edge a flowerbed or decorate a rock garden with its low rosettes of lacy blue-green foliage, salad burnet, or pimpinella, remains evergreen throughout a snowless winter. Only the youngest leaves go into salads or "green sauce," a German specialty. In the market stalls, German vendors hawk bundles of mixed fresh herbs wrapped in damp paper. The contents of the bundles change with the seasons, but besides parsley, borage, sorrel, dill, chervil and chives, there is usually salad burnet in a supporting role. Shoppers snap up the green-sauce ingredients and, once home, finely chop the herbs to fold into *quark*, a simple dairy product not unlike yogurt mixed with fresh cream cheese. This fast and flavourful sauce is traditionally served over boiled potatoes and hard-boiled eggs for a nourishing lunch. The young leaves have a subtle flavour: mildly cucumber, a little tart, a little hot. Older leaves are as stringy as grass and taste about the same. In early summer, up come slender reddish stems topped by small balls of crimson blooms that make decent cut flowers; cutting flower stalks encourages new leafy growth.

Burnet does not transplant well, so the seeds are sown in the open garden around the last spring frost date and seedlings are thinned to 6 inches apart. Alternatively, a few weeks earlier, start them indoors in 3-inch peat pots or the equivalent. This elegant little

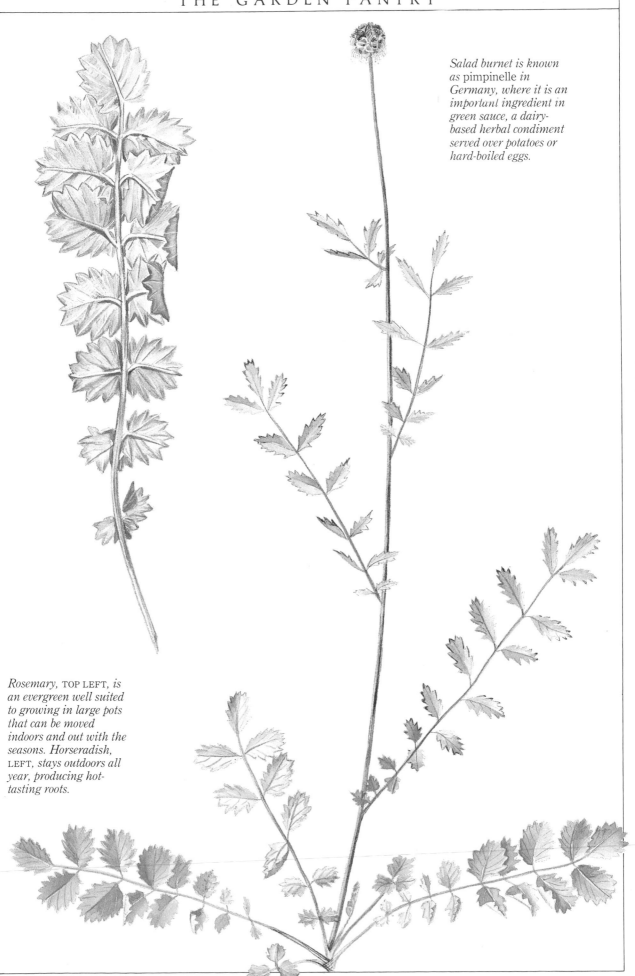

Salad burnet is known as pimpinelle *in Germany, where it is an important ingredient in green sauce, a dairy-based herbal condiment served over potatoes or hard-boiled eggs.*

Rosemary, TOP LEFT, *is an evergreen well suited to growing in large pots that can be moved indoors and out with the seasons. Horseradish,* LEFT, *stays outdoors all year, producing hot-tasting roots.*

herb tolerates dry ground but, like most things, grows better with a bit of fertility, moisture and sunshine. If it is left to seed itself, little burnets are sure to appear.

Burnet is one salad herb that seems to have been overlooked despite the current interest in unusual greens. As long ago as 1934, Maud Grieve (in *Culinary Herbs and Condiments*) noted that "burnet, once in every herb garden of older days, has now gone out of fashion and as a kitchen herb is much neglected." But the didactic words of an old Italian proverb warn, "*L'insalata non e buona e bella, ove non e la Pimpinella,*" the salad is neither good nor fair, if pimpinella is not there.

SORREL

Rumex acetosa

The species name tells of the acidic bite of this herb, called *Sauerampfer* by the Germans and sourgrass by the English. Now, having scaled the heights of haute cuisine, it is known as French sorrel, with cultivars such as 'Blonde de Lyon' and 'Nobel' available. Easily grown from seeds sown outdoors a month before the last spring frost, or indoors about four weeks earlier, a few plants provide a long harvest of young leaves. It is recommended that flower stalks be removed to prevent seeding and to

encourage tender basal growth. In any case, sorrel is at its best in spring or early summer and again during the moist days of fall; it is stringy and less flavourful during summer heat. Space the plants 8 inches apart in peat-enriched soil in a sunny corner where they can remain undisturbed for some years. Like tarragon, the same sorrel plants return year after year in this garden, but one writer says it is "grown as a hardy annual throughout most of the north." Experimentation is the essence of good gardening – I can only say, try and see.

Besides giving a tang to the soup that bears its name, acidic sorrel tarts up a lettuce salad or, with a bit of lovage and fennel

Gourmet herbs need not be difficult to grow. Tarragon, RIGHT, is surprisingly easy, requiring only ordinary garden soil and some sun. Watercress, however, demands a special environment. Without a constant supply of moisture, its roots, LEFT, will wither.

added, seasons a cream sauce for poached fish. It is also good finely chopped with lovage and stirred into sour cream or thick yogurt to dress boiled or baked potatoes.

TARRAGON

Artemisia dracunculus sativa

Another culinary herb adopted by the French as their own fills out the corner of perennial essentials: French tarragon (*Artemisia dracunculus sativa*) – "little dragon," the French estragon. Tarragon seed is always suspect, producing a tasteless sprawler of no use in the kitchen or garden. True

French tarragon, of more moderate growth and simple linear lines, has a sweet taste of anise and a brief analgesic (numbing) effect on the tongue if nibbled alone. A clump in the garden keeps a cook in fresh tarragon for more than half the year, and the branches freeze or dry easily for winter.

Tarragon responds to sun, warmth and ordinary garden soil that does not stay too wet for long periods. This herb has lived in our garden over many winters, but others say its hardiness is not ironclad. No doubt the persistent snow here protects it; often snow arrives so early that the ground beneath never freezes but stays as soft in winter as in summer. Each spring, just as the tips of tarragon are showing above ground, we take a morning to divide the clumps (for selling). A plant is pried out of the ground with a spading fork and the spaghetti-like runners are split by hand or with a small knife into three-to-five-shoot rooted divisions. The roots are trimmed a bit to fit 6-inch pots without bending, and the divisions are planted firmly in a mixture of sandy loam flecked with peat moss and bone meal; the pots are then well soaked, and fresh green soon sprouts. But except for propagation, tarragon need not be divided. As long as it is thriving, let it be.

The taste of tarragon is sometimes featured in a dish: tarragon chicken, eggs *à l'estragon*, omelettes, tarragon mayonnaise, hollandaise or tartar sauce. Tarragon vinegar is a pricey but delicious culinary cliché easily concocted by anyone with a plant in the garden. Push a little bundle of fresh tarragon tops into a bottle of cider, wine or white vinegar, and leave it to steep, in the sun if possible, for a week or so – *c'est ça*. Forget the instructions that call for heating the vinegar, shaking the bottle twice daily or straining out the herbs – but a few cloves and a bit of lemon peel can be added for extra élan.

This vinegar, with oil, salt and pepper, produces the simplest of elegant salad dressings. More elaborate is tarragon vinegar

added to half-and-half sour cream or yogurt and mayonnaise, mixed with plenty of chopped chives; a pressed clove of garlic is optional. Spread this over slices of cooked beets, hard-boiled eggs and still-warm boiled potatoes arranged on a bed of lettuce and garnished with tarragon leaves. Such a salad might well include cooked, chilled green beans, chickpeas and crunchy steamed cauliflower.

Tarragon butter seasons vegetables wonderfully. And, for a nice change from regular tomato juice, to every pint of fresh or canned juice, add a teaspoon each of minced tarragon, chives and basil, one-half teaspoon of lemon thyme, the juice of half a lemon, a dash of cayenne pepper and a pinch of salt if starting with fresh juice. Allow the mixture to stand for an hour or two in a cool, not cold, place, and strain before serving.

THYMES – See pages 74-79

WATERCRESS

Nasturtium officinale

Watercress is among my favourite salad herbs. Water-crisp leaves are sharp and peppery and, if grown in fresh flowing water, are always succulent and clean-tasting, never too hot or bitter. I have tried to grow watercress in my dry garden several times, going to some trouble to prepare a special spot of rich soil near the pump or under a faucet, only to harvest a few pale shoots and then watch plants disappear during the heat of summer.

Now, I content myself with the free harvest from the wild. Like asparagus, watercress lasts for a month or six weeks in late spring. In many places, this best of wild foods grows thickly along the margins of shallow streams. My sources are rather different – one patch crowds the mouth of a large metal culvert that keeps a spring-swollen swamp from flooding the road; in another place, watercress hangs in heavy, green mats from the sheer face of a high limestone cliff – a piece of the Niagara escarpment – just where a spring seeps and trickles from the rock crevices. Since watercress absorbs whatever is in the water, foragers should find out what goes on upstream. It is important that the water be as clear and uncontaminated as possible.

The Chinese stir-fry watercress or simmer it in soup, but I find that this crisp herb becomes stringy with cooking. Watercress sandwiches, of course, are considered de rigueur in England, and in late May, nothing could be finer than a salad of fresh spinach, the first leaf lettuce, crisp radishes, green onions and lots of peppery watercress tossed with a simple oil-and-vinegar dressing well flecked with tarragon or chervil. What could be better for you? Rich in minerals, tonic watercress is also a famous antiscorbutic – a potent source of vitamin C.

WINTER SAVORY

Satureja spp

Two perennial savories belong at the edges of a herb bed. Winter savory is *Satureja montana,* "from the mountains," a slowly widening, upright (to 10 inches), shrubby counterpart to the annual summer savory. Branches are clothed in dark green needle-like leaves, hot-tasting and aromatic; the small-lipped flowers are white, faintly flushed with mauve. Loveliest of dwarf herbs is creeping savory (*S. repandra*), which looks like a trim little heather when the green nests bristle with tiny white flowers in late summer. Creeping savory tumbles gracefully over the edge of a raised bed or sprawls in a small way in a rock garden. It likes to bask in the sun for at least six hours a day. Margot Barnard, a gardening neighbour, is so enthusiastic about this herb that she has turned a single plant into 20 in three years. The soft mats

now festoon the length of a 30-foot herb-and-flower bed raised with railway ties. One fall, they were still in full bloom as of Thanksgiving – something to be thankful for indeed during the long season of frost and farewells.

Gardeners with small sunny places to furnish ought to investigate the two hardy savories, persistently green, dwarf, decorative in a quiet way and useful for seasoning. As long as they are not crowded, shaded or sitting in damp places, they look after themselves. Seeds are offered for both, but started plants are a shortcut, and they can be propagated from cuttings or, more easily, layered. They can also be created from slips: to produce new plants of creeping savory in spring, I ease away – fingers are the right tool here – some of the emerging shoots from the outside of a clump. These slips invariably have a few thread-like roots attached, and they can either be potted up or planted firmly elsewhere, away from strong-growing neighbours. If a clump is large enough, I sometimes take a little wedge of crown and roots with a sharp knife and trowel; but this must be done carefully, or one is left with a mangled plant and no division. Branches of both these savories layer nicely if held to the ground with a hairpin or bit of bent wire and further anchored with earth.

Purists insist that the flavour of winter savory is inferior to milder summer savory. Agreed, but the winter sort returns year after year and is usable fresh from early spring until December, while summer savory is a June-through-August herb – see page 73. In Germany, savory, both summer and winter types, is called *Bohnenkraut* – the bean herb. Winter savory is the perfect complement for soups or casseroles based on dried legumes, but the more delicate annual is the one to use on fresh green beans. Savory also flavours homemade pizza, stews and meat loaf. The flavour is similar to both oregano and thyme. In my cooking, they are interchangeable.

Herbal soups such as watercress, ABOVE, *can be prepared cold or warm from ingredients available just outside the kitchen door. At Larkwhistle,* BELOW, *the culinary garden includes nasturtiums and, in the raised bed, sage, thyme, trailing rosemary, parsley and fruit sage.*

Pretty and versatile, creeping savory, RIGHT, is a hardy herb that blooms from summer through fall and is as suitable for complementing beans, pizzas, stews and meat loaves as its taller cousins.

SOUP-HERB TEA BAGS

With dried herbs, consider making what I call soup-herb tea bags, homemade mixtures for cooks, who often do not want to open six different jars of dried herbs for a pinch of this and that. To make winter seasoning more convenient, blend together two parts dried leaf celery or lovage with one part each of dried marjoram, thyme, and summer savory. If the dried herbs are still in whole leaves, crumble them coarsely and blend them thoroughly. Put a heaping teaspoonful of the blend into a 4-inch square of cotton or cheesecloth and add half a bay leaf and a couple of cloves. Gather the fabric up and tie it tightly with white string. Store the seasoning bags in a closed canister. In winter, drop one or two into a potful of soup during the last half hour of simmering. Needless to say, a jar of one's own superb soup-herbs makes a wonderful gift and gives the recipient a taste of the perennial bounty of homegrown herbs.

CHAPTER FOUR

SUMMER SEASONINGS

Annual and biennial kitchen herbs

Making temporary appearances in the garden are the movable herbs—the annuals and biennials. The culinary equivalent of marigolds and petunias, annual herbs accomplish a full cycle of growth from seed to seed, by way of leaf and flower, in one year. They can fill all kinds of odd spaces, between perennial herbs or even among flowers. Biennials grow leafy basal rosettes their first year from seed; they then overwinter, flower and produce seeds the following spring or summer. Often, both annuals and biennials are relegated to the vegetable garden, where the soil can be tilled or turned each fall after the plants have gone to seed or have been killed by frost.

Among the ranks of annuals and biennials are those judged hardy, half-hardy and tender. The first will withstand almost any amount of cold; dill and chervil seedlings, for instance, routinely make it through the winter unscathed. The second group withstands light frosts but succumbs to a hard freeze, while tender annuals such as basil wither at a hint of frost and even sulk during cool spells. Putting up with their varying tolerances is worthwhile, however, for the annuals and biennials provide some of the essential seasonings of summer.

ANISE

Pimpinella anisum

Fresh homegrown anise seed is far more potent than the stuff of the spice racks and worth the bit of work to grow it. An annual, anise grows best in moderately rich, well-drained loam in a warm, sunny spot. Sun is important to hasten the herb to seed production. Sow the seeds in the garden about the time

Typical annuals, lemon basil, LEFT, *and coriander,* RIGHT, *grow from seed to flower in a single season, yielding a fleeting harvest of delectable fare.*

tomato plants go in, and thin the seedlings to 8 inches apart. In short-season areas, starting seeds indoors, timed as for basil, ensures a crop. Use small peat pots to avoid disturbing the roots in planting out. As seeds begin to ripen in late summer, cut the stalks, tie a paper bag loosely over the seed heads, and hang the stalks upside down; in short order, the seeds will dry and drop. Save a few for next season's garden.

Anise seeds are a reputed digestive aid, hence their use in liqueurs such as anisette, pernod, ouzo and sambucca. Since alcohol extracts the medicinal properties better than water, the seeds may be steeped in brandy—two ounces to a pint—to make what one old-timer near here would call a tasty "tunick." This herbal drink can be embellished with the addition of pieces of angelica and sweet cicely stems, snippets of hyssop, a few common yarrow flowers and tiny bits of wormwood and rue to create a homemade brandy bitters reminiscent of one of those aromatic monastery liqueurs. Baked into bread, cakes and cookies or sautéed with scallops, anise seeds impart a delicate licorice scent and a hint of sweetness. In a trusty hand mill, my partner John grinds soft wheat kernels, anise seeds, sesame seeds and sunflower seeds into a fragrant flour that is mixed with oil and water to pie-dough consistency. Bits of dough are rolled into paper-thin wafers that are slapped right on the surface of the wood stove to "bake" into crisp unleavened crackers, a favourite breakfast with herbed butter or cream cheese.

BASIL

Ocimum spp

Fresh sweet basil is the very essence of summer, with an aromatic scent and flavour hinting of cloves. Dried bottled flakes can never match the fresh herb, but since basil is one of the best herbs to grow in pots, containers and window boxes,

anyone with even a tiny bit of space in the sun can easily grow a summer-long supply—and a few indoor winter plants besides.

I have learned one secret about growing good basil—patience. In seasons past, in haste to harvest the earliest plants, I have seeded a flat indoors in early April. In the pale spring light, growth was slow and slender; plants from a May sowing always caught up and outpaced the earlier seedlings. Now I wait and time basil as for melons, seeding it between May 1 and 10, setting plants in the garden three or four weeks later, with an ear to the long-range forecasts; basil not

only succumbs to the least whisper of frost but sits still during cool weather. Seeds can also be sown directly in the garden as soon as the soil is warm and the danger of frost has passed. (Ancient Greeks and Romans uttered curses when sowing basil to ensure its germination, hence the French *semer le basilic*, meaning to use abusive language.)

City gardeners can often find boxes of nicely started basil, or even full-grown plants of the tiny-leaved bush basil, at corner greengroceries in spring. Leafy basil grows especially lush in warm ground enriched with old

manure or compost, bone meal and a sprinkling of wood ashes if available.

One spring, in an effort to outwit voracious earwigs at ground level, I planted basil, summer savory, marjoram and parsley in a wooden half-barrel filled with nourishing soil. The results were so good—beautiful as well as useful—that several herb barrels have become permanent features of our landscape. If a sunny apartment balcony or a city patio were my lot of land, I would grow basil by the barrelful for summer pestos (page 85) with plenty left to freeze or dry for winter. The most delicious way to keep basil over winter is to blend batches of pesto and then squirrel away small jars or bags of the green, garlicky sauce in the freezer, to bring back the flavours of summer in frigid February.

The fantasy of actually picking cupfuls of basil for a February pesto is probably just that, unless indoor light conditions are nearly perfect. It is possible, however, to extend the fresh season for several months. Do not try to transfer summer's basil plants—picked over, seedy and insect-chewed—from the garden to the house (unless you have extra fine specimens already growing in containers). What you want are vigorous young plants, and a second seeding is the way to go. Sometime during early August, sow a dozen seeds of large-leaved basil in a 10-inch pot of good soil, and water well. In summer's heat, the seeds are up and away within a week, growing rapidly. In several weeks, thin the plants to five, evenly spaced around the pot. By mid-September, but before the first frost, bring the basil pot into the very sunniest spot indoors. Harvest the leaves as needed without stripping the plants. Some sort of artificial lighting—fluorescent is best—will bring basil through the dark days of December and into the new year.

Gardeners searching for basil seed may be confused by the choices; one company lists 15 different kinds. For insatiable "curious seekers after outlandish things"—an old but apt description of gardeners—there are basils smelling of anise, cinnamon, camphor and, best of all, lemon. Lemon basil (*Ocimum americanum*), a slender herb sharply scented of citrus, is one I like to have in the garden or basil-barrel just for smelling. But it is also fine for salads, fish sauces and herb teas; perhaps lemon pesto? Bush basil or 'Picollo,' dwarf-to-medium-sized strains, are the ones for smaller pots, window boxes in sun or trim little hedges for flowerbeds. One friend insists that only bush basil (*O. basilicum minimum*) makes proper pesto. My grandmother still grows a tall crinkled *basilico*, probably the "lettuce-leaf" type, from seed she has saved from her crop for many years; a leaf or two seasons each jar of home-canned *pomodoros*, and dried basil and oregano adorn her thick-crusted pizzas. Others, no doubt hoping to have their ornamentals and eat them too, grow 'Dark Opal' basil, a cultivar with dull wine-coloured leaves and (they say) showy spikes of pink flowers. I have never found this plant very pretty, perhaps because its growth is not enthusiastic in our garden, nor is it as tasty as the green basils. For most purposes,

"The very essence of summer" is fresh sweet basil, which can be purchased in a gratifying range of shapes and colours, including lettuce-leaf and opal basil, LEFT.

including container growing, just plain sweet basil, large-leaved and prolific, will do nicely.

"The most sacred plant in all of India" is *Ocimum sanctum*, holy basil or *tulasi*. Consecrated to the Hindu gods Vishnu and Krishna, this herb grows by almost every Indian temple and dwelling as a protective talisman. Hindu dead are washed with basil-water and carry a leaf of basil with them on their afterlife journey through the corridors of transmigration.

CARAWAY
Carum carvi

Like parsley, caraway is a hardy biennial that grows a leafy rosette the first season and then runs to flower and seeds the next. As much as I appreciate its delicious seeds, however, I am always tempted to banish caraway from the garden entirely. Every last seed left unharvested falls, sprouts and grows into a well-anchored rosette of carrotlike foliage and produces yet another crop of seeds. "Weed," I say, extracting the interlopers from among the vegetables, herbs and flowers. A friend grows caraway in a segregated, shaded spot behind a hen house where it fights (like any weed) with encroaching grass and nightshade. "Thrives on competition," says she.

The only trick to growing caraway is getting it started in the first place. Typical of umbelliferous plants, which include dill, carrots, parsley, sweet cicely and many others, caraway produces seed that is viable for a short time only; by spring, it may not sprout if it has been badly stored over winter. Putting seeds in the freezer for a few days before sowing may wake them up. The hardy seeds are then sown at the same time as spring lettuce and radishes. Three or four plants will be enough. To harvest, cut the heads when the first seeds turn brown; hang the stalks upside down over newspaper or a dish pan, or enclose the seed heads in a paper bag; any seeds that do not fall are easily rubbed off by hand. Be sure the seeds are thoroughly dry before storing them away in jars. Leave one or two unharvested seed heads in the garden to perpetuate the crop – if you dare.

I like to use caraway in split pea or lentil soups, in creamed cabbage or ground with wheat kernels into the flour for homemade crackers, but new to me is caraway soup. "The queen of pot herbs to all Norwegians is Karvekal, caraway," wrote Sigrid Undset in an informative article in the 1945 *Herbarist*, journal of the Herb Society of America, "and in Norway, it is the commonest weed – first thing to sprout from last year's withered grass." Here too. She went on to describe harvesting "some 2 inches of the fleshy taproot with the rosette of leaves – a lovely way to spend some hours of a sunny May morning." The brown skin is scraped from the roots, and the plants are carefully rinsed, then finely chopped and tossed into hot broth that is kept just under the boiling point, but not boiling, for five minutes. The soup is thickened with anything that is on hand, such as leftover meats or cubes of fried bread, and ladled over a poached egg in each bowl. "We may have Karvekal soup every day as long as the plant is in season until early June, when the leaves grow coarse," Undset concluded. Nice how a recipe like that can turn a chore of weeding into a spring harvest.

CHERVIL
Anthriscus cerefolium

To have a supply of chervil in the kitchen, one needs to grow the herb oneself; it is so perishable that it never appears in markets. Once established, however, the pretty annual sows its hardy seeds and reappears in the garden every season. Chervil will not transplant. To start a first patch in May, simply scratch the long, shiny black seeds shallowly into rich soil in, if possible, a partly shaded spot. Keep the ground moist until the

Caraway seeds, ABOVE, *and roots,* BELOW, *impart the distinctive flavour popular in North American rye breads and in Norwegian caraway, or Karvekal, soup.*

Decorative but fiery, small versions of chili peppers, BELOW, *will survive several years in indoor pots. Most chilies, however, are grown as outdoor annuals in the north.*

Summer savory, ABOVE, *is generally regarded as having more flavour than its winter counterpart and is best appreciated as a complement to all types of beans.*

seeds sprout, thin the seedlings to 6 inches apart, and harvest the outside leaves, always leaving the central crown intact to keep growing. Lacy umbels of pinkish white flowers—"like exquisite bits of enamel work," says one observant writer—are followed by seed in midsummer. Allowing chervil to seed itself saves the gardener the work.

"The leaves put into a sallet give a marvellous relish to the rest," said John Parkinson in his 1629 "speaking garden," *Paradisi in Sole*. Later, in the 1699 *Acetaria*, John Evelyn added his assent: "The tender tips of chervil should never be wanting in our sallets, being exceedingly wholesome and cheering of the spirits." Indeed, the herb's name comes from the Latin *chaerephylum*, "a joy-giving leaf"; chervil equals "cheerful."

I like plenty of minced cheer with chives and a bit of lovage in new-potato salad (warm) or green salads or with parsley in tabouleh. Chervil is the right herbal complement to gentle soups such as cream of carrot or purée of fresh green pea. Tasting mildly of anise, tender leaves of chervil are combined with fresh parsley, chives and tarragon to create the classic French fines herbes that make such a splendid omelette. Or its flavour may be featured in a cream soup on its own, a quantity of minced leaves being stirred in during the last few minutes of simmering. That, in fact, is about all the cooking this subtly flavoured herb will stand. Chervil makes a delicate herb butter or flavours cream or cottage cheese alone or with chives or dill; leave out the tarragon here, or you will overwhelm the chervil flavour.

Dill weed, ABOVE, *is a summer treat seldom available in markets. It is best served when fresh. Chili peppers,* RIGHT, *dry easily, retaining enough fire to warm winter foods.*

CHILI PEPPERS

Capsicum spp

I am a fan of hot herbs. I like the breathtaking rush of heat from jade-green horseradish sauce with sushi; I like hot herbed mustards and tear-producing curries. Seldom have I bitten into anything my taste buds found too hot to handle. For day-to-day fire, my favourite herb is cayenne pepper, which I sprinkle on anything from eggs to fruit—a taste acquired during a visit to Mexico where *salsa* Tabasco spices *huevos rancheros* (fried eggs) and street vendors smear slices of pineapple and papaya with a lemon dipped in ground chili and salt. More traditional uses for chili pepper are in chili con (or *sin*—without) carne (meat), tomato juice, homemade barbecue and chili sauces, relishes and chutneys, summer ratatouilles, spaghetti sauces and many other dishes, from potato salad, hot or cold, to quiche to macaroni and cheese.

Those who grow their own know that not all varieties of hot peppers are created equal—degrees of heat range from pleasant to blistering. I recall the first season we grew hot peppers. One afternoon, I brought to the table the first red-ripe fruit of what promised to be a bumper crop of the cultivar called 'Ring of Fire.' During lunch, I took a big bite out of the little pepper and went into an immediate fit of gasping and tears. Water—I had the presence of mind to remember—does not extinguish this kind of fire; bread or another starchy food helps absorb the oils responsible for the heat. Thereafter, I treated the little devils with cautious respect. The seed catalogues had not been

A pepper frame is a bottomless glass box made by fastening four storm windows together at their edges with nails or wood screws. Pairs need not be the same length as long as their vertical dimensions are all equal. Four identical windows make a square frame, two matching pairs a rectangle. A vertical dimension of 2½ to 3 feet is best. A cover, important to hold heat, is either a single large storm window or several smaller ones. If nothing on hand provides a tight fit, a lid is easily made by covering 1-by-2-inch lumber with heavy, clear polyethylene. A more permanent frame cover is made by fastening a sheet of rigid, clear acrylic to the wood. Both of these lids must be hooked down, or they will fly away with the wind. We leave the pepper frame out over the winter, only storing the lid under cover. In the garden, orient a rectangular frame so that one of the long sides faces as close to south as possible.

Like any cold frame, this oddly shaped one warms both soil and air, buffers chilling breezes and creates a microclimate of tropical humidity, making a world of difference to a pepper crop in the north. With this protection and extra warmth, the plants grow waist-high and set plenty of fruit, most of which ripens red from mid-August through September.

Long and thin, as a rule, most hot peppers dry easily. The bulk of my first crop of 'Ring of Fire' was skewered with a darning needle, threaded onto fishing line and hung for several weeks above the wood stove—one answer to the sun-drenched adobe roofs and walls of Arizona and Mexico. I add dried chilies whole to simmering chili or tomato sauce and fish them out before serving. Ground in a hand mill, they are sprinkled over pasta dishes, pizza, bean-vegetable stews, lentil soup and the like. With garlic, onions, ginger and soya sauce, bits of hot pepper (fresh or dried) also give tofu some spark.

Jethro Kloss, in his classic (if a little cranky) 1939 book on herbal medicines, *Back to Eden*, devoted a full 14 pages to

indulging in the usual hyperbole when they had described 'Ring of Fire,' a "short, smooth, pencil-thin cayenne type," as "very hot." The next summer, 'Ring of Fire' gave way to 'Crimson Hot' on the seed list. This productive sort has just a hint of heat and pleasantly warms any dish calling for green or red peppers.

Most nurseries sell sweet pepper plants in May, but not all have chilies or cayenne; starting plants from seed—easy in any warm, bright indoor spot—opens the door to garden-grown fire. Hot peppers grow just like sweet ones, except that they produce more prolific crops of smaller fruit on somewhat larger plants. Some, the ornamental peppers, produce tiny scorching chilies on plants small enough to spend all

year in 6-inch pots of fertile soil on a window ledge. Others, large perennial shrubs in their warm and native lands, can be disappointing as garden annuals in short-season areas, especially if a gardener is after ripe fruit—I have about as much interest in green peppers as I have in green tomatoes—precious little.

After seasons of setting out house-grown seedlings in early June, only to watch them sit still until July and seldom ripen fruit, my partner devised a simple heat-holding pepper frame. Basically a mini-greenhouse made of storm windows, the frame holds nine plants for their entire garden life—late May until long after the first frost, at least a month longer than in the open garden.

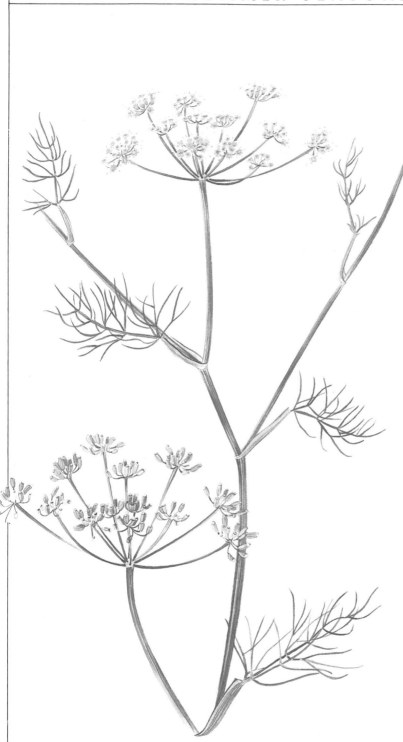

One of several related plants that have a delicate licorice flavour, fennel can be used in its entirety—leaves, stems, flowers and seeds—in salads, with cooked vegetables or chicken or in a delicious tea.

Capsicum—from the Greek *kapto*, I bite. Calling it "one of the most wonderful herb medicines we have," Kloss praised cayenne's curative properties for external wounds—"smarts a little" but is "very healing instead of irritating"—stomach ulcers, chills, coughs, colds and congestion, cramps and stomach pains, cold feet—"a little capsicum sprinkled in the shoes will greatly assist"—and hangovers. Virtually every other treatise on plant medicines echoes Kloss's enthusiasm. "There are many languid people," says one, "who need something to make the fires of life burn more brightly. Capsicum . . . is the thing to do it."

CORIANDER

Coriandrum sativum

As Mexican and Peruvian restaurants open their doors and family cooks try their hand at Latin American cooking in all its simple goodness, many northerners are tasting cilantro, the essential coriander, for the first time. On the tables of every Mexican eatery are small ceramic saucers—one of coarse salt, one holding wedges of green-skinned *limóns*, one of *salsa picante* and a fourth of chopped onions and cilantro. No taco—traditionally a soft tortilla rolled around bits of beef or chicken, cheese or refried beans—is complete without a sprinkling of coriander and onions and a splash of *salsa*. At home, I have come to relish the taste of fresh coriander leaves in a version of refried beans made with kidney beans or tucked into a grilled cheese sandwich, which, come to think of it, is just a variation on a *taco de queso*.

If the leaves are traditional in Latin cooking, Egyptian cooks use the seed to flavour bread and soup; as early as 75 A.D., Roman botanist Pliny the Elder wrote that the best coriander came from Egypt. In India, coriander seeds go into curry powders; and in Russia and Scandinavia, into liqueurs. But not everyone who tries the herb likes it; coriander, like garlic, seems to provoke either a rave or a definite thumbs-down. The name is derived from *koros*, Greek for bedbug, "in reference to the foetid smell of the leaves," wrote Mrs. Grieve in *A Modern Herbal*. Having never sniffed a bedbug, I can only say that to my nose, the scent of coriander is a little like french fries or the smell that hangs in the air of a greasy spoon restaurant, but hardly "foetid."

As a garden plant, coriander presents no difficulty. Bugs turn up their noses at it and move to the cabbages. Seeds sown in mid-May sprout with encouraging speed and grow to usable size quickly, too quickly for those intent on an extended harvest of leaves. Soon, lacy white flowers appear, and the plant suddenly goes to seed. A native of lands where day length remains fairly constant all year, coriander's internal clock is thrown off by the waxing, then waning summer sunlight of the north; hence its rush to mature its seeds. For a longer harvest of leaves, sow the seeds in succession every three weeks, like radishes or leaf lettuce. Giving plants 8 inches of space all around will delay flowering a little; good garden soil also helps produce lusher leaf growth. In this garden, coriander seeds itself from the previous season's crop to provide an early harvest.

CUMIN
Cuminum cyminum

Like coriander, cumin seed, the fruit of *Cuminum cyminum*, gives a distinctive flavour to Latin, Indian and Middle Eastern cuisine. Ground cumin is a large part of curry powder. The garden culture of cumin seed is like that of anise seed, with the important note that cumin, a native of the hot Middle East, must have four warm months for a crop of seeds to mature. Start it indoors in peat pots or other small containers about a month before the last frost date. Then set the plants out a month later,

making sure to place them in good soil, in sun, and to keep the delicate herb weed-free.

DILL
Anethum graveolens

There is never enough dill. Some gardeners will likely disagree as a tide of green and yellow sweeps over the garden, but even though dill sows its hardy seed everywhere – the feathery seedlings spring up under our young plum tree and through the phlox – the plants insist on running right back to seed in short order, producing only a few sparse leaves. And it is the leaves I want. Others may prize the flowers and seed heads for pickles, but the cool, aromatic dill foliage, often called dill weed, is among my favourite fresh herbs.

For its own perverse reasons, dill is always better if left to find its own way around the garden. Year after year, we seed a careful patch, usually the improved tetraploid 'Aroma,' in hopes of having a dense harvest of dill weed in one spot. But each year, half-wild dill appears in outlying corners of the garden, while the planted seeds, for all their extra chromosomes, often come to nothing. My suspicion is that, like angelica and sweet cicely (and other related members of the family Umbelliferae), dill grows best from just-ripened seeds sown in late summer. This, of course, is the pattern the herb follows on its own, but seed purchased in spring may have lost some of its spark over winter. While I appreciate the free harvest, the season is too short.

One gardener told me that in the Ukraine, the appearance of dill seedlings signals the arrival of spring, like the first robin here. The tiny leaves are harvested eagerly, along with young blades of chives, then the two are sautéed in sweet butter for a sauce "to pour over everything." My own taste buds imagine pasta, potatoes, baked trout and especially asparagus. I use finely chopped dill weed in

tossed salads and coleslaw; with lovage and Spanish onions for potato salads dressed with yogurt; with parsley over buttered new potatoes; blended with lemon thyme and chives in cream cheese to spread on homemade crackers; in any recipe for stuffed, baked fish; or tossed by the handful in traditional Greek *tzadziki*, a summer salad of cucumber, yogurt, pressed garlic, olive oil, lemon juice, salt, pepper and a pinch of cayenne, the whole left to marry until it is redolent of garlic and green with dill.

FENNEL
Foeniculum vulgare

Among the licorice-sweet herbs, there are two kinds of fennel. One is Florence fennel, or *finocchio*, an aromatic vegetable as tricky to grow as celery, given its need for extra-rich earth and constant water. A selection of the common fennel, it is not unlike a fat celery in appearance, with wide-ribbed leaf stalks overlapping to form a bulbous base. This "bulb" is the edible part but must be harvested before it is overly large and stringy. Throughout Italy, where it is almost a staple vegetable, small mountains of *finocchio* are sold in market squares. The taste of fennel is less appreciated in North America – but tastes change.

Boiled fennel is bland and soggy, but chunks baked with a creamy chicken casserole make a tasty vegetable accompaniment that pervades the dish with a mild flavour of anise. Slivers of fennel stir-fried with onions, garlic and any other fresh vegetables, but especially red peppers and broccoli, make one version of *pasta primavera*. Some may prefer Florence fennel raw, sliced thinly with apple, celery and grated carrot as a salad or served with other crudités to be dipped in any number of herbal sauces.

Looking much like dill or a skinny, elongated version of Florence fennel, the common sweet fennel (*Foeniculum vulgare dulce*) that is a perennial in milder climates is grown as an annual in northern gardens. Thread-fine leaves are minced into salads and butter sauces for steamed carrots or bland summer squash. Fennel and fish are often paired, either using fresh leaves to stuff fish before baking or adding leaves and stalks to the water for poached fish. According to the starstruck Nicholas Culpeper, a 17th-century herbalist and astrologer, fennel suits fish "because it is a herb of Mercury, and under Virgo, and therefore bears antipathy to Pisces and consumes the phlegmatic humour which fish plentifully affords."

The seeds, whole or crushed, are used in a similar fashion to anise; a relative of mine adds a teaspoon of fennel seeds to a kettle of homemade spaghetti sauce with the usual basil and oregano. I put all parts of sweet fennel — leaves, stalks, flowers and seeds — into the teapot with lemon balm and spearmint for a good-tasting herbal brew that is meant to calm nerves and aid digestion. Fennel tea, according to one herbal, "stayeth the hiccup and taketh away wind, nausea or an inclination to sickness."

Once, in an English garden, I saw a beautiful, tall fennel with feathery foliage tinted shades of Indian red and green decorating the centre of a herb bed; a fine contrast to the wheel-like umbels of yellow bloom. The gardener parted with a handful of seed, and this colourful fennel has proved hardier than the green kind in our cold garden. So far, it has returned for three seasons and has begun to seed itself in a modest way. If seeds of 'bronze fennel' ever appear in a catalogue, they are worth a try for a herb that is both useful and decorative.

Incidentally, if you see an impressive caterpillar — tiger-striped green, cream and black with some orange spots — on any of the Umbelliferae, including fennel, please let it be. The so-called parsley worm is the larval stage of the swallowtail butterfly, a species that is becoming scarce. It is worth taking the time to plant a patch of dill, anise, carrots, fennel or the like just to encourage butterflies to visit.

LEAF CELERY

Apium graveolens secalinum

Real celery is notoriously difficult to grow in the average garden, needing rich, moist soil and just the right temperatures. But for flavouring purposes, the easier leaf celery, grown like parsley, is a fine substitute. It gives celery flavour to potato, egg, salmon or other salads and can be featured in a green creamy celery soup or any other soup. Since leaf celery is full of mineral salts and natural sodium, it is a good seasoning for salt-reduced diets.

Fresh herbs are an easy — maybe the only — way to make canned soups more lively. That old standby, cream of mushroom, is much better for a generous handful of minced leaf celery tossed in during cooking. Dill and lemon thyme are for canned tomato soup; parsley for vegetable or chicken noodle; caraway seeds and thyme or savory for split pea . . . and so on.

MARJORAM

Origanum majorana

Although closely related to oregano, marjoram is definitely tender and very different in scent and flavour. This is a herb I like to smell but not taste. The fragrance is piny and sweet — I don't get the "blend of mint and nutmeg" that one writer suggests — a little too perfumy for foods, I thought, even before I learned that it has been used in French soaps and pomanders. In the past, marjoram was an ingredient "in all odoriferous waters and powders that are for beauty and delight," wrote one herbalist. Altogether, it is more of a cosmetic than a culinary herb.

But the German *Wurstkraut* says that marjoram is the sausage herb, and according to Ontario herb grower Waltrout Richter, "It is a must in German potato soup." Italians use marjoram in sweet spinach fritters and in a stuffing for chicken. Tea made from marjoram, mint and lemon balm is a pleasant way to avail oneself of the reputed antiseptic power of the herb.

A Mediterranean native, marjoram grows from April- or May-sown seeds that sprout in 10 days or so in a warm place. Set the seedlings (or nursery plants) in a sheltered, sunny part of the garden about the time tomatoes go out. A small 8-to-10-inch sprawler, marjoram

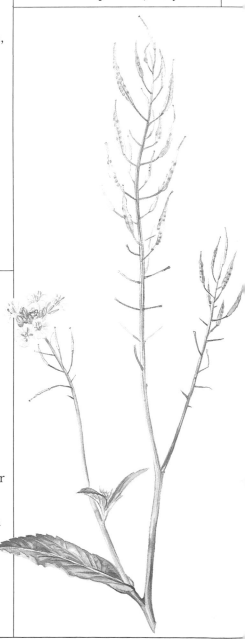

rambles over the edge of a half-barrel herb garden or raised bed. As an indoor winter herb, it is better than most if transferred to and 8- or 10-inch-diameter pot of light loam before frosts; grown in the sunniest window and snipped occasionally for use. It is a sweet little houseplant that may even go on for several seasons; in mild climates, sweet marjoram is a perennial.

MUSTARD

Brassica spp

A neighbour tells a story of how the weed inspector, on the lookout for noxious thistles, campion and pigweed, visited her carefully tended suburban garden on the edge of prime farmland. "Everything's fine," he said after a tour, "but you'll want to get rid of that mustard."

"Get rid of it?" she countered, a little indignantly. "I planted it."

In an attempt to set down a herbal "who's who," one writer suggested that "quasi-vegetables, herbal weeds and medicinal what-nots are not herbs and never will be; clumsy food plants, curlicue salad messes and roots belong in the kitchen garden and not with the herbs." Roquette, watercress and mustard, a trio of "quasi-vegetables" and "curlicue salad messes" if ever there was one, can nevertheless be considered herbs because they are far too hot to be primary "salletings." Like any herb, they are added to salads for their special flavours.

Quick-growing, cold-resistant mustard is always the first seed I sow in spring and among the last to go in the fall. A cold frame seeded with mustard as soon as the snow subsides is usually filled with peppery greens by daffodil time; a late-August sowing yields an October harvest. Cultivars include 'Green Wave' and 'Florida Broadleaf.' Plant seeds several inches apart, in shallow furrows 8 inches apart; thin seedlings to 6-to-8-inch intervals, using the thinnings for salads. Harvest leaves as long as they are tender and not overly hot, but when the plants begin to send up seed

The seeds of cultivated mustard, LEFT, *display the herb's close kinship with its wild forebears, but the leaves of cultivars such as 'Green Wave,'* BELOW, *have been bred for size and tenderness. Also valued for its pungent leaves is a massed planting of summer savory,* RIGHT.

stalks, pull them to make room for another crop. At its best during cool, moist weather and the shorter days of spring and fall, mustard grows tough, hot and seedy (not to mention flea-bitten) in summer.

The leaves, flowers and seeds of this radish relative are all edible, but it is primarily the greens a gardener wants, to spark up spinach and lettuce salads or stir-fried vegetables; the small broccoli-like buds are used like the leaves, while sprays of yellow flowers are as decorative and edible as blue borage stars or fiery nasturtium flowers. Seeds, of course, make the ubiquitous yellow condiment slathered by the ton on hot dogs and hamburgers. But recently, mustard has moved from the realm of fast foods and picnics into the fickle world of food fashion. Silver-spoon eateries feature mustard sauces with meat, poultry and game, and gourmet-store shelves are lined with jars and fancy pots of mustard, smooth or grainy, wine-soaked or honey-sweet, hot as Hades or gently piquant and, best of all, flecked and flavoured with different herbs.

JOHN'S OWN HERB & HONEY MUSTARD

2 cups ground mustard seed (purchased as a flour-like powder from gourmet or health food stores)
1 tsp. salt
1 tsp. turmeric
2 cups apple cider vinegar
⅓ cup water
¼ cup honey
3 Tbsp. each of minced chives, parsley, lovage (more or less to taste)
1 tsp. each of minced tarragon, lemon thyme, savory (more or less to taste)

Combine mustard powder, salt and turmeric in a stainless steel, glass or enamel saucepan. Slowly add the vinegar and water, stirring all the while to make a smooth mixture. Add the honey and herbs. Bring the mixture to a boil, stirring to prevent scorching. Simmer very gently for 10 minutes, stirring constantly. (The vapours from heated mustard can be irritating. Open the kitchen window, and keep your face away from the rising steam.) Pour the hot mustard into sterilized half-pint jars and seal. Let sit for several days before using. Makes three half-pints.

PARSLEY

Petroselinum spp

Intensely green, always vigorous, parsley looks every bit the nutritional powerhouse it is. It is a mistake to relegate this herb to the side of the plate as a garnish alone—eat it. According to Rodale's *Encyclopedia of Organic Gardening*, one tablespoon or a good-sized sprig supplies the daily minimum requirements of vitamins A and C. If I am feeling a bit enervated after a long day's gardening, I pick a few stalks of parsley, shake off the sand and graze on the tonic greens.

There are four types of parsley. Most common is the curly-leaved variety that shows up on the edge of a plate of fish and chips. Italian, or flat-leaved, parsley looks more like a small-leaved celery but has the same flavour as the curly type. In her admittedly "cantankerous and opinionated" book *Green Thoughts*, Eleanor Perenyi commented that "today, no food snob would consider using any but the flat-leaved parsley." She prefers, however, the tightly curled, jewel-green mossy sort— more my idea of what parsley should be—but Italian parsley is full of flavour and as easily grown. Some seasons it may bolt to seed in midsummer, especially if dry or crowded, while curled parsley is always biennial.

Hamburg parsley supplies flat leaves all summer and a storage crop of white roots, like skinny parsnips, that are just the thing to flavour any soup or stew. This delicious dual-purpose vegetable/herb ought to be more generally known and grown; it is especially suited to small or city

There are more types of parsley than those appearing regularly as restaurant garnishes, and one of the least familiar to North Americans is Hamburg parsley, LEFT, whose thick white roots flavour soups and whose leaves are as edible as those of any other parsley.

SAUCE PERSILLADE

Thicken a simple oil and lemon juice dressing with mashed, hard-boiled egg and plenty of minced parsley for a sauce to serve with cold meats, especially lamb; to season mild vegetables such as cauliflower or fresh lima or soy beans; or to spoon into soups.

"partly shaded situations." In our cool garden, it is fine in the sun. Mitsuba is the appropriate herb to stir-fry with vegetables and tofu, to float on miso soup or to season a sauce for Japanese soba (buckwheat) noodles. It can also substitute for other types of parsley in many dishes, but take into account its stronger taste. Every cook likes to have a plant of parsley on the windowsill over winter, but after the first harvest or two, a single plant provides slim pickings. A friend reports that mitsuba is far more prolific indoors if moved into an oversized pot of rich earth in October.

All parsley seed is notoriously slow to germinate, travelling, according to legend, to hell and back in the three-week process. Some gardeners suggest soaking the seed in water overnight; "but," notes one author, "you end up with a gelatinous mess that sticks to fingers and everything else and is impossible to sow properly." Freezing the seed briefly helps to break dormancy by signalling that "winter" is over. Another approach that results in an even stand of seedlings is to soak the seeded flat or furrow with a kettleful of boiling water. And then there is always patience: I generally seed a 4-inch-deep flat indoors around April 10 and leave it in the vicinity of the wood stove for the few weeks it takes the tiny green backs to show through. Then I grow the slow seedlings, thinned to several inches apart, in the sunniest window—they are less light-demanding, however, than tomatoes or peppers. In mid-May, parsley goes into our garden; light frosts leave it unharmed. A soaking with fish emulsion once or twice over the summer keeps the pest-free parsley lush.

"I haven't planted parsley in years," one gardener told me, "and the same plants keep coming back." The same patch, perhaps, but not the same plants. Biennial parsley stays green and usable late into the fall; the wise gardener leaves the parsley row undisturbed during the October cleanup. Often, the hardy plants survive the winter and resprout

gardens because it takes up little space—thin the seedlings to 6 inches apart—and is usable from leaf top to root tip, from midsummer until well into winter if stored or mulched in the garden. We keep a sharp eye on the fragile seedlings, a favourite food of earwigs; a whole row has disappeared in a night. Insecticidal soap kills the pests, but you must hit them

directly, and that means a foray into the garden after dark with a flashlight.

Japanese parsley, mitsuba (*Cryptotaenia japonica*), is an unfamiliar perennial herb that grows from seed to usable size the first season. Looking like an especially robust, large-leaved Italian parsley, aromatic mitsuba grows best in rich, moist ground and, says one herb grower, at spring's first encouragement. If left to flower and set seed, parsley perpetuates itself, but the original plant disappears after seeding. We use spring leaves from the previous year's plants until the current crop thickens up and so have an eight-month garden-fresh harvest.

There are many ways to carry the goodness of parsley to the table. The easiest is to mince a half cup or so and toss it into any and all mixed salads, coleslaws and potato salads. Tabouleh, a cold Lebanese salad that starts with cooked bulgar wheat, is green with parsley; egg or tuna salads can be well flecked, and simple white sauces are better for parsley, a little lovage and chervil. Stir sweet butter, minced parsley and chervil (or basil) into plain cooked rice, and season the mixture with plenty of freshly ground pepper and Parmesan cheese. A garnish of sweet red pepper and slivered almonds makes this easy dish festive. I sprinkle almost every soup generously with parsley just before serving.

ROQUETTE

Eruca vesicaria sativa

Also called rocket, rugola and arugula, roquette is a pretty herb whose lobed rosettes spread out over the spring-dark earth. An absurdly easy salad herb to grow, it is hardy even into the Far North. Seeds of this cabbage cousin are sown in October or November – small seedlings survive the winter – or first thing in spring. Within a month after a spring seeding, leaves are ready to pick. But note – roquette is a favourite forage for flea beetles, and leaves can become riddled and unusable in short order. For the earliest crop of undamaged leaves, I like to sow roquette in a cold frame (as for mustard) soon after the snow has gone – mid-April here. For an extended picking, take a few outside leaves from each plant before they grow coarse and bitter. Toss the leaves with other early salad fixings, or use roquette as a watercress substitute in stir-fried

dishes; add leaves to soup, or cream them like spinach. The harvest lasts until about mid-June, when roquette, along with spinach, mustard and other early greens, responds to the lengthening days by going to seed. If a few plants are left to flower and seed, half-wild roquette will spring up here and there in the garden for years to come—a bit of work saved, a free harvest. Not an essential seasoning herb, roquette is easy, early, hardy, quick and an unusual touch in spring salads.

SUMMER SAVORY

Satureja hortensis

This annual plant does not self-sow but grows quickly from spring-sown seed into wiry branching bushes (to 12 inches tall) covered in narrow, warmly aromatic leaves. I start the tiny seeds in small peat pots in early May to be sure of getting plants past infancy indoors and then set them out, 8 inches apart, when frosts are over. Some people believe that herbs thrive in poor ground. This may be true of the thymes and grey-leaved herbs native to stony, sun-baked slopes, but last season, I planted summer savory seedlings in a new garden bed prepared with one-third old manure, one-third peat moss and a generous helping of bone meal. The plants grew to great size, supplying fresh leaves all summer to toss with butter, garlic and lemon juice over green or yellow beans. Just as the flowers appeared, I pulled the leafy bushes to hang them to dry.

Besides its classic role, fresh with snap beans, dried summer savory is better (to my taste) than oregano or thyme in all of fall and winter's hearty cooking: vegetable and pea soups, lentil casseroles, chili, scalloped potatoes, tomato sauce, cheddar cheese sauce for vegetables, or with dried lovage in stews. The flavour is pungent and, well, savoury but never overpowering.

Among the most unusually scented culinary annuals are marjoram, FAR LEFT, whose sweet fragrance is suited to soaps and pomanders, and coriander, ABOVE, whose botanical name suggests that the plant smells like bedbugs.

FRESH CORIANDER OR MINT CHUTNEY

This condiment is served with Indian curries. Pick, wash and chop coarsely enough fresh coriander leaves (or mint—spearmint is best) to fill 2 cups when packed down. Blend ½-cup batches with ¼ cup of either lemon juice or good vinegar, adding just enough water to keep things running smoothly. When all of the herb has been puréed, add salt to taste (about 1 teaspoon), one or two chili peppers (stems and seeds removed), 2 tablespoons of grated, fresh ginger, and the same amount of chopped green onions. A little sweetener and/or grated coconut may be added.

CHAPTER FIVE

ON THYME

This plant, too, is of the essence

Last spring, a friend handed me a catalogue listing no fewer than 27 variations on the theme of thyme. No child in a candy store ever surveyed an inventory as eagerly: there were orange-balsam, lemon and lavender thyme; 'Moonlight' and 'Silver Needles' thyme; thymes flowering pink, crimson and white; others with leaves flecked with gold or splashed with silver. When it comes to thymes, I am an inveterate collector. If a new species appears in a nursery (rarely), I bring it home; if I spy an unfamiliar thyme in another garden, I am not too proud to beg. Fruity or medicinal, sweet or savoury, tall or short, thymes are friendly, lovely plants that fit well in any garden and add their distinctive flavours to all kinds of cooking.

Nor do these treasures gobble up garden space in the manner of mints or certain artemisias. At present, 21 species and varieties of *Thymus* grow in our garden.

Home for fully 10 of them is a narrow bed, 10 feet long and a foot and a half wide, raised with two rotting barn beams along a southwesterly foundation wall. But thymes need not be in a special herb garden – they easily spill over the limestone rocks that edge flowerbeds, creep between paving stones or carpet the ground around a garden bench. These accommodating plants are tiny, in scale with the smallest garden.

When it comes to knowing which thymes are which, the one note of agreement among botanists is that they are a hard lot to pin down. Even England's august Royal Horticultural Society, champion of botanical clarity, concedes that thymes are "notoriously difficult to classify and identify; and as specific limits are not well defined and local variants are numerous, accounts by botanists disagree widely."

Let the botanists puzzle. I never met a thyme I didn't like. There is something about thymes that seems to encourage contact. Visitors invariably stroke the mossy spreads of creeping thyme or the furred backs of woolly thyme. Few resist tousling the wiry shrublets of lemon thyme and silver cooking thyme or inhaling their scents, sweet or pungent.

For the gardener, it is enough to know if the thyme in question is good to eat – all thymes are edible, but some are quite delectable – and how it will grow, so the gardener will know where to put it. Thymes grow in one of three ways. Some hug the ground closely and send out little searching shoots that root as they go, to make pleasant pools of grey, green or gold – these are the creeping thymes. Others, lemon thyme for one, form small mounds of wiry, procumbent branches clothed with larger, shining green or variegated leaves. Several of these, the

Adventurous gardeners may find more than a score of thyme varieties, including the citrus-flavoured lemon thyme, RIGHT *and* BELOW, *and* Thymus doerfleri *'Bressingham Seedling,'* FACING PAGE, *a British selection.*

mound-makers, mimic the fragrance of lemon, lavender, camphor or oregano. A third group grows into small upright shrubs, 10 to 15 inches tall, that eventually develop a woody central trunk and side branches that rarely root unless given the hint of a hairpin holding them to the ground.

Whatever their size, thymes cannot cope with crowding – pressed by pushy neighbours, they either die or send some stringy runners into the light and air in an effort to survive. That new corner of herbs that looks so well ordered in May – everything in its place and given plenty of space – can grow rather tangled later on. By July, the thymes will be scrambling for their little lives to get out from under a shoving sage or toppling tarragon. If possible, give thymes a place of their own – a rock garden in full sun is just their notion of home – but take care, in any case, that neighbouring plants are in scale.

COOKING THYMES

Thymus vulgaris

These taller, shrubby thymes include the common cooking thyme (*Thymus vulgaris*) of spice racks and supermarket shelves. Usually the first of the tribe to find a place in a garden, cooking thyme grows easily from seed started indoors about a month before the last frost date; set out a month later, late May in our garden, the herb becomes a usable bushling by midsummer the first season. Good thing too, because this Mediterranean native, safe only in very well drained or gravelly ground, does not winter as well as other thymes. Even when given its choice of gritty soil, the small woody shrub, evergreen in its native land, does not take kindly to a four-month spell under soggy snow and has proved short-lived in our garden. Gardeners on the milder West Coast, however, will have little trouble keeping cooking thyme

flourishing all year long. Every season or two, we raise a few plants from seed or avail ourselves of started plants from a nursery.

A hardier, variegated sport of cooking thyme and one of the most decorative of all is silver thyme (*Thymus vulgaris argenteus*) with pale green leaves edged with white. In our garden, this low shrub comes back year after year in sandy soil along the edge of a raised iris bed. No doubt, the excellent drainage and the warm cushions of limestone upon which it rests keep the pretty silver thyme comfortable.

Rodale's *Encyclopedia of Organic Gardening* calls cooking thyme "the universal herb" and suggests its use with fish, poultry and meats, vegetables, egg dishes, soups, stuffings, cheese sauces and chowders. The small, arrow-shaped thyme leaves are pungent and peppery, not unlike but milder than oregano and winter savory. Sprigs tied together with parsley and bay leaf (and I would add lovage) form a classic bouquet garni to simmer in soup stock and stews. This herb dries easily, but the flavour becomes more pronounced as the moisture evaporates, leaving only the aromatic oils. I like to be lavish with fresh herbs all summer, but with dried herbs, it is easy to tip the balance from pleasant to overpowering.

LEMON THYME

Thymus × citrodorus

Lemon thyme is at its best only when fresh. The delicate bouquet of citrus and spice is lost through drying or anything more than the briefest cooking. Even though some people recoil from a whiff of eau de cologne mint, rue or even sage, almost everyone reacts with a surprised smile to the fruity fragrance of lemon thyme. Our garden grows three variants of this species: lemon thyme (*Thymus × citrodorus*) is upright and bushy, with

uniformly green leaves and a sprinkling of lavender flowers well into September; variegated lemon thyme (*T. × citrodorus* 'Aureus') is shorter, has leaves flecked along the edges with cream and is more prone to sprawl in a small way; and nicest of all is 'Doone Valley' thyme, shorter yet, with small, green leaves marbled with yellow, cream and red, especially in spring. Seeds will not produce lemon thyme, and I have even seen plants tagged with the name that gave no hint of the plant's notable citrus tang; so although several mail-order nurseries list this herb, it is best, if possible, to let the nose judge to be sure.

As useful in the kitchen as they are beautiful in the garden, lemon thymes are perfect small plants for a sunny spot among rocks, along the edge of a flowerbed or spilling over the sides of a raised bed or half-barrel high-rise herb garden. Once settled in the garden and sprawling nicely, lemon thyme is

complaints so far about a sauce of sautéed onions, garlic, ginger, minced lemon thyme, lemon juice and tamari, which, after fillets of whitefish are cooked in it, is thickened with arrowroot powder and poured over the fish.

CARAWAY THYME

Thymus herba-barona

Like the strange and wonderful scented geraniums that borrow for their own the fragrances of pine, rose, nutmeg, lemon, mint and other plants, many thymes have learned the tricks of mimicry. When crushed, the tiny, pointed leaves of *Thymus herba-barona* smell of caraway. The name is derived from the plant's traditional use in seasoning a baron of beef.

CREEPING THYMES

Green-leaved English thyme and its variegated sport silver thyme, ABOVE, *are beautiful plants whose foliage is accentuated when alternated as an edging,* LEFT.

easy to increase. Often, the plant does the preliminary work: side-shoots that touch the ground send out tentative roots, and these branches may be snipped off and planted elsewhere. To hasten this process, called layering, press any number of shoots against the ground with stones or, better, hairpins or small wire hoops. Earth tossed over the contact point of the layer is a help. When roots have formed, the new plants are ready. I have turned a single straggling plant into six thrifty new ones by layering the shortened branches around the plant's centre, like the spokes of a wheel.

Lemon thyme (and most others except the very flattest) grow more compactly and winter better if sheared back by at least half — but not to the woody framework — in mid-August, in time to allow the plant to make new growth during fall's cooler weeks. Sharp scissors are less cumbersome than garden shears for this work.

Like parsley, chives and chervil, fresh lemon thyme is a pleasantly mild herb that can safely season most foods. All summer and well into fall, we harvest lemon thyme for kitchen use. I encourage experimentation.

¶Sprinkle finely chopped lemon thyme and parsley over any soup — the full aroma of the herbs is released when they hit the hot broth. I can think of no better way to bring canned or powdered soups to life.

¶Stir minced lemon thyme and chives into cottage cheese, blend them with cream cheese, or toss with buttered boiled potatoes; chervil is a good third here.

¶Shake lemon thyme, tarragon and a snip of lovage with a crushed clove of garlic, cider vinegar, olive oil, a daub of homemade herbed mustard (see page 70) and a little salt and fresh pepper to dress summer's romaine and bibb lettuces.

¶Lemon thyme is a natural with baked fish or minced into the floury coating for fried fish; no

Five years ago, my partner John Scanlan and I built across the front of our house a raised porch of flat stones laid over several feet of well-tamped sand. A flight of low stone steps, also set in sand, leads up to the porch. When the work was done, John tucked a sprig of the lowest of the low creeping thymes in the steps. In short order, a stream of green was following the narrow gaps between the stones, and by June, the flat greenery had become a flowery patch of bright lilac humming with honeybees. Lovely — and the next spring, bits of green tracery appeared between the porch stones and spread out to soften the rock-hard lines; again in early July, green was lost under lilac. A perfect picture, this, and all the better because it happened on its own. Maintenance consists of now and then extracting the few weeds and grasses before they grow large enough to do any damage to the thyme mats.

Most of the creeping thymes in our garden have tiny, faintly scented foliage and expand slowly by means of delicate rooting runners. Although they prefer carpeting the ground to moving over stone — far easier to root in earth and take up nutrients — I have noticed that when I lift the leading edge of a mat of thyme off a rock, there is a rubbly substance, like the thinnest layer of damp compost made from the plant's own spent leaves and tiny twigs. This meagre ration is apparently all the plants need; those that carpet the porch are nourished somehow by sand and stone.

It is no wonder that creeping thyme, shepherd's thyme or hillwort (*Thymus serpyllum*, the French *serpolet*), is also dubbed mother-of-thyme. This nonculinary species has given rise to a whole tribe of trailers, most, it must be said, far better than their parent for the garden. Grown from seed, the original creeping thyme is a tallish, lax sprawler with round, glossy green leaves and a sprinkling of pale flowers. The scent is suggestive of turpentine but not unpleasant. Nice enough, but better are the flat-growing, mat-making, free-flowering varieties of creeping thyme that create cascades of green and grey over rocks, or little rugs of pink and white along the edges of a sunny path. Their names are legion and confused: *T. serpyllum* appears in some lists under the alias *T. praecox*, with or without a subspecies name *album* (white) or *coccineus* (crimson). Creeping thymes flower mauve, lilac or crimson, and we have a patch of a white-flowering variety, *T. serpyllum album*.

The grey-leaved woolly thyme (*Thymus pseudolanuginosus*), aptly christened "mousy thyme" by a neighbour, spills over a rock-edged bed or carpets the driest, sunniest ground. We had some trouble with this herb until we moved small clumps of it to a hot, sandy border that bakes in the afternoon sun. Here, it grows thick and springy. Ants and earwigs like to build their mazes under a woolly rug of thyme — they cannot be blamed, but they should be discouraged, or they will undermine the mats and kill the roots, with obvious consequences. Woolly thyme flowers very sparingly — just a twinkling of mauve here and there over a patch — but, as one writer observed, "its silvery soft foliage is somehow flowerlike in appearance."

Very hardy, enduring and pretty for contrast with the green and grey thymes is golden creeping thyme (*T. serpyllum* 'Aureus'), which is sometimes clipped into tiny hedges woven through with silver santolina and green germander in a knot garden or trained to spell something in a formal park bed. Clipping in spring and again in August keeps it tight and leafy, but otherwise, golden thyme is undemanding. Its green-gold mounds, to 5 inches tall, persist from spring until the snow flies, and through the winter in milder climates.

An easy garden picture includes a patch of golden thyme edging a few tufts of *Achillea*

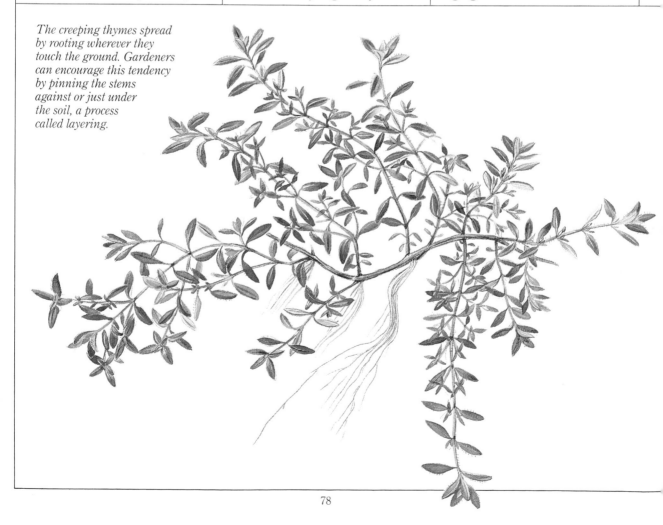

The creeping thymes spread by rooting wherever they touch the ground. Gardeners can encourage this tendency by pinning the stems against or just under the soil, a process called layering.

'Moonshine,' with clumps of creamy yellow and sky-blue bearded iris behind, contrasting grey, blue-green and golden foliage all season, a burst of late June bloom and yarrow flowers until fall.

We have a spread of creeping thyme in front of a garden bench that is a perennial pleasure, green for 12 months, a perfect setting for the tiny wild tulips that poke through in spring and wildly floriferous for three weeks each summer. Less work is a sunny slope planted with the stronger-growing mother-of-thyme, seeded for economy's sake, and the golden creeping thyme; these will create a dense cover but are still no match for stubborn grasses.

I have heard of thyme lawns and think they might work well if the soil is very well drained and absolutely free of perennial weeds—twitch grass, bindweed, horsetail and the like; the patch, not too large, is in full sun; flagstones, or something else to step on, are sunk level with the ground along the most travelled route; the thymes do not suffer the abuse of constant traffic, barbecuing, kids playing or dogs digging; a gardener is prepared to get down on hands and knees and weed.

Our treasure trove of thymes was enriched this summer with half a dozen new species from Tansy Farms in British Columbia (see Sources, page 166). Orange balsam thyme (*Thymus vulgaris* 'Fragrantissimus'), the "most fragrant" of the selections, smells sweet and tastes mildly of artemisia without the bitter tang. Moonlight thyme (*T. leucotrichus*), an upstanding small shrub 8 to 10 inches tall, densely clothed with narrow, silvery, sweet-scented leaves, looks at home on the sunny side of a small shoulder of limestone. There is also a low, green tuft labelled *T. doerfleri* 'Bressingham Seedling.' After seeing pictures of Bressingham, English horticulturist Allan Bloom's magnificent garden, I am willing to bet on anything so named. Intriguing and different from the others is a bit of silver tagged *T. nieceforii* 'Silver Needles,' with prostrate, woody branches just beginning to feel their way over the stony surface in front; imagine a spreading, silvery juniper gone Lilliputian, and you have a picture of 'Silver Needles' thyme.

These unproven thymes had a light covering of cedar or spruce boughs laid over them in late November and left in place until spring settled (at least mid-April in our garden) to keep them from being dried by chilly winds or sunburned after a long season sleeping under the snow.

And still there are thymes to explore, thymes for cooking, thymes for garden decoration. Few plants are as friendly or as easy, given their modest demands of full sun, sandy, gravelly or otherwise well-drained soil, light winter protection and the occasional cutting back. Theirs is the charm of fragrance, persistent green, grey or golden foliage, a gently spreading habit and tiny abundant flowers buzzing with bees in the summer sun.

Ingredients for a bouquet garni, ABOVE, *clockwise from top, include chervil, parsley, bay and thyme, but not all thymes are appropriate. June-flowering* Thymus serpyllum, RIGHT, *is better for pathways than it is for soup pots.*

CHAPTER SIX

SWEET AND FAIR

Alliums for flavour and colour

You plant an onion, you get an onion. Like most gardeners, my first experience with alliums was just that, pushing papery miniatures into the friable spring ground, planting sets of cooking onions (*Allium cepa*). Success with those onions sent me searching for seeds of chives and bulbs of shallots, begging a cluster of top-onions from a neighbour and, soon after, scouring bulb catalogues for ornamental alliums. A decade later, a score of different species, both edible and ornamental, grew in the garden – some in a border of perennial vegetables, many more in the flowerbeds, a few dwarfs in rocky places, and garlic in a vegetable garden bed of its own. And after all these years, there is a wide field of allium possibilities to explore.

The genus *Allium* is a vast and varied race of more than 300 species. In the wild, some species grow on high, grassy slopes from China to California; others spring up in stony, sunbaked meadows throughout the Middle East and southern Asia. Some hide away in the olive and citrus groves of the Mediterranean and others even cluster among maples and birches in the shaded woodlands of North America. Indeed, throughout the temperate regions of the northern hemisphere, alliums of one sort or another flourish. Among them are some of the best seasoning herbs: chives, shallots, garlic chives, garlic; some of spring's first edible greens – Welsh and Egyptian onions and wild leeks; and a handful of flowering onions, not strictly herbs but plants that enhance the ornamental or herb garden.

All alliums share a family resemblance in root, leaf, flower and, of course, scent – even some of the ornamentals exude a whiff of garlic if their leaves are crushed. All are hardy bulbous (or occasionally, rhizomatous) plants. Bulbs varying from pea-to apple-sized yield vertical, straplike leaves, which may be flat, triangular or hollow, grass-narrow or as broad as those of tulips. A sure sign of allium kinship is the sunburst flower head: radiating from a central point are many thread-like stems bearing star-shaped flowers, often several hundred packed onto a head, arranged in either a perfect sphere or a loose umbel. In some species, small bulblets appear amid the flowers; in others, flowers give way entirely to a cluster of top bulbs. Rosy purple is the predominant flower colour, but allium blooms are also white, crimson, greyish lavender, sky-blue and lemon-yellow.

All onions are partial to a light-textured, organically enriched soil of moderate fertility, warm and well drained. As a rule, they thrive in full sun, but I have dug the bulbs of wild leeks from the dense clay of a nearby woods, and pretty *Allium moly*, the golden garlic, shines in light

The ornamental and edible alliums such as garlic, LEFT, *are most easily grown from bulbs or rhizomes, but many onions produce flowers that in turn yield clusters of seeds,* RIGHT, *which can also be used to produce new plants.*

Garlic chives, BELOW, *and chives,* RIGHT, *are among the most popular herb-garden residents, and rightly so. They are easy to grow from seed or bulb and can be used in any dish that would benefit from a mild onion or garlic flavour.*

shade. Alliums are easily grown and give returns in flavour or flowers far exceeding their modest demands.

CHIVES

Allium schoenoprasum

Best known and most often grown of the seasoning alliums are chives, anyone's herb in perpetuity for the mere sowing of a few seeds in a sunny, fertile place. Better, however, to start seeds in spring in a small pot of good loam and wait until the stripling onions have grown a bit in height and girth before setting them in nourishing loam outdoors. The six fat clumps in our garden are descendants of skinny seedlings started 12 years ago and 200 miles away – they are among the more portable of plants. Alternatively, buy nursery-grown plants, or divide an outside bit of an established garden clump, pulling away five or six of the thin, tightly packed bulbs again in spring.

Once in the garden, the indestructible chives, "a good sawce and pot-herb," as early English herbalist John Gerard wrote, will be in constant demand for flavouring any dish improved by a mild tang of onion. "In the Ukraine," Guelph, Ontario, gardener Mary-Ann Robinson told me, "the appearance of dill seedlings and the first shoots of chives signals spring – just like the first robin here; we sauté minced dill and chives in butter very briefly, and pour the sauce over everything." I envisage the sauce on pasta, asparagus, boiled potatoes and baked fish. Along with chervil, parsley and tarragon, chives are a fourth constituent of the classic French fines herbes so good for omelettes. Snip small bundles of chives to flavour cream or cottage cheese, salad dressings (especially yogurt-based), green or grain salads, herbed butter, hot or cold soups or eggs or potatoes in any guise.

Spiky-leaved mauve-flowering chives are also pretty enough to edge a bed of flowers or decorate a rock garden.

Always, there is a drone of honeybees and a flutter of butterflies around the nectar-rich flowers. Pink vinegar tasting mildly of onions is easily made by steeping a handful of chive blossoms in a quart of white vinegar, with a sprig of tarragon or lovage for extra flavour. We give the chives a close shearing each year after flowering is past to encourage a new crop of tender leaves.

Chives freeze well, dry poorly; but since this is the earliest herb to rise in spring and one of the last to retire in fall, we enjoy the extended fresh-from-the-garden season. But chives are better candidates than most herbs for the winter windowsill garden, as long as their need for a dormant spell is met. Sometime in late August or early September, pot up (in 6-to-12-inch pots) small divisions from a garden clump – you will need to trim the roots in the process. Set the pots in a cold frame or cool place protected from freezing and thawing until early in the new year. Then, bring the pots indoors to the very sunniest window, or place them close to grow lights, and fresh greens will soon sprout.

GARLIC CHIVES

Allium tuberosum

Most decorative of the flavouring alliums are garlic chives. All through late August and September, loose umbels of fragrant white stars bloom on foot-high stems above flat, narrow, arching foliage. In a bed of perennial flowers and herbs, garlic chives are well placed in front of clumps of *Sedum spectabile*, the showy stonecrop known hereabouts as Liveforever or Frog's Bellies. The two bloom simultaneously, and both the allium flowers and the sedum's flat heads of reddish blooms encourage congregations of butterflies.

I use the minced leaves of garlic chives in the same ways as chives, only taking into account their mild garlic flavour. In

Chinese markets, I have seen small bundles of the herb alongside Chinese parsley (coriander) and watercress sold for stir-fried dishes; in some nurseries, *Allium tuberosum* is sold as Oriental garlic chives.

This hardy perennial is easy to grow from seed – too easy, in fact. I snip off the faded flower heads to avoid forever rooting out stripling garlics. Divisions taken from established clumps in spring soon settle in the garden, and the plant is content in ordinary garden soil, in sun or light shade – all in all, an essential garden or container plant for both flavour and flowers.

WELSH ONIONS

Allium fistulosum

A well-travelled onion, this species moved west from Siberia, was dubbed the *welsch* (or foreign) onion in Germany and eventually entered England as the inappropriately named Welsh onion. *Allium fistulosum*, easily grown from seeds sown in the same way as chives, provides tender foliage and narrow underground bulbs for early spring seasoning. Our slowly expanding clump has been in place for seven years in a perennial border that also grows horseradish, rhubarb and a few clumps of Jerusalem artichokes. Its grey-white flower heads, the size of tennis balls, dry easily for winter bouquets if hung in an airy, shaded place.

WILD LEEKS

Allium tricoccum

This North American woodlander, described by Roger Tory Peterson in his guide to wild edibles as "our best wild onion," is to my taste the strongest of onions, wild or tame. Known also as ramps, wild leeks have ramped in profusion through our local woods and, says Peterson, throughout southern Canada and the northeastern United States. Early in spring, as hepaticas fade and trilliums blossom, the broad, deep green leek leaves emerge by the thousands from slender scallionlike bulbs. I have learned to take a sharp trowel along to pry the tenacious plants from the soil in the dense woods.

After the blandness of stored potatoes and shrivelling rutabagas, I welcome May's robust salads: frankly bitter, intensely green, a tonic mixture of dandelions, violet leaves, young asparagus, snippets of lovage, chives and sweet cicely, with perhaps the first cold-frame-grown greens and radishes, and always wild leeks. To prepare this best of wild foods, wash soil from the leeks, peel off a layer or two of skin, pare off the roots, trim the leaves a bit, and wash again. Then simmer in water until tender, drain well, and toss with butter and salt for a simple side dish. Even better is a pungent cream of wild leek soup that I like to flavour with the first fresh lovage. Pickled leeks (the bulbs only) are for those who like their food to bite back.

EGYPTIAN ONIONS

Allium cepa viviparum

"A vegetable triffid," one visitor called our Egyptian onions, and indeed, the gangling plants, also dubbed walking onions or top-onions, do seem ready to take giant steps across the garden. No other plant proliferates in quite the same way. From the crown, fat stalks arise, hoisting not a head of flowers but a cluster of small bulbs, some of which also grow green shoots topped with yet another storey of bulblets. When the whole is too top-heavy to stand, down tumbles the stalk, top-onions and all. In short order, the fallen bulbs are rooting and raising a new crop, and so on *ad allium infinitum*. With no work on the gardener's part, this species provides spring's first

fresh green onions, and in midsummer, the peeled top bulbs make perfect pearly pickles or an easy seasoning popped whole into summer ratatouille, soup or tomato sauce. The hard top bulblets store well into winter. Start a plantation of perennial Egyptian onions in spring, midsummer, fall or anytime a plant or a handful of bulblets comes your way. These surface-rooting bulbs are easily dug up if they stroll out of bounds.

GARLIC

Allium sativum

For many years, we grew no garlic, assuming that this Mediterranean native needed a

long, hot season to mature. Instead, we made do with store-bought bulbs, often shrivelled or mouldy. Then, one propitious September day, a friend brought some bulbs of the best garlic I had ever seen and surprised us with the news that they had been grown not in California but by a market gardener only a few miles south. The friend left with our request to send enough garlic to plant a 4-by-25-foot intensive bed, and we have been revelling in the "reeking rose" ever since.

Garlic is as hardy and as easy to grow as any allium. I am always surprised at the generous return—plant one clove, harvest ten—for so little work. Garlic is one of the few crops best planted in fall. Sometime in mid-September, perhaps

The Egyptian onion, RIGHT, is also appropriately named the top-onion or walking onion for its habit of producing, at the stem tops, clusters of bulbs that topple and root. However, a decorative onion, Allium kartaviense, *FAR RIGHT, spreads by seed if allowed. Its early blooming is as eye-catching as the Egyptian onion's gangly eccentricity.*

after the beans have been blackened by frost, I turn a 6-inch dressing of very old cow manure and a dusting of bone meal into the garlic bed, which is in full sun, rake the ground to a fine tilth, and push the largest cloves saved from that season's crop several inches deep into the loose earth. (In heavy ground, trowel out a little planting hole.) I set the cloves at 6-inch intervals in rows 8 to 12 inches apart. Very soon, thin blades of garlic grass emerge and continue to grow into fall, until checked by severe cold. One garlic grower near Point Pelee, Ontario, a region of fickle winter weather, suggests mulching the garlic beds with straw at this time to prevent repeated freezes and thaws from heaving the

bulbs, but since consistent snow cover is the winter rule here, I skip this step. As soon as the snow has receded in the spring, the flat, arching garlic foliage begins to grow strongly—several visitors have looked at the garlic beds in June and wondered why the "corn" was so far advanced. Some attention to weeding and a deep drink of fish emulsion in a droughty season are all that garlic requires for good growth. Needless to say, insects give the bed of garlic, which has pesticidal properties, a wide berth.

As its foliage begins to ripen in August, I harvest the bulbs as needed to blend with basil, olive oil or butter as a sauce for pasta or rice; to mince with summer savory and toss with buttered

French-cut green beans; to slice, sweet and raw, on buttered dark bread; or to sauté with yellow crookneck squash seasoned with tarragon, lemon thyme and fresh tomatoes. The abundant use of fresh green herbs, especially lovage, parsley or celery leaves, helps mute the "sulphurous stink" that is garlic's chief virtue in the kitchen but a liability in some company.

By late August, after most of the leaves have yellowed, I harvest the crop; bulbs left in the ground much later, especially in a wet fall, will continue to fatten and are apt to split their protective husks. Bulbs are dried in an airy, rain-free place for a week or so, soil is brushed off, the roots and tops are trimmed, and the cache is stored someplace dry and cool in open baskets—I have yet to learn how to turn out those decorative braids. Thus treated, garden-grown garlic keeps firm and fresh all winter long.

Pesto is the very breath of summer, redolent of garlic, green with herbs and creamy with pine nuts and Parmesan cheese. Pine nuts are traditional; they are also expensive and, in this region, very scarce. But why let tradition stand in the way of creativity? Pesto begins with lots of fresh basil, olive oil and garlic; pine nuts make for creaminess, but ground toasted sesame seeds do nicely. Parmesan cheese gives a salty tang as does a splash of tamari. If the basil is on the wane or not yet ready, I simply substitute other herbs—fresh dill makes an appetizing pesto; parsley is good alone, better with a sprig of lovage. I have made a pesto with summer savory, lemon thyme or chervil, alone or in various blends. Since we have already broken a few rules, why restrict the use of this tangy sauce to pasta only? Any variation using garlic is good stirred into rice (especially the delicate Indian basmati rice) or other cooked grains; a dollop transforms minestrone or lentil soup into a rare treat. One pesto fan I know spreads the leftover on bread and breathes a (garlicky) sigh of contentment.

Today, as in times past, garlic

excites either ardent admiration or definite repugnance. Few plants are as lauded in the old herbals, few as damned. "When Satan stepped out from Eden after the fall," says one ancient legend, "garlick sprang up from the spot where he placed his left foot, onion where his right foot touched." And several centuries ago, English herbalist John Evelyn pronounced a complete censure of garlic: "We absolutely forbid it entrance into our Saleting, by reason of its intolerable rankness, and which made it so detested of old. To be sure," he continued, " 'tis not fit for Ladies Palates, nor those who court them." Times have changed. I suspect that more than a few romantic liaisons have begun over a shared dish of garlic-laced escargots or Caesar salad. "In Spain," Evelyn did admit, "they eat Garlick boil'd which taming its fierceness turns it into nourishment, or rather medicine."

It is in part for its medicinal properties (both preventive and curative) that garlic has long been and continues to be praised. Besides being a proven antiseptic, garlic has some effect on the regulation of blood pressure and may help prevent the formation of tumours.

ELEPHANT GARLIC

Allium scorodoprasum

"Produces huge bulbs, sometimes exceeding one pound each; flavour is sweeter and much milder than regular garlic," rhapsodizes one herb catalogue of elephant garlic. Sorry, but I have not been impressed with either the flavour or the growth of this allium. Planted side by side with our crop of regular garlic, the supposed giant failed to mature any larger bulbs, and to my taste, a disagreeable bitterness underlies the faint garlic flavour. The off-putting taste disappears with cooking, but then the bulbs are bland. We maintain a small stock of

elephant garlic in a corner of the vegetable garden for the sake of the pleasant, round, lilac-tinted flower heads that appear in late summer and dry easily for winter bouquets, but I would never trade our patch of the real thing for this disappointing novelty.

ORNAMENTAL ONIONS

If elephant garlic has fallen – or ascended, some might say – to the role of an ornamental plant in our garden, there are other alliums that are meant to nourish the eyes only. Some may be edible, but all are too expensive and too cherished to eat. However, if they share garlic's reputation for deterring insects, they may be practical, to some extent, by helping to keep the roses free of aphids or by chasing some other small plant predators from the garden.

Allium albopilosum: Even if it had no pesticidal properties and did nothing but be its lovely, outrageous self, I would still grow this plant. A literal translation of the Latin is "white shaggy onion"; *A. albopilosum* appears to be from quite another world, a sort of vegetable alien. Its six-pointed star-shaped flowers, apparently cut from some ghostly lilac-tinted metal, radiate from a common centre on thread-like stems to form large, gleaming globes that seem ready to hurtle skyward.

Most plants, herbs or otherwise, are improved (or spoiled) by the company they keep. Our space-age alliums grow with a colony of old-fashioned roses, masses of swaying foxgloves and spritely coral bells, the whole a blaze of pink, white, crimson and lavender for many weeks in July. This picture, both imitative and flattering, we borrowed from Vita Sackville-West's famous garden at Sissinghurst Castle in Kent, England. Even a sunny corner of a tiny garden may achieve a similar flowery juxtaposition.

Allium aflatunense: Less other-worldly but just as striking is this ornamental onion, recently dubbed 'Purple Sensation' by one bulb hawker perhaps worried that buyers would be put off by the botanical name. By any name, this is one of late spring's best gifts, with grapefruit-sized spheres of countless, tightly packed purple stars swaying on 3-foot stems. Of them all, this is my allium of choice for several reasons: the flowers appear here during late May and early June, after the departure of spring bulbs but before the arrival of June's colourful crowds; the flowers last in good condition for as long as three weeks and, even after their colour has faded, remain decorative to the paper stage, when the jet-black seeds have ripened. Furthermore, the hardy *A. aflatunense* increases its kind in a modest way from year to year – our original patch of six bulbs now hoists 16 to 18 flowering stalks after four seasons without any attention whatsoever.

In our garden, the bulbs grow in front of a shrub of honeysuckle (*Lonicera zabelli*) in a close harmony of pink and mauve, with a neighbouring patch of pearly *Iris florentina*, source of the herbal fixative orrisroot. This allium is at home anywhere in sun or light shade; few gardens are too small for its slender growth.

Allium giganteum: Resembling 'Purple Sensation' but taller (to 6 feet), larger altogether and later flowering (mid-July here), this species is native to high Himalayan slopes. I would like to see this giant onion increase or at least maintain its original numbers in our garden. But for whatever reason, whether lack of hardiness (doubtful in a Himalayan) or some quirk of diet – what do giant onions eat? – the big fellow frequently stalks off after one season of bloom or sometimes waves a few pale tantalizing leaves as a reminder of past glory. Unfortunately, too, as befits a behemoth, the bulbs are far too expensive to be treated as annuals. All things considered,

Despite its supermarket price, regular garlic is exceedingly easy to grow in perpetuity from cloves saved from the previous crop. At the top of the plant, RIGHT, *grows a cluster of small bulblets rather than seeds.*

Garlic cloves, BELOW, *used for both planting and cooking, vary in size and pungency with variety, soil and culture. Smallest and often most strongly flavoured is wild garlic, left, with regular garlic, centre, and elephant garlic, right, increasingly large in size and mild in flavour.*

AIOLI

This is the most famous of the French Provençale sauces, often described as the butter of Provence. It is traditionally served with cold salt cod and potatoes but also complements any cold fish or hot vegetables such as broccoli and cauliflower, or it may be stirred into thick vegetable or bean soups.

Press three or four large cloves of garlic into a bowl, and further mash with a little salt. And two egg yolks and plenty of freshly ground pepper and whisk well. In a thin stream, add 1¼ cups of olive oil (as for mayonnaise), whisking rapidly to blend and emulsify the ingredients – it can also be prepared in a blender set on a low speed.

the reliable and much cheaper *A. aflatunense* – the price of one *A. giganteum* bulb will buy a dozen of the lesser – is a fit substitute for this inconstant giant. But our experience may not be typical; an experiment would be worthwhile for the sake of the splendid lilac-coloured balls of bloom towering at the back of a sunny herb bed or waving in light shade amongst ferns and wildflowers.

Allium moly: From the tallest of onions, we come to a veritable dwarf. *A. moly* is just 8 inches tall and trades the usual rosy purple of the clan for bright yellow flowers. This inexpensive, hardy bulb may be drifted along the edge of a sunny herb bed – I like to plant it in front of the glowing violet of *Salvia superba*, best of the ornamental sages, or massed in a slightly shaded bed beneath shrubs. Both the bulbs and leaves of *A. moly* are strongly garlic-scented, an odour that is undetectable unless the parts are crushed. The long-lasting yellow flowers appear in June, and although this pretty allium does not self-sow, the bulbs make a steady increase.

Dubbed golden garlic, this species has lived in gardens for centuries. Legend has it that it is one of the best floral talismans. A black cat may cross your path, you may walk under ladders, do what you will on Friday the 13th and be blasé about voodoo dolls being made in your likeness if only *Allium moly* grows in your garden. And, the teller of the tale goes on to say, many gardeners are unaware that the presence of this "assiduous vegetable" in their gardens is responsible for their "astounding good fortune and prosperity."

Less deserving of fortune are current catalogues that assume the right to rechristen golden garlic 'Sunny Twinkles.' Besides being confusing, this tampering with plant names strips away the pleasant association with gardens and gardeners of the past.

Allium sphaerocephalon: Globe-headed garlic blooms in July or August and carries many smallish heads of deep wine-coloured flowers, like showy red clover, on 2- or 3-foot stems. This plant is easy to grow in any sunny place, is good for cutting and drying, is apt to seed freely and is inexpensive. If this or any other allium threatens to become a nuisance by scattering seed in all directions, it is easily checked by nipping off the faded flower heads.

Allium karataviense: This eye-catching central Asian native has decorative broad foliage, blue-green edged with red. Softball-sized flower heads of pale lilac, almost grey, appear on 6-inch stems. Our bulbs grow very well and seed freely in almost pure gravel.

Allium caeruleum: The only blue-flowered onion I know, this is pretty but slender and of delicate constitution. Our dozen bulbs have not increased but have dwindled after several seasons.

Allium cowanii and *A. oreophilum* are dwarfs, white and mauve, respectively, for nooks in the rock garden.

Ornamental alliums make very few demands on a busy gardener's time or skills. All of them grow from bulbs that must be planted, like any tulip or daffodil, in the fall. In general, plant the larger bulbs deeper than the smaller; a covering of earth to twice the height of the bulb is an easy rule of thumb. Like their edible kin, these alliums revel in a light, warm, well-drained soil enriched with old manure, compost and/or bone meal. Once settled in the garden for a few seasons, any of the colourful onions that show signs of increasing can be propagated by lifting and dividing the clumps of clustered bulbs from late summer through fall. All that I have grown have proved hardy in central Ontario. These ornamentals are not strictly herbs, yet their kinship with a genus rich in flavouring plants and their similarity to the edible onions in growth, flowering and amount of cultivation required renders them perfectly suitable to a bed, border or garden of herbs.

SHALLOTS

Allium ascalonicum

So often are they linked with gourmet fare that ordinary folk may be excused for thinking that these small alliums require as much effort to grow as pale Belgian endive or white asparagus. The fact that shallots seldom crop up in markets, and only then at a high price, keeps alive the illusion that this is a difficult bulb. Gardeners know better – nothing to it but to push single pink-skinned sets into loose, fertile earth up to their necks, about 6 inches apart. High-rise gardeners should know that shallots can be successfully cultivated in containers, six bulbs to a 12-inch pot.

Early spring is the usual planting time, but shallots are hardy enough that they can be fall-planted like garlic in most northern gardens and will sail through winter unscathed if snow-blanketed or mulched with 6 inches of straw or rough compost. One shallot bulb yields an aggregate of six to ten in a season. Harvest this carefree crop in late summer as the tops yellow and begin to dry; lay the clusters in the sun for several days to cure. This process is especially important if one hopes to keep shallots free from mould for any length of time. Stored in net bags or open baskets in any place dry, cool and airy, shallots keep until spring providing the family cook does not rob the cache to season salads, salad dressings and sauces or to make shallot butter or vinegar with what has been called "an ideal blend of onion, garlic and scallions." In France, where shallots are widely used in cooking both *haute* and *du jour*, each region has its own prized variant of this allium. On this side of the water, we mostly make do nicely with a generic "French shallot" – but do note that shallots are distinct from the yellow-skinned multiplier onions sold by the bagful alongside plain old onion sets in spring.

At home in a sophisticated English garden is Allium albopilosum, FACING PAGE. *The confusingly named Welsh onion,* BELOW, *can also be decorative, while the strictly ornamental* A. giganteum, BOTTOM LEFT, *and* A. aflatunense, LEFT, *have garlic-like cloves in proportion to the relative sizes of the stems and blooms they will produce.*

CHAPTER SEVEN

TEA LEAVES

Herbs to blend and brew

Larkwhistle garden grows a score or more of tea herbs. An essential step in the tea ceremony here – at least during the seven-month growing season – is to take the teapot into the garden and fill it loosely with an impromptu blend of fresh herb leaves and sometimes flowers or seeds as well. One morning, it will be a citrus-sweet mixture of lemon balm, lemon verbena and anise-hyssop leaves, with sprigs of spearmint and unripe seeds of sweet cicely. Another day, it will be a tonic, slightly bitter brew of sage combined with a bit of rosemary, a smidgen of rue and a few flower heads of common yarrow. A favourite blend has lemon balm, spearmint and orange mint as the dominant flavours, with a leaf of sage and a sprig of rosemary and a few leaves of anise-hyssop or sweet cicely for sweetness. Into the pot may go calendula flowers, the fragrant petals of old-fashioned roses, leaves of scented geraniums or spikes of flowering lavender. In the evening, we have a sleepy tea of catnip leaves and chamomile flowers, with a little mint to temper the medicinal edge. Sometimes, I brew a bouillonlike tea of parsley, lovage, savory, dill seeds, chive blossoms, thymes or other potherbs salted with a few drops of tamari or a daub of miso paste.

Blends vary with the seasons – summer teas often include lemon or cinnamon basil or leaves of the tender tropical sages or a bit of one of the milder-scented geraniums. Seldom is one pot of herb tea just like another. But besides their endless variety, herb teas have a lot going for them. They are homegrown and hence can be free from the pesticides and other chemicals routinely used in the raising, processing, packing and shipping of commercial herbs. They cost nothing beyond a small sum for seed or starter plants and, best of all, the plants themselves are among the easiest in the garden to grow.

MINT

Mentha spp, *Pycnanthemum pilosum*

Growing with such abandon that they need occasional restraining, some mints are distinctly pushy plants, moving in on neighbours by surface runners or underground rhizomes. A few, however, are worth growing in corners of the garden where they will not menace other things. One

Mints are excellent tea plants, but varieties such as curly mint, spearmint and peppermint, BELOW, from top, have pushy tendencies best checked by growing the plants in a confined space, RIGHT.

member of the family, peppermint, makes the most familiar of all herb teas. But if the reaction of visitors to a whiff of the head-clearing fresh leaves in our garden is a clue, few gardeners know the true peppermint (*Mentha piperita*), which smells, as might be expected, like those red-and-white-striped Christmas candies or a peppermint patty – it is sometimes sold as candy mint. *M. piperita* may also be labelled black peppermint in reference to its purple-brown stems and top leaves suffused with deep violet. Still, it is wise to taste before buying. Even a nibble of true peppermint will fill the mouth with the characteristic mentholated coolness that identifies it.

Peppermint is a hybrid plant. "Seeds sold as peppermint," states one herb catalogue, "are never true to name; quality strains can only be grown from cuttings or divisions." In our garden, peppermint is the least expansionist of mints; our small clump barely maintains itself in a corner of a raised bed where six other species jostle for root room. But in a neighbour's garden, a slip from our plant has covered a wide swath of ground in the shade of some old apple trees. Peppermint craves partial shade, good black loam and moisture – one parent is water mint (*Mentha aquatica*), a vigorous plant that grows beside streams throughout Europe.

"Peppermint will stimulate like a glass of whiskey," Jethro Kloss says in his book of herbal medicine, *Back to Eden*. An overstatement, but there is no doubt that strong peppermint tea is a potent drink. I have heard several people say that they cannot take their mint tea strong and straight – "it goes right through me." All the herbals agree that the active constituents of peppermint act on the organs of digestion; the tea (or oil, which contains about 50 percent menthol) is recommended to allay stomach cramps, nausea, abdominal pains and the like.

Peppermint's other parent, spearmint, is far more common in gardens. It can be distinguished from peppermint by its leaves, which are uniformly green, pebbled, longer, more pointed and toothed along their margins – spiked, in fact, as the Latin *Mentha spicata* tells us – while peppermint leaves are smooth-edged. Southerners call it julep mint; alternate names, lamb mint and pea mint, indicate that this is the plant for general culinary use in sauces and jellies or minced over boiled potatoes, steamed carrots or fresh peas. A little spearmint clipped into green, grain or potato salads dressed with yogurt is a cooling touch. The scent and flavour of spearmint, milder than peppermint, blends well with other tea herbs, such as balm, anise-hyssop or chamomile, whereas peppermint would overpower them.

A pretty sport of spearmint is curly mint (*Mentha spicata crispata*), whose leaves are twisted, waved and crimped along the edges. Gardeners with limited space might grow curly mint in preference to its parent for the sake of its decorative

foliage. I have noticed, too, that curly mint never succumbs to the spotty fungus disease that sometimes bothers other species.

Different from other mints is one with the fragrance of eau de cologne. Orange mint (*Mentha citrata*) is also called bergamot mint because of its resemblance to *Monarda didyma*. Too perfumed, for my taste, to make a good tea on its own, a few sprigs of orange mint will add a unique bouquet to a blend that may include lemon balm and anise-hyssop. Attached by short stalks to the square stems typical of all mints are broadly heart-shaped leaves; these and the unusual fragrance identify orange mint.

For sheer beauty of leaf, no mint can match the variegated form of apple mint (*Mentha rotundifolia variegata*), also called pineapple mint. Apple-green, woolly rounded leaves smelling of apples and spice are flecked and bordered with creamy white. Not as determined a spreader as some, apple mint is an easy herb for massing in a lightly shaded corner of a city (or any) garden where height – about 3 feet – and highlights are needed. I have seen it given a prominent place toward the front of English perennial beds as an effective foliage accent.

Equally decorative is golden ginger mint (*Mentha gentilis aureo-variegata*), sometimes called American apple mint. (Given the many and similar common names, it is easy to see how useful the Latin can be.) Smaller, serrated (botanically called toothed or dentate) green

Chamomile, LEFT, *after painstaking harvesting, yields one of the most popular teas from tiny flowers. Anise-hyssop,* RIGHT, *far less known, is also a delicious tea plant that provides weeks of summer colour.*

For sheer beauty, no mint can match the variegated form of apple mint, which is less pushy than some of its cousins and sufficiently ornamental for a lightly shaded corner of a flower garden.

leaves are shot through with yellow and cream. To my nose, the scent resembles tangerines. In our garden, a clump of American apple mint grows at the side of a concrete watering pool, where it seems to appreciate the shade and dampness.

Mints are the easiest plants to propagate—and, in fact, are more likely to need curbing. Any shoot eased from the ground is likely to have a few roots. Planted firmly in a new place, it soon takes hold and starts to travel. Gardeners go to great lengths to confine mints: sinking sheets of metal, even used licence plates, around a patch; hauling old tires into the garden; planting in containers of all sorts. Wooden wine-barrel halves are my choice for mints and most other herbs because they are not porous like clay, being designed to hold wine, so far less watering is required—nor have I ever seen clay pots as large. A half-barrel will grow three species of mint comfortably. But each spring, the tangled mat of roots that will fill a barrel in a season must be pried and pulled out just as growth begins, and three to five shoots of each type replanted. If a single species grows in a half-barrel, it can be left for several seasons.

With mints, one can have one's tea and bathe in it too: the long branches of any fresh mints (but especially orange and peppermint) swished vigorously back and forth in a tub of hot water, then left to swirl under the faucet, make a fragrant bath; or simply empty a teapot full of a strong, minty brew into the tub. The practice is an old one. John Parkinson, apothecary to King James I and author of two 17th-century herbal classics, wrote, "Mints are sometimes used in the bath with balm and other herbs to comfort and strengthen the nerves and sinews." Since mint is a reputed anodyne—an agent that soothes pain—and is also recommended to relieve itching skin conditions, a mint bath may be as therapeutic as it is pleasant.

Far too small to be easily picked for tea, let alone a bath, the ground-hugging half-inch-tall Corsican mint (*Mentha requienii*) is nevertheless a sweet plant that will creep between paving stones or carpet a shaded slope of the rock garden, if it is not harassed by stronger plants. This herb has the tiniest flowers of any plant in the garden—a little pale lavender galaxy—but honeybees crawl eagerly over the small-leaved mats. Native to a warm Mediterranean island, Corsican mint is not as easy as some to keep over the winter—the herb lady who sold us a starter plant pronounced it "definitely tender"—but under the snow, small patches always squeak through and grow over the summer to fill in the bare places. A springy mulch of evergreen boughs (not matted leaves) is recommended protection where freeze and thaw is the winter pattern. Some gardeners recommend removing the mats of Corsican mint to a cold frame or even indoors over winter, but I confess that my interest in a plant wanes if I have to move it twice a year. Only the decidedly

tender rosemary, lemon verbena and several tropical sages (all good tea herbs) receive that attention.

Despite its name, mountain mint (*Pycnanthemum pilosum* or *Koellia pilosa*), a hardy American native, is not a species of mint at all, although it is a member of the same family, Labiatae, to which mint, bergamot and several other herbs belong. Its crushed leaves are redolent of peppermint and may be used in the same ways. Three-foot-high mountain mint does not creep but returns each spring wider by just a shoot or two. Nectar-hungry insects are drawn to the dowdy whitish flowers; I have counted four species of butterflies feeding at once, as well as a bevy of bees and smaller flying things. The flowers must brim with an unusually sweet nectar. Grow this plant from spring-sown seed or starter plants; our specimen lives in sandy ground in full sun but would probably respond to soil enrichment with more lush growth.

CHAMOMILE

Chamaemelum nobile, Matricaria recutita

A sprinkling of seed scratched lightly into any piece of sunny ground in spring will provide chamomile in perpetuity. What you sow, you reap. The choice is between the creeping perennial Roman chamomile (*Chamaemelum nobile* or *Anthemis nobilis*), a colonizing species that grows so thickly it has been used as a ground cover for paths or as a lawn substitute—"so that being trod upon, the scent is set free to regale and invigorate the passerby," wrote one gardener—and the annual German wild or sweet-false-chamomile (*Matricaria recutita* or *M. chamomilla*), sometimes judged better for tea.

I grow annual chamomile, or rather it has grown itself for years, with no attention except thinning (to 3 or 4 inches apart) the dense crop of fine-leaved seedlings that springs up every

The annual German wild or sweet-false-chamomile reappears every year from seedlings so dense that they must be thinned to 3 or 4 inches apart in spring.

season and weeding out their increasing kind from the paths (maybe I should leave them) or from the crowns of pinks and dwarf catnip edging a bed opposite. It is wise to grow chamomile (both the self-seeding German and the creeping Roman) in the vegetable garden – perhaps at the end of an intensive bed or in a corner where seedlings may remain undisturbed. Grown anywhere near other small herbs or perennials, seedlings become a nuisance, lodging where they will.

In preparing chamomile tea, remember that it is easy to oversteep the flowers past pleasant and fruity to bitter; equal parts chamomile and spearmint or lemon balm leaves make a more mellow brew, and a scant teaspoon of dried chamomile makes a cup of tea. Once dubbed "the plant physician," chamomile produces one of the most venerable herbal brews, long popular in the home medicine chest to soothe and strengthen stomachs and to calm restless or feverish children. In her book, *A Modern Herbal*, published in 1931, Maud Grieve says of the plant, "It has a wonderfully soothing, sedative and absolutely harmless effect." This is another herb tea to pour into bathwater; a little can be reserved for rinsing the hair to bring out highlights.

Chamomile has a reputed influence not only upon "frail humanity in distress," as one herbalist put it, but also upon other plants; grown near "weak or ailing plants, it exerts a strengthening influence." Cooled tea sprayed over a flat of seedlings, or dried chamomile flowers scattered between them, is said to reduce the risk of damping-off, a fungus that can lay low a batch of small plants in short order.

There is but one difficulty in growing chamomile: harvesting the flowers is like picking wild strawberries – it takes forever to fill a teapot or to gather enough to pack dry into a jar for winter teas. This is work for a sunny

Bergamot is one of the most decorative of the tea herbs and is often grown strictly as an ornamental. 'Croftway Pink,' RIGHT, *has been selected for blooms that are pink, rather than the usual bright red.*

Sunday when one is content to sit in the chamomile patch, under the shade of a wide-brimmed hat, and just pick. We harvest chamomile flowers first when the patch looks to be in full flower, taking small button buds, the wide-open flowers and everything in between. Soon, this generous herb is full of blooms again; three or four successive pickings are possible if patience, ever a virtue in gardening, persists. To dry chamomile flowers for tea, spread them in a single layer on a screen in an airy, shaded place out of the way of rain or dew, stirring and turning every few days until the flowers appear desiccated. Then store for a

while in a punctured paper bag to ensure that drying is complete, lest the bulky flowers mould in closed jars.

BERGAMOT

Monarda spp

Goodness and moisture, too, are needed for *Monarda didyma*, another herb of many names— bergamot, bee-balm, monarda, Oswego tea. This is a favourite of mine on several counts. The whole plant—flowers and leaves (and roots, says one writer, although I have not investigated that claim)—smells deliciously of oranges and spice; the leaves add a special bouquet to a tea blend, similar to the flowery essence that pervades Earl Grey tea.

Bergamot is a North American native. In 1744, so the story goes, Virginia farmer and amateur botanist John Bartram collected seeds from stands of red bergamot found growing near Oswego, New York—both the town and the tea received their names from the Oswego Indian tribe that lived in the region and apparently used several species of *Monarda* to flavour their food. Bartram sent seeds to English horticulturist Peter Collinson who recorded that "plants flowered the next year, and by 1760, there were plenty in Covent Garden Market." Two centuries later, there are plenty in this garden, too, and I wouldn't want it otherwise.

Crowns of tubular flowers, sometimes one atop the other, may be shades of purple or rose-pink. For curious gardeners, seeds of the 'Panorama' strain will flower in a range of colours the first season. But better are the named varieties of plants: 'Croftway Pink' is one cultivar to look for, and best of all is the glowing red 'Cambridge Scarlet,' always alive with hummingbirds performing their aerial acrobatics. Bergamot colours for weeks in July and early August. Each season, I find a new corner that would be brighter for a plant of bergamot, perhaps behind a cloud of baby's-

breath or in front of the reaching spires of delphinium or dusky blue aconite. With tall lilies and day lilies of any colour, 3-to-4-foot-tall red bergamot makes a fiery picture.

Bergamot is amiable enough if its few specific needs are met. Give it organically enriched ground that does not dry out, or it will lose its lower leaves and become stunted. Give it elbowroom and good air circulation, or it will become lanky and mildewed. Divide it first thing in spring or early in autumn, or it will spread, mintlike, into a choked mat of weak shoots. Division is easy— all the roots are near the surface—but the gardener must ruthlessly toss out the spent centre of the clump and retain three-shoot segments from the outside as new plants. Set these firmly, and a little deeper than they were growing, in the best ground you can manage in sun or partial shade. Thus treated, bergamot will be the jewel of the July garden, and its leaves will make many a cup of fragrant tea.

The delicate lavender flowers of wild bergamot (*Monarda fistulosa*) decorate roadsides, thickets and clearings throughout parts of eastern Canada and New England. At one time, native people steeped the leaves into a medicinal tea for mild fevers, headaches, colds and sore throats; other herbalists speak of bergamot, a general tonic, as a specific for stomach ailments. The genus is named for Spanish medical botanist Nicholas de Monardes, author of a book pleasantly titled *Joyfull Newes out of the Newe Founde Worlde*.

ANISE-HYSSOP

Agastache foeniculum

Although it is little known and seldom grown, anise-hyssop is good company for balm in both the garden and the teapot. This 3-to-4-foot-tall easy plant, always surrounded by honeybees and butterflies when in flower, ought to have a place toward the back of a bed of tea herbs. Leaves scented of anise and mint—licorice-mint is another common name—clothe square stems topped with short but showy spires of bright lavender flowers. If hung upside down in an airy, shaded place, the flower spikes dry as easily as yarrow (see page 120) for a winter bouquet. Since the shrivelled leaves are not decorative, they can be stripped for tea.

Just once have I seen these plants for sale; and anise-hyssop does not spread by runners as do plants of the genus *Mentha*. But spring-sown seed grows usable anise-hyssop in a season; left to seed, it scatters a colony of young plants at its feet. In hot, starved soil, this hungry herb grows stunted and weedy-looking, but given moisture and goodness (old manure, compost, peat moss and the like), anise-hyssop is an ornamental that provides weeks of late-summer colour and months of fresh licorice-mint leaves for tea.

COSTMARY

Chrysanthemum balsamita

In old abandoned farm gardens near my home, costmary has stood its ground against encroaching field flowers and grasses for half a century or more. My elderly neighbours know the herb as "sweet Mary," but none can recall just what their parents or grandparents used it for—"probably tea," is the usual guess.

A close botanical relative of the feathery, dark green tansy (*Tanacetum vulgare* syn. *Chrysanthemum vulgare*), costmary, in contrast, grows smooth, elongated, oval leaves, toothed along their edges and lightly silvered with a coating of countless minute hairs. Its flowering stems support clusters of small, yellow tansy-like button flowers (actually the central disc of a composite or daisy flower minus the surrounding petals) on 3-to-5-foot stems. Given costmary's persistence in old gardens, it is no surprise that the

herb takes to sun or light shade, dry or moist ground and forms an enduring clump in a season or two.

To my nose, the scent of costmary is a mixture of mint and wormwood, an aroma once described as "vaguely reminiscent of 'morning bitters,' whiskey with bitter herbs." Bitterness is all that comes through if costmary is nibbled, yet the herb was once included in every "Sabbath posy," a nosegay of aromatic leaves and flowers carried by churchgoers to amuse the nose and titillate the taste buds during drawn-out sermons. At meeting's end, the long leaves were tucked between the pages of the Good Book, a custom reflected in the name Bible leaf.

Today, this stalwart old herb, "once very common in all gardens," according to a 16th-century writer—and amusingly listed as "new for '86" in a recent

herb catalogue—is appreciated (again) by herb-tea fanciers for the balsamic bite it gives to a blend of milder herbs. The licorice sweetness of anise-hyssop or sweet cicely, or the citrus taste of any of the leafy lemons—balm, verbena, thyme and geranium—all temper costmary's edge. In any case, the bitterness of a nibbled leaf is considerably mellowed by several minutes' brewing. Ordinary black tea can be spiced with a bit of costmary (and any other tea herb for that matter). But, like the early New World settlers, I sometimes enjoy a cup of costmary tea straight.

HOREHOUND

Marrubium spp

If costmary can be pleasant on its own in tea, horehound cannot. Whether brewed or chewed, this

is a bitter herb that tastes as if it just might be as good a medicine as it has been reputed to be. An infusion of horehound is meant to remedy a weak stomach or lack of appetite, while horehound tea, syrup or candies have alleviated coughs, colds and sore throats for many centuries.

In our garden woolly, silver-green tufts of horehound appear here and there, like catnip; grown originally from seed, it can be counted on to naturalize itself. It is pretty enough for a corner of a flowerbed—its 2-foot height can be attractive in dry places where other plants are reluctant to grow.

ROSES

Rosa spp

Among the most exotic flowers for the teapot are roses, although it is the fruit of the rose—the vitamin-C-rich hip, or hep—that is most often brewed. The species *Rosa rugosa* and its many named selections produce some of the biggest and most prolific hips. Unlike modern hybrid tea roses, lanky prima donnas which demand that a gardener keep them warm in winter, fend off pests that might annoy them and generally keep them in good health, rugosa roses flourish even in sandy ground, are ignored by insects of all sorts and are hardy without protection even in the northlands and on the Prairies. Rugosa is a rose that yields fragrant flowers from mid-June through July, then opens a blossom or two until September when it regains a rosy fall glow.

Why doesn't every garden grow at least one bush of *Rosa rugosa*? Perhaps the tag "shrub rose" has frightened some gardeners who envisage a space grabber, but this prickly beauty needs less room than a suckering lilac or a straggling (and none-too-hardy) forsythia. Some gardeners feel that any rose more exuberant than a spindly hybrid tea has gone wild—and indeed, *Rosa rugosa* has created weedy thickets in parts of New England and farther south—or that a rose is only a rose if its petals spiral formally into a tight, high-centred blossom, beside which the blowsy rugosa bloom seems not quite elegant. The colour of the wild rugosa rose is magenta, sporting simple, open, five-petalled flowers. Let us call the rugosa flowers informal and appreciate the plant's many good qualities.

Canadian hybridizers have always been keen on improving the Japanese native *Rosa rugosa* as well as the numerous wild single-flowered rose species that grow across the country. During the 1920s, in Ottawa, Isabel Preston turned her considerable skill from lilacs, lilies and the

Any roses, including the wild natives, BOTTOM LEFT, *will produce hips that can be used for tea, but the largest hips,* LEFT, *come from certain cultivars of* Rosa rugosa. *Lemon verbena,* RIGHT, *has the strongest citrus flavour of all the herbs.*

Pineapple sage is a perennial but so frost-tender that it must be grown in a pot which can be moved to shelter during the winter. Its aptly named foliage may flavour teas year-round.

Siberian iris to *Rosa rugosa* and left as a legacy a willowy (to 5 feet) amber-cream cultivar named 'Agnes.' More recently, gene jugglers in Morden, Manitoba, and in Ottawa have introduced a bevy of hardy beauties, many of which have double blooms—that is, flowers with at least twice the normal number of petals.

Along a 75-foot stretch of rail fence, we have planted a selection of rugosa hybrids. The two fall days given to digging holes (18 inches deep and wide), removing subsoil, piling in a nourishing mixture of old manure, topsoil, peat moss and bone meal, well stirred with a spading fork, and finally setting in the stripling bushes have yielded perennial returns in flowers, fragrance and fruit. The dense hedge also buffers westerly winds that would otherwise chill the vegetable garden.

If one is after a crop of rose hips for tea, the rugosa roses are among the best, but understand that not all cultivars are created equal. 'Martin Frobisher,' listed as a rugosa hybrid, produces no fruit in this garden, nor does 'Agnes.' 'Hansa,' 6 to 8 feet tall, well known and overly vigorous in most gardens, has loose wine-coloured flowers and only a few large hips. 'Jens Munk,' 5 to 6 feet tall, opens pure pink semi-double flowers followed by lots of marble-sized crimson hips. Most productive of large, orange-red hips is 'Scabrosa,' a restrained and elegant 4-foot shrub carrying wide-open single flowers, mallow-pink with a centre of creamy stamens. Of those we grow, the latter two are my choices for hip production.

Pick rose hips when they are plump and red but not softly over-ripe; trim the stem and blossom end, cut the hips in half, scoop out the seeds and fibres with a small spoon, and dry the halves on a screen in an airy, shaded place indoors. Dried rose hips are as hard as coffee beans; to make tea, pulverize a handful in a blender, grinder or mill, and steep for at least 10 minutes with other herbs, dry or fresh, for more flavour.

LEMON BALM

Melissa officinalis

"Comforts the heart and driveth away melancholy and sadness," wrote English herbalist John Gerard of balm, in the 16th century. Almost every potful of fresh herbs I pick for tea includes a generous helping of lemon balm leaves. Few herbs are as sweetly cordial–the scent is citrus but not sharp, much like the bland, refreshing *limón dulce*, or sweet lemon, eaten like an orange in Mexico and points south. Here is the perfect tea herb. The mild flavour blends well with all other herbs; it offends no taste buds; and the plant, a completely hardy perennial, grows willingly in any good ground, in sun or shade. True, lemon balm is a mover, but much less so than mints; three clumps have been in place in our dryish garden for seven years with no tampering or attention. Its spread–faster in rich, moist earth–is easily checked with a sharp trowel; and if the maturing seed stalks are cut back, no seedlings will spring up. Two plants will meet most needs, but beekeepers might want more.

Melissa is Greek for bee; *Melissa officinalis*, "medicinal bee," is the botanical tag for lemon balm. Balm and honeybees belong together. Not only do the worker bees seek balm nectar, but leaves rubbed all over a hive seem to calm a colony that has just endured the trauma of a trip through the mail. In preparation for working with our bees, my partner, John Scanlan, rubs his hands with balm and brushes his clothing with the branches–better safe than sorry. This little ritual slows him down and, one hopes, makes the bees take more kindly to the intrusion. I read that the Greeks once stuffed their skeps–those picturesque beehives made of coiled straw–with branches of balm in hopes of attracting a passing swarm.

Balm is just as appealing to humans. In all herbal literature, the plant is described as soothing and useful for "nervous problems, hysteria, melancholy and insomnia." Equal parts of lemon balm, chamomile and catnip make an effective nightcap tea; balm, mint and anise-hyssop create a delicious breakfast brew.

Fresh balm leaves also add a mild citrus tang to green salads or other light summer dishes. My preference is fresh balm for tea as well; the flavour, subtle even when fresh, barely survives drying (although we dry a few branches for a winter blend). In any case, fresh frost-hardy balm can be harvested during at least half the year here, longer on the "balmy" West Coast.

OTHERS

Herbs discussed in detail elsewhere in the book, which I like to add to a blend in lesser quantities or brew alone as a medicinal tea, include:

Rue (*Ruta graveolens*): Use the fresh leaves, a tiny smidgen only because of the bitterness and because rue, although beneficial if properly used, is powerful; large doses are capable of producing mental confusion and can even be toxic. Rue is an abortifacient and so should not be consumed at all by pregnant women. Also, handling the plant can cause allergic reactions in susceptible people.

Hyssop (*Hyssopus officinalis*): Bitter but decorative, hyssop, whose tea is also not recommended for continual use, is an old country remedy for rheumatism. A leaf gives body to a blend of sweet herbs.

Sage (*Salvia officinalis*): Fresh or dried, a little adds depth and highly praised health benefits to blends of milder-tasting herbs.

Mullein (*Verbascum* spp): Flowers, fresh or dried from wild or garden mulleins, add flavour and body to mixtures.

Catnip (*Nepeta cataria*): This produces a very soothing tea; sleep-inducing if strong, made from fresh or dried leaves alone or blended with chamomile, balm or mints. It tastes pleasant if sweetened with honey.

Lemon Thyme (*Thymus × citrodorus*): The fresh leaves have the scent and flavour of citrus and spice. Use other thymes for tea, as you like.

Sweet Cicely (*Myrrhis odorata*): This is an excellent tea herb, whose Latin name means "fragrant perfume." The leaves or crushed green seeds add sweetness and a taste of anise to a blend; used alone, sweet cicely tea is said to act as a "gentle stimulant for debilitated stomachs." The sweet seeds of anise or fennel, both of which taste of licorice, may also go into the teapot.

A few flowers can be added to the tea blends. Lavender (*Lavandula vera*) flowers perfume a mixture and, according to John Gerard's 16th-century herbal, are of "especiall good use for all griefes of the head and brain and comforteth the stomach." Petals of the old-fashioned fragrant roses and the ray, or outside petals, of bright orange and yellow calendula (*Calendula officinalis*) are good for tea. Use flower petals fresh or dried.

The leaves and flowers of yarrow (*Achillea millefolium*), fresh or dried, were commonly brewed by North American native people into a general health-building and digestion-aiding tonic. A good addition to a blend, yarrow also makes a pleasantly bitter and aromatic brew on its own, although large doses can produce headaches and vertigo. A mineral-rich tea made from the dried leaves of alfalfa (*Medicago sativa*) has been described as "helpful for every condition of the body, whether maintaining or regaining a healthy state." Blend bland alfalfa leaves with more aromatic mint, lemon balm, anise-hyssop and the like.

WILD INGREDIENTS

The best source of rose hips may be a tangle of wild plants growing in a field or an empty lot beyond one's garden. Many of the native species have good-sized fruits, and the hips of all roses are edible, although not all are large or numerous enough to be worth seeking. Farther afield, meadows and woodlands provide other forage for herb tea aficionados. A tea made from wild strawberry leaves is a reputed "blood cleanser," while raspberry leaves brew a delicately flavoured beverage with mild medicinal effects. Both of these are best blended with more aromatic herbs from the garden. A tea of red clover (*Trifolium pratense*), the ubiquitous pasture plant, is said to be very soothing to the nerves; gargled, a strong infusion helps soothe a sore, inflamed throat.

Also blended for beverages is St. John's wort (*Hypericum perforatum*), a common roadside and meadow flower recognizable by its clusters of small but showy sunburst yellow flowers in late summer. The flowers and leafy tops of *Hypericum* species were once found in almost every Old World country household, where they were used medicinally, both externally and internally, to improve sleep, blood circulation and the working of the gastrointestinal system. Now, the plant is usually blended with other herbs simply for use as a beverage.

While it is a good mixer in a blend, yarrow also makes a pleasantly bitter and aromatic brew on its own. Mineral-rich alfalfa, on the other hand, is best blended with more fragrant mint, lemon balm, anise-hyssop and the like.

TENDER TEA HERBS

"What does this smell like?" I asked a 5-year-old visitor, tucking a crumpled leaf under his nose.

"Suckers," he said without hesitation and, after another sniff, "yellow suckers."

Of all the herbal lemons — lemon balm, thyme, basil, scented geraniums and verbena — the latter (*Lippia citriodora*) is the sweetest and the closest to the real thing. The trouble is that lemon verbena, a small shrub native to Chile and Peru, demands heat and full sun to flourish and shrivels at the first breath of frost. Two sweet-smelling tropical sages — the names pineapple sage (*Salvia elegans*) and fruit sage (*S. dorisiana*) say it all — also thrive in heat and sunlight but struggle and become spindly in low light and chilly places. It is best not to grow the tender herbs if conditions are wrong, but one is tempted for the sake of their ambrosial scents.

The tender tropicals are best grown in large (10-to-12-inch-diameter) clay pots that can be shifted outdoors into the sun when summer has settled and brought in again before the first fall frost. The soil mix must be porous but nourishing and moisture-retentive without staying soggy. I like roughly equal parts of good garden loam (but not clay), sifted compost or

Homemade herbal teas are best not only because they can consist of personally chosen blends of flavours and properties that marry well but also because they can be made from fresh ingredients. Even made with dried herbs, however, these teas are often distinctive and delicious.

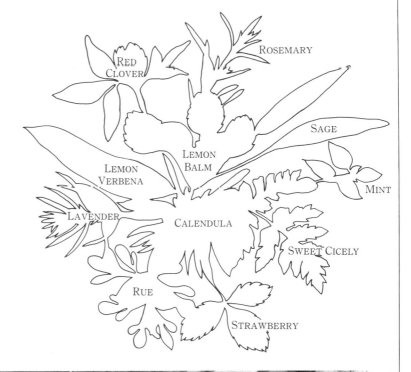

RED CLOVER • ROSEMARY • SAGE • MINT • LEMON BALM • LEMON VERBENA • LAVENDER • CALENDULA • SWEET CICELY • RUE • STRAWBERRY

bagged manure and perlite – several double handfuls of peat moss and a handful of bone meal are a help. Set small nursery plants directly into the large pots to get them going and to avoid time-consuming potting up later.

There are two options for wintering lemon verbena and the tender sages. Either keep them in active but slowed growth all winter by placing them in the sunniest place indoors – a south-facing bay window, sunroom, greenhouse or equivalent – or, lacking such a spot, store the tender herbs after their late fall pruning as one does geraniums, in a cool low-light place (by a basement window or in a protected shed), keeping the soil nearly, but not totally, dry. The herbs will be semi-dormant and need not be disturbed until about a month before the last spring frost, when they are brought again into warmth and light to gear up for summer. In either case, one never feeds a plant that is not actively growing. Potted herbs respond to a drink of half-strength fish emulsion, or the equivalent, two or three times from May through August only.

Pruning twice a year is necessary: once to reduce spindly winter growth by half or more before plants are set out for the summer – less if the herb has been pinched back during the winter; again, but more moderately, in early November as daylight wanes (this is a good time, too, to dry the late summer's growth of leaves).

Sooner or later, tender potted herbs, which are shrubs in their native lands, will outgrow the confines of a container. This is the time to start new, small plants from cuttings. Sometimes I do this in spring but more often during August, when sturdy (as opposed to winter-spindly) new shoots are available. (See Chapter 13 for details about propagating from cuttings.)

BREWING

Summer is the time for cold teas made from the fruity tropicals, fragrant drinks so much more refreshing than syrupy soft drinks. Nothing could be easier; it is not even necessary to brew the herbs first. Pick a handful of each of lemon verbena, pineapple and/or fruit sage, a sheaf of spearmint, some leaves of lemon balm or anise-hyssop, perhaps a sprig of lemon or cinnamon basil. Put the works into a pitcher with a cup or two of water, then crush and macerate the leaves with the back of a wooden spoon or the end of a wire whisk. Add the juice of a lemon, fill the pitcher with water (sparkling water is a good variation), sweeten to taste – if using honey, dissolve it first in a little of the tea before adding to the pitcher – then let it stand out of the refrigerator for at least half an hour. Strain into glasses over ice, and garnish with borage flowers or a few leaves of the herb. This recipe can be varied by crushing some strawberries or raspberries with the herbs or by using pineapple or orange juice (omit the lemon juice) in place of water. Keep in mind that the less elaborate the mixture, the more evident the herbal tastes will be.

A word about brewing the hot herb teas: "doesn't taste like anything" or "too strong" are frequent reactions. The good-tasting middle ground between insipid and medicinal can be found only by trial and error and, in fact, varies from herb to herb and taste to taste. Be guided by the scent and flavour of the herbs themselves in determining the amounts to brew and the duration of steeping: mild leaves of lemon balm, spearmint and

MARGOT'S TEA BLEND

2 parts each of raspberry leaves and
red clover flowers
1 part each of strawberry leaves,
St. John's wort flowers, crushed rose hips,
common yarrow leaves and flowers, garden sage,
horsetail leaves, black currant leaves, lemon
balm, bearberry leaves, twitch grass roots,
common plantain leaves, common or lemon
thyme and dried apple peel
½ part of bergamot leaves
¼ part each of oregano leaves, violet flowers,
rose petals, chamomile, mullein and calendula
flowers.

Strawberry leaves, ABOVE, and lemon balm, RIGHT, are among a score of herbs in Margot Barnard's custom tea blend.

anise-hyssop, for example, are used alone or blended in larger quantities as the predominant flavours, while stronger or more bitter flavours—a leaf or two of sage or a bit of rosemary—will add body and complexity to a blend. Most herb teas are steeped longer than black tea—5 to 10 minutes on average—but taste to be sure. It is possible to almost fill a teapot with fresh herbs and still brew a delicious tea that is not overpowering; just use proportionately fewer dried herbs. One teaspoon per cup is about right.

Each year, a neighbour, Margot Barnard, patiently gathers from her garden and the wild the 20 or so ingredients that make up her own tea blend. "This is the only herb tea my husband will drink," she says.

"He doesn't even want his morning coffee anymore." I can attest that the tea is delicious, and given the extraordinary list of ingredients, it must be a potent health-promoting drink.

"It's not difficult to get the herbs together," says Margot, although "they are not all ready at once. I dry little batches of this and that all summer and blend them in the fall."

STORAGE

The foregoing herbs alone or in varying combinations fill a teapot from day to day during the growing season. All are easy to dry for winter use: hang bundles of three or four branches (many more and drying is uneven due to bulk) anywhere out of sun where the air circulates freely. Attic rafters or a garden shed will be fine if there is ventilation. I hang bunches from a dowel suspended over the wood stove; the dry rising heat crisps them in short order. When the leaves are crackling-dry, strip them onto a sheet of newspaper, pick out bits of twigs, and funnel the herbs into jars or any containers that can be closed tightly. Store clear glass jars out of light, opaque containers anywhere. Screen drying (as described for chamomile flowers and rose hips) works for leafy herbs if fresh leaves are plucked from stems and laid in a single layer on the screen; if the screen is propped on clay pots that sit directly on the surface of a gently radiating wood stove or over a hot-air vent or register, drying is swift. Oven drying (the oven turned to its lowest setting, the oven door slightly ajar) has its proponents, but I cannot speak from experience.

I wonder if herbal teas—I'll avoid the cumbersome but more accurate term tisane—will ever catch on as a day-to-day drink in the manner of coffee and black or green tea. Probably not, yet because they soothe without sedating and refresh without the nerve-jangling effects of drinks with caffeine, herb teas are gaining popularity. Any restaurant worth its sea salt and demerara sugar now lists, in addition to black tea flavoured with everything from strawberries to almonds, alternative teas—at the very least, chamomile, mint and rose hip. Ironically, this narrow range may be the reason that some people turn up their noses at herb teas in general and opt for yet another cappuccino. To my taste, the best herb teas, like the best regular teas, are blends. Unlike "real" teas, however, some of the best herbal drinks are made with fresh ingredients. Teas composed of garden-grown herbs (see page 41 for a plan of a tea garden) are as varied as the imagination; a little experimental brewing and sipping are sure to result in a special blend or two.

CHAPTER EIGHT

IN LIVING COLOUR

Beyond the green herbal horizon

The herb garden of most imaginations is filled with modest plants, plain green or soft grey, that scarcely draw one's attention until a touch or gentle breeze sets free their fragrance. Aromatic leaves, we are apt to feel, are what herbs are all about — not colourful flowers.

But the definition of a herb has changed with the times. If one were to turn to the old herbals and compile a list of plants deemed useful 300 or 400 years ago, the result would be an impossibly long list and would result in a garden resembling not only our usual notion of a herb garden but one that is part flowerbed, part meadow and part woodland as well. Green and grey foliage would be well represented but so would every floral colour. Centuries ago, virtually all plants, from the loftiest pine to the lowliest violet — including such common-place garden flowers as peonies, irises, primroses and carnations — were used in some way, whether for food or medicine, brewing or strewing, cosmetics, baths, dyes or simply for fragrance. Among these legacies of ancient gardens are species that add sparks of colour to otherwise subdued plots of potherbs. Mingled freely with less showy plants, the colourful ones help make an entire garden or a single backyard bed as lovely to look at as it is useful.

Many of the colourful herbs are discussed in other chapters: the flowering alliums, yarrows, bergamot or bee-balm, anise-hyssop, lavender, roses, primroses, violas and more. However, there are a few additional ornamental plants that are historically suited to a place in the herb garden.

FOXGLOVE

Digitalis spp

Perhaps the best known of the colourful herbs, this staple of the ancient herb garden is an elegant biennial or perennial almost lost in the trend toward instant floral gratification and bedding annuals. Until the 19th century, foxgloves were used medicinally as a purgative — something that "goes right through you" — and to treat ulcers and dropsy. The plant remains important in medicine today as the source of digitoxin, a chemical that reacts directly upon the muscles of the heart, slowing the pulse, raising

Herbs need not be green or grey. Nasturtiums, RIGHT, *and saffron crocuses,* FACING PAGE, *are herbs in good standing that contribute bright colour to the garden.*

blood pressure and increasing blood circulation. So potent is it that digitalis or its constituents must only be used when prescribed by a doctor.

In the garden, tall spires of foxgloves hung with white, pink or rosy purple bells, the "fingers" – hence, *digitalis* – freckled inside with darker colour, are the perfect vertical contrast to rounded bushes of old-fashioned roses that bloom at the same time. To this duo, I like to add the spreading silver of wormwood (*Artemisia absinthium*), an edging of coral bells and a few of the eerie onions *Allium albopilosum* to create a picture to satisfy any gardener's soul. Foxgloves may be allowed to seed at will in less cultivated corners of the garden. Many years ago, we grew a few foxgloves from seed, and they have been in and around the garden ever since. Sometimes they lodge between the hand-squared timbers, salvaged from a tumbled barn, that raise a herb bed; or they may sprout from the sides of the stone steps. I seldom have the heart to remove a foxglove unless it is actually blocking traffic.

Like the related mulleins (*Verbascum* species, also members of the family Scrophulariaceae), most foxgloves, including the common *Digitalis purpurea* and its cultivars, are biennials that grow leafy basal rosettes the first year from seed, send up 5-to-6-foot flowering stalks the next and then disappear. An exception is the shorter cultivar 'Foxy,' which blooms the first year from seed. To have 8 to 10 well-grown foxgloves flowering behind the old roses each July, I salvage some of the plentiful seedlings in spring, grow them to greater size in a vegetable garden bed and transfer the rosettes to their flowering position in early September, in plenty of time for the plants to become well anchored before winter. Moving a full-grown foxglove rosette should not be done lightly; the plant must be lifted carefully, with a root ball of undisturbed soil, and set in an oversized hole; earth is then tamped firmly

around the roots and water flooded in to settle the ground.

Consistent snow cover is all the winter protection foxgloves need, but a springy mulch of evergreen boughs is useful in cold areas where the snow comes and goes. Given their woodland origins, foxgloves grow to greater heights – I have seen them 8 feet tall – in humus-rich, moist earth; compost, leaf mould, peat moss and old manure all help.

Well-grown plants of the common *Digitalis purpurea* are all one could ask for in foxglove beauty, but the cultivar 'Excelsior' has larger bells all around the stalk rather than just on one side. Only fans of oddities should grow the variety *monstrosa*, which opens a saucer-shaped flower at the tip of the stalk, totally spoiling the plant's graceful taper. As one old-time writer says, "As well top a cathedral spire with a cartwheel and ask for praise." Worth praise, however, is the hard-to-

The foxglove has a venerable medicinal reputation, but its properties are too powerful for it to be used as anything but an ornamental at home.

Nasturtiums, RIGHT, *whose peppery seeds, leaves and flowers are all edible, have been bred into cultivars of many colours.*

find *D. mertonensis*, a hardy perennial foxglove with lightly furred, strawberry-pink flowers that bloom on majestic 4-to-5-foot stalks for many weeks in summer.

VALERIAN

Valeriana officinalis

The species name *officinalis* indicates that a plant was once medicinally used, or "of the apothecaries." Until synthetic tranquillizers were fabricated, roots of valerian or garden heliotrope were made into an effective sedative, allaying pain, calming nerves and promoting sleep without narcotic side effects.

In the garden, the lacy umbels of valerian produce much the same airy effect as baby's-breath or coral bells and flood the air with fragrance. The scent is a little musty, but it is obviously evocative. "What's that smell?" one visitor muttered as she walked through the garden. "I know that smell." Like a bloodhound, she traced the invisible trail to a stand of valerian. "That's it," she said. "It grew in my grandmother's garden. Takes me right back."

The hardy valerian grows in any soil and spreads, but not too quickly. The shallow spaghetti-like runners are easily pulled back if they threaten to grow out of bounds. Start valerian from seed or from a bit borrowed from a neighbour's garden. A tall herb (to 5 feet), valerian is well suited to the back row. One plant is plenty for most gardeners.

MONKSHOOD

Aconitum spp

Although this is one of the most poisonous of garden plants, one that should not even be tasted, monkshood, or wolfsbane, has long been a resident of the herb garden; it was once medicinally valued – in very small doses – as a sedative or a pain killer. But aconite is extremely dangerous; the ancient Celts and Chinese alike used to smear their lethal arrowheads and spear tips with aconite, and the sorceress Medea included it in her panoply of poisons. "Without question, there is no worse or more speedie venom in the world," wrote John Gerard.

Still, the tall spikes of slate-blue or violet flowers provide pleasing colour for the very back of a herb bed. Gerard described these hardy perennials as "so beautifull, that a man would thinke they were of some excellent vertue." Perhaps the most decorative monkshood is the two-colour sport of *Aconitum napellus*, a species native to mountain slopes from the Himalayas to eastern Europe. The 6-foot spikes of blue-and-white hooded flowers create a favourite July picture when grown behind clumps of red bergamot with a cloud of baby's-breath nearby. This aconite is also good company for the curious orange of tiger lilies or behind tall yellow yarrow (*Achillea filipendulina*).

The two-toned aconite (*Aconitum napellus* 'Bicolor') is not often seen. We found a few exhausted clumps standing guard over an old grave site in the woods behind a nearby farmhouse. Our old neighbour recalled that "before my time," the family living in the house had suffered a tragedy: one day during target practice, the father had accidentally shot and killed his son. Wanting to keep the boy close, the family had buried him under the maples and planted the grave site with aconite.

The tall fall-blooming species *Aconitum autumnale* is one of the last perennials to bloom, colouring coldly blue into October. A shorter June-flowering species, *A. henryi*, competes with day lilies for root room beside the steps of many of the local farmhouses and provides a pleasing blue for the middle of a herb bed or flowerbed. And a few hybrids occasionally crop up on nursery benches. One with deep violet flowers arrived at our garden as a single shoot, but it is so pretty and useful for August colour that I can't resist dividing it down to the last stem each fall and spreading it around the garden, interplanting it with phlox or pink bergamot.

Although all aconites grow slowly from seed, a clump pried from the ground with a spading fork falls readily into separate divisions and can be further eased apart by hand. Each stem ends in a little rooted tuber that detaches with a gentle tug and is soon established in a new place. Well-enriched moisture-holding ground supports this thirsty herb best, in sun or partial shade. If starved or dry at the root, aconites lose their lower leaves and grow stunted and yellowish. Although a mulch of compost, manure or old straw is a help, it is no substitute for good soil in the first place. In leaf and habit, monkshood resembles the related delphiniums; however, aconites are enduring perennials, while the others sometimes disappear after a season or two.

SALVIA
Salvia superba

Often, when planning a new bed or renovating an old one, I cast about for a medium-tall plant (of about 2 or 3 feet) for the middle row – something self-supporting, so I won't have to bother with stakes or string, drought-resistant (given this garden's sandy soil), long-flowering, bug-proof and hardy. A tall order, but *Salvia superba* fills the bill. A relative of cooking sage, it returns year after year with no designs on more garden space. Each June, it grows a crop of violet flower spikes that remain in good colour while the irises and poppies come and go.

Like the related clary, much of this salvia's colour is in its bracts, modified leaves under each flower. Even after the flowers have faded, the bracts continue to be decorative. If the stalks are cut back to the ground in midsummer, a second batch of flowers may appear during a warm fall. Seeds will grow this hardy sage, but look for nursery plants of the bright cultivar 'East Friesland.' Once in the garden, *Salvia superba* is easy to split into three- or four-shoot divisions in early spring or fall.

PEONY
Paeonia officinalis

This hardy perennial has roots, mythic and historic, in herbal medicine; its name comes from Paeeon, the Healer and student of Aesculapius, who, according to Greek myth, used a poultice of peony to heal wounds inflicted on Hades by Hercules. Some species were and are still appreciated as medicinal plants in their native Orient. At one time or another, the peony has been thought to cure madness, persistent coughs and epilepsy in children; some centuries ago, children wore necklaces of peony roots as a protective talisman and to guard against the "falling sickness." Because its seeds are slightly phosphorescent, the peony was supposed to ameliorate what 16th-century herbalist John Gerard labelled "the disease called the Night Mare" and "melancholie dreames." But a caution: the peony, especially the flowers, contains poisons that can cause severe gastric disturbance. It is just as well that this herb has traded its medicinal role for an ornamental one.

In any case, if beauty is curative, peonies are as effective as ever. Purchase peony roots and plant them in fall with the topmost eye, the red bud on the root, no more than an inch and a half below the surface of the ground, in good fertile soil. Support the flowers with stakes or in wire cages.

HYSSOP
Hyssopus officinalis

Much like 'East Friesland' salvia in height, habit and ease of tending is hyssop, a decorative medicinal herb with dark green, narrow foliage that tastes sharp and bitter and smells of pine or balsam with a hint of turpentine. A member of the family Labiatae, the vast herbal group that includes mints, balm, thymes, savories and a score of others, hyssop sends up 2-foot spikes of small, ink-blue flowers in midsummer. It is well placed in front of tall yarrows or the lanky stems of lilies. Seeds sprout with encouraging speed. Spring cuttings soon form roots, but this low shrub cannot be divided.

Hyssop is used by some people, not by me, as a culinary herb to flavour fatty meats. This may be a holdover from distant days in Europe, when meat and game composed almost the whole diet, and bitter herbs were needed to aid digestion. I can think of no other reason one would welcome the taste of hyssop. But the herb has its uses; a tea of hyssop and sage is a recommended gargle for sore throats. I once used crushed hyssop leaves, reputedly antiseptic, to make a poultice that included thyme, comfrey,

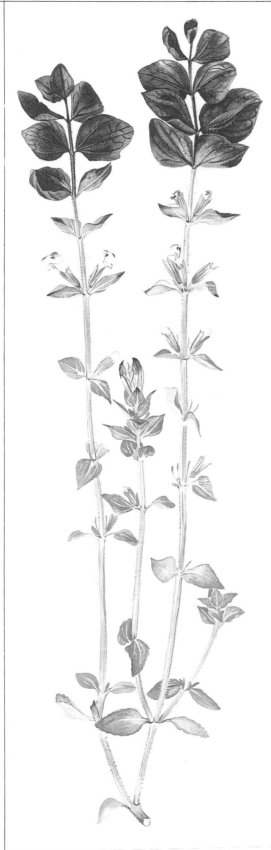

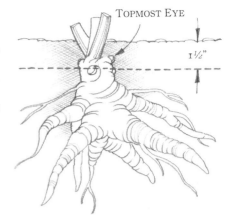

Plant peony roots in fall, with the topmost red bud, or eye, no more than 1½ inches below the surface of good fertile soil. Cage or stake plants in spring.

TOPMOST EYE

1½"

Requiring little care are the self-seeding purple-top sage, ABOVE, much of whose colour is in its bracts, and the musk mallow, RIGHT, whose wild forms often spring up uninvited.

Close cousins of musk mallows and bearing similar but larger flowers, hollyhocks were once called "holy hocks" because they grew against the walls of monastery gardens.

cayenne, garlic, olive oil and the juice of aloe vera for some nasty scrapes incurred by a young neighbour when he tumbled from his motorbike onto the gravel road. "Smells like stew," he said, but it did the trick.

HOLLYHOCKS

Alcea rosea

Behind hyssop might grow clumps of purple coneflowers and, behind them, hollyhocks. Once, tall "holy hocks" grew against the walls of every monastery herb garden in Europe, where the flowers were used in medicinal preparations. Today, scorned as weeds by some, they linger in city lanes or are allowed to spire up against rail fences and house walls in country gardens because "they've grown here since my grandparents had the place."

Visitors often ask us for a few hollyhock seed pods; it seems that this erstwhile favourite has been ousted from the seed catalogues by flashier newcomers. Seeds, preferably sown outdoors where they are to flower, are the best route to hollyhocks in the garden. Even though young plants move fairly well, the earth occasionally falls away from the thong-like roots, and they are set back. Besides, seeding in situ saves the work of transplanting.

If established hollyhocks are left to seed, they will stay in a garden indefinitely and surprise the gardener by flowering in colours unlike those of the parent plants, from white to all shades of rose (to be expected on a plant with the species name *rosea*), crimson, peach, pale yellow and plum – some with zones of darker colour. For many years, I preferred the fat doubles but now find them congested and graceless next to the simple singles, perhaps because of the comment that the doubles look "like those toilet paper decorations on wedding cars" – enough to put one off any flower.

Hollyhocks would likely be more popular if they did not succumb so easily to rust, a fungal disease whose nasty orange spots soon render a clump totally leafless, if still bravely flying its colours. One possible remedy is garden sulphur sprayed on the leaves soon after they appear. Another solution is to plant hollyhocks at the very back of a border, where their stems will be hidden by the tall growth of other plants in front. And since young plants are likely to be healthier, we remove badly infected older clumps and leave new seedlings to carry on. Hollyhocks respond to the rich earth of the perennial border. So treated, they often reach 10 feet and flower for many weeks from July to September.

MUSK MALLOW

Malva moschata

Close cousins of hollyhocks – both belong to the large family Malvaceae, which includes plants as diverse as the exotic southern hibiscus and a lowly garden weed known hereabouts as "cheeses" (*Malva neglecta*) – the musk mallow was once one of Gertrude Jekyll's favourite flowers and an ornamental in good standing. Its ease of culture recommends it for today's low-maintenance gardens.

I first saw musk mallows gleaming shyly in the shadow of the tangled briar roses and old apple trees that had grown up, like a Sleeping Beauty garden, around a windowless, decrepit farmhouse long abandoned to time and weather. Although variations of this pretty pink or white flowering herb crop up in fields and along roadsides throughout most of arable Canada and the United States, it is not a native, but a naturalized descendant of escapees from old gardeners. Early colonists first brought musk mallows, tamed English wildflowers, to remind them of home in their New World gardens; the enterprising plant soon set about colonizing new territory on its own. Every garden grows its share of

surprises. I do not recall ever seeding musk mallows, but for years the satiny, funnel-shaped flowers, like small mauve or silver-white hibiscus, have appeared here and there in flower borders, along a path or among the vegetables to colour a corner of the potato patch. For gardeners not as fortunate, seeds of *Malva moschata* are available from specialty seed houses, and *Lavatera*, the closely related annual tree mallow, can be purchased almost everywhere; simply sow the seeds where they are to grow around the last spring frost date. Plants are self-supporting, grow to 2½ feet tall and flower for many weeks in midsummer. Musk mallows are elegant enough to decorate a flowerbed, tough enough to hold their own in half-wild places; light shade or sun, dry soil or damp are all the same to them.

Mallows of all kinds are known for their soothing and softening action on inflamed skin and persistent sores. "In inflammatory conditions of the external parts," wrote Alma R. Hutchens in her *Indian Herbalogy of North America*, "the bruised herb forms an excellent application, making as it does a natural emollient cataplasm. Our Indians used leaves, soft stems and flowers steeped and made into a poultice for running sores, boils and swellings."

SAFFRON CROCUS

Crocus sativus

Saffron, the fiery red stigma snipped from the heart of a small lilac-coloured crocus, is the costliest of spices. And no wonder – 4,500 flowers are plundered to yield a single ounce of dried saffron, much of which finds its way into Eastern rice dishes, confectionery, medicines, perfumes and liquors in minuscule amounts. This ancient herb crops up in the writing of Homer and Solomon, among others. "An odour of perfect ambrosia," was the fragrance of

saffron; theatre benches and banquet halls were scented with saffron-water, and the cushions of the high and mighty were stuffed with the crocus petals. Persian kings wore saffron-yellow shoes, and the gods on Mount Olympus were robed in saffron hue – not unlike contemporary Buddhist monks in the Far East.

Persia, Greece, the steamy Orient . . . . I should have known that this famous flower would not take kindly to a northern garden. Unlike the familiar crocus of spring, saffron produces its fragrant blue, lilac or purple blooms in fall after its bulbs have had a good baking over summer. Fall is an uncertain season here, apt to be cut short by the chilly blade of winter, and since central Ontario is not the Middle East, a summer baking is not a sure thing either. Bulbs of *Crocus sativus* planted in our garden five years ago have so far steadfastly refused to flower. Likely, I would not have the patience (or the heart) to pinch the stigmas if they did appear.

Our experience with saffron crocus is echoed by Louise Beebe Wilder in her informative 1936 book *Adventures With Hardy Bulbs*, in which she says of the plant, " . . . it is sadly disappointing in the garden . . . indifferent to your best efforts in its behalf, flowering sparsely and seldom . . . . Save for its antique interest . . . it seems to me the saffron crocus is not worth growing." Hear, hear, I say.

BORAGE

Borago officinalis

I do not pretend to understand the subtle links between herbs and human emotions, but for as long as people have written about plants, borage has been linked with both courage and joy. Pliny called the plant *euphrosinum* because it supposedly made people happy, and John Gerard wrote in the 16th century, "Those of our time do use the flowers in salads to exhilarate and make the mind glad . . . . The leaves and flowers put into wine . . . drive away all sadness, dulness and melancholy." Perhaps it was the wine that did most of the driving.

I have not noticed a mood-elevating effect from eating borage, although the lovely pink or bright blue star-like flowers are cheery enough throughout the summer. Not only do bees love them, but they can decorate any of summer's cold dishes or stud a cream cheese ball flecked with herbs. The rough, hairy leaves are often said to taste of cucumber, but my taste buds detect a hint of fish oil, which disappears if they are minced into a salad. Cooked young borage leaves are a palatable spinach substitute, and Turid Forsyth tells me that she uses borage leaves "almost more than any other herb, especially to mix with other herbs into sour cream or yogurt as a dressing for potatoes or vegetables – and lots in a salad."

A hardy annual and prolific self-seeder, borage is easily grown from large seeds planted in full sun in half-inch-deep furrows about two weeks before the last spring frost. Although it can be started earlier indoors, it resents transplanting and so must be moved with a good root ball. Borage is a rather sprawling plant that grows about 2 feet tall.

ANCHUSA

Anchusa italica, syn. *A. azurea*

I always think of anchusa (pronounced an-*coo*-suh) as the herb that stopped a bus. One June morning some years ago, 20 or 30 people came tumbling out of a tour bus passing our place and swarmed into the garden, all wanting to know the name of "that incredibly blue plant." Searching the back roads for birds and wild orchids, the group of naturalists had spotted the clumps of flowering anchusa from 100 feet away. This showy but seldom-grown, bristly leaved relative of comfrey and borage produces, for at least a month in

early summer, panicles of flowers shaped rather like overgrown forget-me-nots of the most intense, bus-stopping blue.

Like those of borage, anchusa flowers are edible floral garnishes; the roots yield what has been described as an "incredible" red dye. But practicalities aside, anchusa earns space in my garden simply for its brilliant blue, for "no plant," notes one old-time writer, "not excepting the delphiniums, decks itself in a more truly azure colour."

Listed as a biennial in the few catalogues that offer it, anchusa is a short-lived perennial here; plants usually reappear for three or four years. But if older clumps disappear in time, there are always seedlings left to carry on the colour. Seed, in fact, is the best way to start with anchusa, since the tap-rooted herb wilts badly if moved. I start seed in 4-inch pots – a few seeds per pot, thinning to one – or dig seedlings from the garden and tuck them into their flowering position when they are still fairly small.

Anchusa, also known as Italian bugloss or alkanet, has but one fault: the top-heavy stems, 3 to 5 feet tall, are prone to topple,

The seed-filled pods of poppies, BELOW, *are often employed in the kitchen, while purple coneflowers,* RIGHT, *have medicinal applications only.*

smothering nearby plants and generally creating confusion in a border. Two or three slender stakes per clump or as many tall twiggy branches (birch limbs are good) pushed firmly into the earth and wound around with strong cord help to corset this showy but untidy herb.

POPPY

Papaver spp

Because of its narcotic connections, the opium poppy (*P. somniferum*) is officially outlawed in most places. Still, it persists, a fugitive from old gardens that haunts the roadside in several places near here. Its leaves are broad, sharply scalloped and silver-grey. The flowers, like scaled-down versions of the flamboyant Oriental poppies, are pale lilac with a dark blotch at the base of each petal. But given the poppy family's willingness to cross and recross, flowers appear that are white and all shades of pink to dull purple-red, single or wildly double. Oddly, the tiny poppy seeds that fill the little pepper-shaker pods seem to contain no hint of narcotic and are familiar ingredients in cakes, strudels and European breads. Look for the cultivar 'Hungarian Blue,' whose name refers to the colour of the seeds, not the flowers.

To grow this poppy, scatter seeds over any sunny patch of ground and lightly rake; this should be done very early in spring or even the previous November. The next step is to thin the seedlings to 3 or 4 inches apart; this slight crowding means the top-heavy but lightly rooted poppies can lean on each other for support.

The seeds of the corn poppy

Borage, RIGHT, and its more colourful cousin anchusa, BELOW, bring a welcome splash of blue to the garden and to summer salads.

(*Papaver rhoeas*) are also edible but less tasty than those of the opium poppy.

PAINTED DAISIES

Pyrethrum roseum

A colourful duo for the June herb garden includes blue anchusa behind swaying painted daisies. From a crown of finely cut, dark green leaves rise slender 3-foot stems topped with showy blooms, single or double, rose-pink or hot crimson. Few flowers last as long when cut for bouquets. Pulverized, these innocent-looking blooms yield a hard-hitting but short-lived (and thus environmentally safe) insecticide; store-bought organic dusts often contain a percentage of pyrethrum. One of the easiest and most permanent of perennials, painted daisies are quick from seed – they may bloom late the first summer if started early enough – and even quicker from plants or divisions.

PURPLE CONEFLOWER

Echinacea purpurea

Visiting herbalists are always surprised to see this perennial in flower, because although they know it as a valued remedy, they do not realize that it is among the most decorative members of the daisy family, Compositae. The 5-inch-wide flowers – down-turning purple petals surrounding a bristly orange cone – appear on sturdy 4-foot stems during August and September, when they bring butterflies to the garden. Like most daisies, coneflowers are easy to grow from seed – the cultivars 'The King' and 'Bright Star' are larger and brighter than the original species – and they sometimes flower the first season if started early indoors. I usually transplant the seedlings a foot apart into one of the

The calendula, or pot marigold, is a common garden flower with a practical use; its petals, like those of many other herbs, can become ingredients in colourful summer salads.

vegetable beds and move them to their permanent place very early the following spring. Here, they have started to seed themselves, a sure sign that the plants are at home in the garden.

GOLDEN MARGUERITE

Anthemis tinctoria

Another colourful daisy, less exotic but far more brilliant, is *Anthemis tinctoria*, called golden marguerite or dyer's chamomile because its blossoms yield a golden orange fabric dye. Sprawling 2-foot mounds of finely cut aromatic leaves are covered with hundreds of bright yellow 2-inch daisies during late June and early July. This plant is good for disguising the lower stems of delphiniums and makes colourful company for *Salvia superba* or hyssop. It can also be planted as a tall, colourful ground cover on a sunny slope. Use seeds or starter plants; anthemis does not divide well but will seed itself once settled in a garden.

FLORAL CUISINE

Many people are a little squeamish about eating flowers, a practice that was very popular in the early days of "sallets." Broccoli left in the garden for a few days past the "edible" stage, for instance, will break into sprays of yellow blooms just as palatable as the green heads. Other little-known flowers for garnishing or snipping into salads include sage, bergamot, rosemary and lavender; better known are nasturtium, borage and chive blossoms. Flowers of *Anchusa italica*, a brilliant blue borage relative, are also good, as are the decorative petals of rose and calendula or pot marigold. In spring, primroses and violets go into the salad bowl; and from the wild come St. John's wort and yellow potentilla or cinquefoil blossoms.

This perennial herb is as decorative as it is useful; mounds of small single or double daisies – 'White Star' is a good cultivar – can tumble over a sunny border edge. Plants set out on 12-inch centres and left to go to seed create a foot-high weed-suppressing ground cover in any soil in sun or light shade. Feverfew grows easily from seed sown in spring, and nursery plants are widely available; the variety *aurea* has yellow-green foliage. A friend reports that this herb is an exceptionally long-flowering house plant grown in a large pot or hanging basket in a bright window, sunroom or greenhouse.

NASTURTIUM

Tropaeolum majus

For some reason, nasturtiums – the name means "nose twister" – colourful annuals that they are, are neglected in gardens today in favour of bedding annuals that nursery growers can squeeze into little six-packs and harried gardeners can plunk into the soil any which way on May 24. But it is sufficient to push the pea-sized nasturtium seeds into any patch of poor, sun-drenched ground in spring and wait six weeks for a crop of flowers, yellow, orange, scarlet or cream. In rich soil, plants grow lush leaves but flowers are few. I recall one summer, hot and dry in the extreme, when all the garden plants were feeling the heat, but the nasturtiums flowered blithely on.

Once, nasturtiums were valued for treating infections. Now, they are appreciated as salad herbs rich in vitamin C. The sharply peppery leaves are good snipped into salads or in a sandwich instead of lettuce, the flowers make edible garnishes, and the unripe seeds can be pickled to substitute for capers.

Clearly if it is colour a gardener yearns for, there are plenty of precedents in herbal lore and literature for including colourful flowering plants among the leafy aromatics.

FEVERFEW

Chrysanthemum parthenium

Recently, medical research has confirmed that a humble ornamental herb, feverfew, really does have beneficial effects. Leaves of this low, white chrysanthemum have been used medicinally, at least since Roman times, as a sedative, abortifacient and all-purpose tonic; in more recent years, people plagued with migraine headaches have been helped by chewing feverfew leaves.

According to the British Medical Journal, laboratory tests with feverfew capsules and placebos have shown that the herb is indeed effective. At the City of London Migraine Clinic, patients on a placebo had recurring migraines, while those using feverfew reported an improvement; and for one-third of the patients, the migraines disappeared entirely after a period of use. Some mouth soreness and temporary stomach upset were experienced, minor side effects compared with those of many drugs and less traumatic than the headaches.

CHAPTER NINE

GARDEN SILVERWARE

Plants with grey foliage

"What can we plant," visitors often ask, "that will come up every year, bloom all summer and look after itself?"

In a word, nothing. Like the birds, plenty of perennials keep coming back, but all need some attention, and none flower nonstop. But that said, it is a fairly simple matter to arrange a garden so that plants whose good foliage persists even after their flowers have passed will mask the departure of those more transient. Plants chosen for good and lasting leaves, when set toward the front of beds, serve to keep the garden fresh despite inevitable declines in colour.

Among the most effective and long-lasting foliage plants are herbs in shades of grey, blue or silver. Although some grey plants are flowerless – notably the artemisias – and others like rue or lamb's ear grow only insignificant yellow-green or purple flowers, the persistent foliage of all adds colour to the garden picture. Woven among brighter flowers, the quieter grey-leaved herbs serve to harmonize discordant elements and create a peaceful atmosphere. Small, sunny gardens or single beds or borders planted solely with silver are for those keen on gardening for pictorial effect.

In her garden at Munstead Wood, influential English gardener Gertrude Jekyll liked to mass grey-leaved plants – among them yucca, *Artemisia stelleriana* or old woman, woolly stachys, rue and tall mullein – at either end of her "long border," to provide a cool, calm place for the eye as both prelude and coda to the hot colours between and to heighten the glow of adjacent colours with a quiet grey contrast. On even the smallest scale, grey foliage does the same. I hope that after all the work of planning and planting to include grey herbs, the gardener will build a bench – "he loses much who has no aptitude for idleness" – from which to contemplate the quiet scene.

The grey colour – *glaucous* is the botanical term – is due to the presence of countless hairs covering the leaf's surface. If the hairs are very tiny and dense, the leaf appears deceptively smooth; a strong hand lens will bring the hairs to light. If they are more substantial, the leaf texture is furry, downy or velvetlike, botanically described as *pubescent*. In nature, most grey-leaved plants grow in dry, sun-baked places. Surface hairs are an evolutionary adaptation that helps plants survive intense heat and drought: first, a woolly covering checks the loss of moisture (transpiration); at the same time, the hairs trap airborne moisture, especially dew, and hold the life-giving water on the leaf surface. While deep matt green is among the most heat- and light-absorbing of colours, silver-grey or metallic blue-green provides a cooling reflection of the sun's relentless glare.

Our garden, converted from an open hay field, lies in full sun; its sandy soil dries almost to dust in a season with little rainfall. Not surprisingly, our search for

In some grey, or glaucous, plants, such as lamb's ear, RIGHT, *the tiny hairs on the foliage surfaces are downy, while the leaves of artemisias,* LEFT, *are deceptively smooth.*

adaptable plants has led us to include the grey-leaved herbs. Most are medicinals of ancient reputation, but even if they do not find their way into home-brewed remedies, all are lovely, easy-going plants that provide quietly decorative silver foils to the more usual garden greenery.

YARROW

Achillea spp

The genus *Achillea* is high on my list of decorative, low-maintenance plants for a herb garden or mixed border. These plants are among the easiest to cultivate in any reasonably good ground, provided their need for sunshine is respected.

When herbalists speak of yarrow, they are referring to *Achillea millefolium*, the common milfoil that weaves its feathery grey-green through a tangle of roadside grasses and wildflowers. Flowers of this species, white fading to grey or muted pink, are clustered in the typical flower head, or cyme, of the genus. These flat umbrella-like heads of bloom might lead one to guess that yarrows are akin to dill, lovage, Queen Anne's lace and other members of the family Umbelliferae, but look again; each cyme consists of many tiny perfect daisies packed tightly together. Indeed, yarrows belong to the daisy family, Compositae.

For centuries, milfoil has been a reputable medicinal herb. Achilles, namesake of the genus, is said to have stanched the wounds of his soldiers with yarrow leaves. Other old names indicate the herb's use as a haemostatic, an agent to stop the flow of blood: soldier's woundwort, staunchweed, sanguinary, Knight's milfoil and, in very ancient times, *Herba militaris*. Nor was its use exclusively external – an infusion of leaves and flowers (a tablespoon of dried herb to one cup of water, simmered, then steeped for five minutes, with lemon juice, honey and a dash of cayenne pepper) is still considered a remedy for feverish colds because it promotes sweating. A stimulating tonic for the whole system, yarrow tea also has a history of use for lack of appetite, cramps, flatulence and other stomach-related ailments. Extra-strength tea may be safely used to wash external wounds, chapped hands and the like. (Those who are allergic to ragweed, asters or other members of the family Compositae, however, should make sure to avoid using yarrow preparations.)

When milfoil is in bloom along the roadsides, I always think it is pretty enough for the garden. If the common yarrow is too invasive for any but half-wild places, 'Cerise Queen' is colourful and only a bit untidy in a bed of perennial flowers or herbs. June is its month; but in our garden, it colours again in fall. Early in the season, its vigorous, ferny foliage can cover for small spring-blooming bulbs such as crocuses, miniature daffodils or species tulips. Both the common yarrow and its fancy sport can be planted on 8-inch centres to create a tall ground cover; mowed, the yarrows can substitute for lawn grasses, but it is a shame to lay low a crop of flowers.

Several yarrows bring both silver and gold to the garden. The big bear of the genus is *Achillea filipendulina*, better known for its cultivars 'Coronation Gold,' 'Parker's Gold' and 'Gold Plate.' Here is a 4-foot-tall silver herb that is decorative from tip to toe from the time the elegant aromatic foliage emerges in spring until the last of many flat heads of yellow flowers have mellowed to autumnal brown.

For the smallest gardens or a rockery, woolly yarrow (*Achillea tomentosa* or *A. aurea*) is a scaled-down version of the aforementioned. Native to high places in Spain, France, parts of the Alps and through Russia to Siberia, this diminutive creeper has densely furred, finely cut, silver-grey foliage. Flat, intensely yellow flower heads top 6-inch stems from late May through June and dry as easily as *A. filipendulina* for winter colour. The hardy woolly

Achillea *'Moonshine,'* RIGHT, *is one of the reputedly medicinal yarrows whose tall, hardy modern cultivars include:* A. millefolium *'Cerise Queen,'* ABOVE LEFT, *and* A. filipendulina *'Gold Plate,'* BELOW LEFT.

yarrow, which tolerates (and even thrives in) dry, gravelly ground, is not adversely affected by drought. It must, however, have full sun for health.

Sooner or later, most gardeners try their hand at plant division, perhaps to increase some treasure too expensive to buy in quantity. Before one tackles a hefty clump of hosta or a tangle of Michaelmas daisy roots, it would be wise to practise with a plant such as woolly yarrow, whose shallow roots fall easily into distinct crowns. A mat of woolly yarrow is composed of many separate plantlets, each with its own roots, the whole woven together by shallow underground stems. Individual crowns are easily detached with clippers and trowel without disturbing the clump, or the entire mat may be lifted and divided. After a season or two, a single starter plant can be conjured into a dozen to edge a herb bed or carpet a patch of sunny ground. For more colour in the same space, I like to push tiny wild crocus bulbs (*Crocus chrysanthus* or hybrids of *C. tomisinianus*) through a silvery spread of woolly yarrow.

Although 'Gold Plate' is a strong contender, my favourite of the taller yarrows is *Achillea taygetea* 'Moonshine,' a cultivar that has inherited silver-white foliage but has traded the burnished tansy-gold of the genus for clear, lemon-yellow flowers. I first saw this herb growing in shining clumps at the Royal Botanical Gardens in Hamilton, Ontario, and searched for it in nurseries and catalogues without success. When finally I spotted a flat of wilting plantlets on a nursery bench, I scooped up the lot, only to find when the time came to set them in the garden that they were badly handled recent divisions with scarcely a root anchoring them in their pots of soggy sphagnum. Careful not to injure any incipient rootlets, I trimmed away a few lower leaves from each one, dipped the ends in a rooting hormone powder and planted the bits of silver firmly in the sandy soil of a shaded cold frame – in essence, treating them as

cuttings (see Chapter 12). Within a week, all were perky and growing. After several weeks, to my surprise, some began a tentative flowering and were still producing their lemony flower heads four months later. 'Moonshine' yarrow would do well in wooden barrel halves on a sunny porch, patio or balcony if given winter protection of evergreen boughs and burlap – certainly its spilling silver and gold would be effective all season long.

With the exception of the hybrid 'Moonshine,' which must be purchased from a nursery or propagated asexually by cuttings or division, yarrows are best grown from seeds sown in spring, either in pots or flats indoors or in an outdoor cold frame or nursery bed of fine earth. Set seedlings in their permanent place when they appear sturdy enough to fend for themselves, or grow them for a season (spaced 8 to 12 inches apart, depending on species) in a nursery row – we use part of a vegetable garden bed – transplanting them to their permanent quarters early that fall or the following spring. All will flower the summer after sowing; for all species, nursery plants are a shortcut to first-season bloom.

ARTEMISIAS

Artemisia spp

A corner of a herb garden might be planted only with different species of artemisia and still be full of variety. Showy flowers are not this family's forte – a wand of dowdy yellow-green buttons is the typical inflorescence – but artemisias compensate with especially fine foliage, silver or frosted grey-green, always delicately incised. When a full moon lights a warm summer night, ghostly artemisias reflect the lunar glow, somehow fitting for a genus deriving its name from Artemis, the Greek goddess of the moon.

There are dwarf artemisias for the rock garden or for edgings, spreading sorts to cover dry,

One of the best-known members of a plant genus that produced the heady brew absinthe, 'Silver Mound' artemisia, BELOW, *grows into 8-inch mounds. Catnip,* RIGHT, *is taller and more apt to spread, but the tea from its leaves is quite benign.*

sunny places with silver, and several tall species for the back of a herb bed. Most famous, or perhaps infamous, is the common wormwood, *Artemisia absinthium*, which gives its name to a bitter 136-proof brew deleterious to both body and mind. *L'Absinthe*, the famous Edgar Degas painting, shows a benumbed, glum figure, head propped on hands, sitting in a turn-of-the-century Parisian café, a glass of milky liquid on the table before him.

For all absinthe's well-deserved bad press – one-half ounce of the plant's volatile oil has caused convulsions and unconsciousness in humans – wormwood has been lauded as a medicinal herb throughout history. Indeed, it "ranks first," according to one herbal, "for conditions of enfeebled digestion, debility and melancholy." The common name wormwood indicates that the herb was used to rid both man and beast of internal parasites. Russian peasants considered wormwood the most bitter plant in the world; their folk medicine

border for a bed of flowers and herbs or create a neat, persistent silver accent in a rock garden. I have seen 'Silver Mound' used as a ground cover on a hot, dry slope (expensive except for small areas) and planted along the top edge of a sunny retaining wall. To be shown at its best, this herb, tolerant of poorish ground, needs full sun and elbowroom; crowded or shaded, it grows lanky and misshapen. A plant may be carefully split in spring, or new plants may be grown from cuttings.

One of the first lessons a gardener learns is that it is possible to have too much of a good thing, even silver. One spring, I planted a single innocent-looking shoot of the grandly named artemisia 'Silver King,' a cultivar of *Artemisia ludoviciana*, the so-called white sage, in a narrow bed of culinary herbs. In a season, all the meek thymes and savories were swamped. Both 'Silver King' and Roman wormwood (*A. pontica*) extend underground runners on all sides and so tend to take over a garden area; still, both are pretty silver ground covers, achieving a height of 18 inches if they are allowed full possession of a dry, sunny bank or other difficult corner. Although aggressive below, Roman wormwood is delicate and lacy-leaved above; its aromatic foliage shines as if veiled with frost.

If a multitude of common names tells us that a plant has long been welcomed in gardens, then *Artemisia abrotanum*, also known as southernwood, smelling wood, lad's love and maiden's ruin, is clearly a fragrant favourite. Hoary, sage-grey, thread-fine foliage suggesting yet another name, old man, smells of spice and bitters. Shrubby southernwood grows high and wide (5 feet by 3 feet); close pruning in early spring and moderate midsummer pruning (as for wormwood) keep it within bounds.

Southernwood is another of the genus useful for herbal wreaths, and its branches can be dried and its leaves rubbed fine to fill moth-chasing cloth sachets for drawers or wardrobes.

theorized that wormwood's taste was due to the herb's "absorption of bitter human suffering, and its properties drive sickness from the body and restore the soul to peace and calmness." Yet all herbalists temper their praise with a caution that wormwood must be used moderately and only in the doses recommended.

Applied externally, wormwood is safer – country folk once used a poultice of wormwood leaves to treat sprains and swellings in horses. Later, an ointment called Absorbine was refined from absinthol, the oil of wormwood, and still later, a less potent "Junior" version appeared, which continues to ease the sore muscles of thin-skinned humans. Pliny gives a more pedestrian use, suggesting that leaves placed in the shoes keep a walker from growing weary.

For the garden, 'Lambrook Silver' is the best variety of *Artemisia absinthium*. Its growth is less exuberant, its foliage far whiter than that of the unimproved species. But even this restrained sport fills a 3-foot space, its girth equal to its

height. Because wormwood is half shrubby (that is, it does not die right back to the ground over the winter), it is best to prune the woody branches to no more than a foot high in early spring. An additional pruning in midsummer keeps it from sprawling into a tangle of weak stems. If cut while still fresh and hung to dry, the pliable flower stalks are among the best foundations for herbal wreaths.

One plant is a drift of silver – in our garden, it mingles with (but does not crowd) groups of yellow and sky-blue bearded iris. For early colour, I have planted a dozen daffodil bulbs around the clump. Wormwood is late to stir in spring, but once up, its quicksilver foliage soon fans out to hide the fading daffodils.

The dwarf *Artemisia schmidtiana* may be the best-known member of the genus. If the Latin does not roll off the tongue, look for this piece of garden silverware under the apt alias 'Silver Mound.' Feathery grey-white symmetrical globes 8 inches tall and as broad as 16 inches make a nearly perfect

Alternatively, clothing can be brushed with branches of the herb that the French call *garde-robe*. Fragrant southernwood once formed a part of every nosegay, and sprigs of the herb with a stem of moss rosebuds did (and still could) create a classic bittersweet lovers' bouquet.

As a race, artemisias do not dazzle with colour, but their scent is invariably refreshing and their silver filigree foliage always distinctive and persistent. Wherever planted, they make their quiet presence felt.

CATNIP

Nepeta spp

Although we have never planted catnip, it has always been in the garden. Cats writhe and revel in a patch of *Nepeta cataria*, a coarse, sprawling herb that springs up around barns, in vacant lots and in neglected corners of the garden. We leave a plant or two to fight it out with the raspberries and harvest the leaves to brew fresh or dried into a soothing herb tea. Just how soothing, I learned one summer afternoon. After drinking a cup or two of a fairly strong brew, I felt myself growing increasingly drowsy until I could hardly keep my eyes open and had to curl up for a catnap. A herbalist friend suggests that harmless catnip tea be given to restless or hyperactive children before bed in place of stimulating chocolate drinks.

Several catnip relatives are decorative dwarf herbs for rock gardens, edgings or large containers. For years, we have grown Persian catmint (*Nepeta mussinii* or *N.* × *faassenii*) and every spring welcome back the grey-green aromatic mounds studded with lavender flower spikes that colour just in time to heighten the glow of pink, crimson or yellow tulips. Siberian catnip (*N. sibirica*) grows about 18 inches tall, is looser and has lipped flowers that are lighter blue.

Not spectacular, the ornamental catnips are nevertheless dependably hardy

herbs that are quietly decorative all season long – prominently veined and pebbled leaves add textural interest. Maintenance entails a single shearing (back by half) in July when flowering is past. The low catnips make good ground covers, spreading by midsummer to cover an area 18 inches in diameter; but since they die back to the ground over winter, crocus bulbs can be tucked all around their crowns for early colour. When the catnips themselves bloom, honeybees, bumblebees and butterflies flock to the nectar-rich flowers.

Like the catnips, plants with grey leaves are as carefree as any I know: gardeners looking for low-maintenance plants take note. All tolerate hot sun without flinching; all are immune (in my experience) to insect pests and diseases. And all persist as drifts of silver from early spring until long after the last chrysanthemums have faded; indeed, some shine on into December, keeping their corner of the garden lively until the snow flies. A garden growing a variety of grey-leaved herbs is well appointed even in the absence of bloom.

MULLEIN

Verbascum spp

Certain plants are unaccountably absent from North American gardens. Mulleins, for instance, hardly ever make an appearance, even though several are silvery and garden-worthy. No doubt the mania for tidy dwarf plants has led to mullein's exclusion. True, most are imposing giants, but since their growth – slender and self-supporting – is all upward, they may be grown in gardens too small for sprawling delphiniums or top-heavy dahlias.

Almost anyone who has travelled an eastern North American country road has seen the conspicuous grey-flannel rosettes of common mullein (*Verbascum thapsus*), whose downy spires are set sparsely with five-lobed yellow blossoms. The mission of this naturalized mullein seems to be to rescue waste places from ugliness – a vacant lot nearby is transformed each June into a fine wild-flower garden when the mullein masts sway in a sea of blue viper's bugloss and rippling daisies. I am almost tempted to repeat the picture back home. Indeed, I know one gardener, as wild and woolly as the mullein itself, who encourages the grey rosettes (or at least overlooks them in his rounds of weeding) in odd corners of the herb garden. As well he might: they have been respected healing herbs for centuries. Specifically, a tea made of leaves, flowers or both (1 teaspoon to a cup of boiling water) is said to alleviate hoarseness and bronchial catarrh. A brew created from the flowers alone is reputed to allay pain and induce sleep. The flannel leaves immersed in water and cider vinegar may be applied to areas of inflamed skin and have been dried and smoked to soothe a cough.

Mulleins have been tagged with a plethora of names, all of which aptly describe this vegetal exclamation mark: Aaron's rod, Jupiter's staff, shepherd's staff, beggar's stalk. Telling of the leaf's texture is another round of names: Our Lady's flannel, feltwort, velvet plant; the common name mullein was 'woollen' in times past. The German *konigskerze* is king's candle, and other names repeat the association with light: candlewick plant, hag's taper and torches. Not only does the plant resemble a lighted torch when in flower, but in mediaeval castles, mullein stalks were dipped in tallow and set ablaze for illumination.

Like a candelabrum when in full bloom, *Verbascum olympicum* is a branching Greek relative of the weedy single-stalked mullein. Here is a herb to shine at the very back of a herb bed or to be naturalized in a wild garden or the corners of a vegetable patch. The first season from seed, wide grey-leaved rosettes develop. The following July and August, the spot is alight with yellow

Wild mulleins, FACING PAGE, are imposing giants, but their history makes them respectable residents for the herb garden. Not only does mullein in bloom, LEFT, resemble a lighted torch, but in mediaeval times the plant itself was dipped in tallow and used for illumination.

flowers crowding the 6-foot branched stalk. Left to seed, Greek mullein finds its own way around the garden. One season, three specimens towered above a bed of green beans in our vegetable garden – we had simply left the rosettes alone during fall cleanup and sowed bean seeds around them in spring. Besides appreciating the gratuitous colour, I like this kind of haphazard companion planting because it allows the garden, usually so orderly, to mirror the randomness of nature. Many herbs, among them coriander, dill, clary, calendula and chamomile, sow their hardy seeds and reappear annually in the vegetable garden, providing a bonus harvest and, no doubt, helping to keep insect pests at a comfortable distance.

Few plants in our garden draw as much comment or as many requests for seeds as the Turkish mullein (*Verbascum bombyciferum*), a species so thickly coated with "wool," both leaf and stalk, as to be entirely silver-white. In the bone-dry soil of a raised iris bed, Turkish mullein grew beautifully into 6-foot spires studded with soft, yellow flowers. Thinking to encourage the herb to greater heights, we moved a few seedlings into a new bed prepared with manure, peat moss and clay loam. The move was unfortunate: the rosettes pined, dwindled and died from too much richness. Clearly, it is sun, sand and drought for Turkish mullein, no doubt a denizen of deserts.

A first step with mullein is to secure seed; after that, they are so easy to grow that, as one old-time garden writer says, "anyone who can achieve zinnias and marigolds may have mulleins." For all mullein's eventual bulk, its seed is as fine as pepper but sprouts thick and fast. Start seed in early spring, six or eight to a 4-inch pot, thinning eventually to a single, sturdy seedling. When the plant fills the pot, set it in the garden where it is to flower. I like to see mulleins in a narrow border, perhaps on the sunny side of shrubs or at the edges of a gravel walk or driveway

(always in the sun) where their silver first-year rosettes show to best advantage. Like foxgloves, to which they are related, mulleins are biennials that grow basal leaves one year and send up flowering stalks the next. Leave them to go to seed. The spent flower stalks are architectural, the seeds are a favourite winter forage for chickadees and the stalks will linger in the garden perennially.

SILVER SAGE

Salvia spp

Two members of the genus *Salvia* are familiar to all: the annual scarlet salvias burn away in park beds and home gardens, and the grey-leaved "turkey-stuffing" sage is, with parsley and chives, among the most popular of culinary herbs. But clary (*S. sclarea*) – a tall, handsome biennial – deserves to be better known. Its leaves, broadly heart-shaped, pebbled and grey with fine hairs, are topped by 4-foot pyramidal flower spikes whose pearly parchment-like bracts are as striking as their lipped violet flowers.

An infusion of clary seeds was once used as an eyewash; hence, the herb is sometimes simply called clear-eyes. Also, clary once flavoured most homemade wines and ales, and tops of the herb were used to give the bouquet of muscatel grapes to wines of the Rhine region; the German for clary is *muscateller*. In the kitchen, clary had its uses too: both John Evelyn and John Parkinson published 17th-century recipes using young clary leaves and flowers in batter-dipped fritters, in soups and "in our cold sallets yet so as not to domineer."

Clary begins to bloom in July, in time to complement clumps of lilies. Even after the flowers fade, the conspicuous silver-pink bracts keep the herb garden-worthy well into September. Clary is easily grown from seed; if left to go to seed, in fact, there will always be a few grey

rosettes in the garden come spring. These I find useful to tuck into the herb or flowerbeds where less stalwart plants have succumbed to winter. Visitors to the garden always react with enthusiasm to this unusual sage. Considering that it practically grows itself, clary ought to find a home in more gardens.

RUE

Ruta graveolens

Next to wormwood, rue – Shakespeare's "herb o' grace" or, more colloquially, herbygrass – is the most bitter of plants. The 16th-century herbalist Thomas Tusser recommended the two for strewing in sickrooms: "What saver be better, if physick be true, For places infected than wormwood and rue." An aura of mystery still hangs about the cool and quiet rue bushes – the strange, acrid scent of the blue-green leaves seems to conjure past associations with witches, magic, spells and incantations.

Rue has always been counted a prime herbal antidote to poisons and plagues, as well as to the less material but no less malevolent evil eye.

I like clumps of rue in the garden for its metallic, lobed foliage, a foil for bright bee-balm or purple coneflowers; rue's unusual, greenish yellow flowers make little show. Like the taller artemisias, half-shrubby rue needs moderate clipping in spring to keep it shapely. Grow this 2-foot-tall plant from seed or from nursery plants – it cannot be successfully divided – in any decent soil in sun.

LAMB'S EAR

Stachys lanata, S. olympica or S. byzantina

Among the whitest foliage in our garden is that of velvety *Stachys lanata* (or *S. byzantina*), and only the Turkish mullein is as densely furred. Commonly called lamb's ear or lamb's tongue, the herb is also known as woundwort from the former practice of using the leaves as bandages, a purpose they seem nicely suited for, given their cottony surface. Although the wands of small, rose-purple flowers, a favourite forage of honeybees, grow to several feet in June, we have a stretch of stachys along the front of a perennial border primarily for its silver colour, which, combined with pink Oriental poppies and blue bearded iris, makes a favourite garden picture.

Hardy stachys is immune to scorching sun and drought, and if the flower stalks are cut away when they become shabby, this herb remains presentable from spring until late fall. Since this mint relative tends to spread in a slow but steady fashion, I pull back the shallow-rooted shoots every season or two. If parts of a clump have died away from age, overcrowding or winter damp, I press in a few of the rooted shoots to renew bare spots. Lamb's ear grows easily from seed and, like all grey-leaved herbs, needs sun and good soil drainage.

Clary, LEFT, and mullein, BELOW, act as gentle foils to the bright greens and varied hues of other herbs.

Rue has an acrid scent that is reputedly useful against poisons, plagues, sickroom odours and the evil eye.

CHAPTER TEN

SHADES OF GREEN

Choice selections for dark corners

Some years ago, while on a bicycle tour of English gardens, I visited one of those grand country places for which England is noted. Although I was a little bewildered by the scope of this garden and its variety of plants, one special "room" in the overall landscape impressed me as a beautifully practical solution to a common garden problem – shade. Besides the picture-perfect herbaceous borders, an alpine terrace, the peony walk and a herb garden so far from the house it must have been "just for show" (as another visitor suggested), there was a little shadowy foliage garden filled with plants of interesting leaf texture and design – many of them herbs. Although, admittedly, this estate employed four full-time gardeners, "the shaded garden," said the owner, "requires very little work indeed to keep in trim." Planting this area rather than abandoning it as impossible to garden was a sound idea perfectly adaptable to a sunless site of any size.

Shade drastically reduces the range of plant possibilities; put aside visions of bright borders of perennials or even beds of ordinary annuals such as marigolds, zinnias, cosmos or nasturtiums – sun lovers all. Avoid, too, the grey herbs, which thrive in full sun; the hotter, the better. Instead, think of green leaves and ground covers. The visual appeal of the shade plants is often subtle, focused as it is in the shapes, shades and textures of their foliage; their flowers are usually small, seldom showy and often white, shades of violet-blue or, in several species, a cool and curious greenish yellow. If a shaded yard were my lot of land – such gardens are almost the norm in city neighbourhoods

where venerable old trees have been wisely left to weave their way skyward through a warp of wires – I would grow suitable herbs there, mingling them with ferns and native woodland flowers. As it happens, a shaded yard is not my lot in life, but I do want to grow these plants, so I situate some of them in the open and some on the lee side of buildings or garden walls or next to taller species – even trees.

Because many of the plants are low-growing and spreading, it is necessary to prepare the area where they will grow by removing every scrap of sod that would otherwise overwhelm these shy greens. Grass may be nice for sunbathing, but it has no place in the shade garden (and unless one is addicted to croquet or lawn bowling, it is not much use in any case, dull to look at and a waste of good gardening time to care for). It is a mistake to think that the different sorts of shade plants must be separated from one another; let them mingle and, in a few cases, fight it out. Given a good start and some encouragement thereafter (that is, weeding), they soon widen to form interlacing carpets of varied foliage with a few taller sorts appearing here and there as bold leafy accents. Ample paths for working in the garden or just watching things grow could lead through the planted spaces to a small clearing toward the back, where I would place a bench or two, perhaps a birdbath or small sunken pool, even a little fountain. For spring colour, hardy bulbs can be tucked right through the carpeting herbs in fall. A conscientious gardener would be well-advised to devote some thought to matching flowers to ground covers so that tiny bulbs do not have to stretch through tall plants, and strong-

growing bulbs such as daffodils do not smother ground-hugging herbs.

SWEET WOODRUFF

Asperula odorata syn. *Galium odoratum*

Grey beeches or white birches within beds of woodruff, snowdrops and bluebells produce pictures reminiscent of Old World woods; the bulbs will flower in increasing numbers each spring. Other bulbs the gardener might consider planting under woodruff are crocuses or dwarf daffodils such as the slender multiflowered narcissus 'Thalia.'

Sweet woodruff is, I think, the prettiest of the dwarf herbs. A single specimen makes little impact, but woodruff en masse forms a carpet of whorled leaves, dark green and glossy, and an earth-borne Milky Way of tiny white blooms in June. Delicate in appearance but tenacious and hardy, this denizen of British and European woods craves shade, a modicum of moisture and, some say, an acidic, sour soil. At Larkwhistle, however, it has done well in soil that is definitely limy, or sweet, and it has taken to the sun as well.

Germany's famous May wine, *Waldmeister-Bowle*, is traditionally drunk on May Day and then all through woodruff season until the plant starts to flower. "There is something of a ceremony involved in making May wine, like brewing tea in Japan," says a friend, recalling her childhood in Germany. "People go into the woods to gather fresh sprigs of woodruff; traditionally, white wine and

woodruff go into an earthenware jug or crock that is then buried in the ground for half a day to chill to earth temperature. The woodruff is strained out and the wine served, sometimes mixed with champagne, from a crystal punch bowl into crystal cups." Woodruff gatherers also bring home extra bunches to hang in wardrobes and linen closets, where the herb dries, pervading clothes and bedding with a summer sweetness.

I remember my first whiff of woodruff in the greenhouse of a commercial herb grower. It was a grey February day, but the scent of a few dry woodruff leaves transported me to a summer meadow. The fragrance, often compared to that of freshly cut hay, is a blended redolence of spring earth and honey sweetness. Only faintly fragrant when fresh, leaves develop their full bouquet when dry and remain fragrant for years. Dried, crushed woodruff leaves are useful in a potpourri, not only for their own fragrance but also for their ability to fix or retain the scents of other herbs and spices in the manner of orrisroot, described in Chapter 11, page 145.

A restrained creeper, not aggressive like mint, woodruff sends small searching runners in all directions. To cover a given area—that is, *after* all perennial weeds have been removed—set out at least five plants, and preferably more, 10 inches apart, and keep the intervening spaces scrupulously weedless until the cover is complete.

Unfortunately, woodruff is slow and difficult to grow from seed—germination can take as long as a year—and plants in quantity are expensive. A generous gardening friend may part with starter clumps, and if patience allows, several plants left to spread for a season will provide good propagating stock. Either take small plugs—pieces of crown with roots attached—from a patch with a sharp knife and trowel, or lift a whole plant and break it into rooted bits to plant elsewhere. Give new plants a trowel or two of a recuperative mixture of damp peat moss, old

Sweet woodruff, LEFT, *is a restrained creeper, and comfrey,* BOTTOM RIGHT, *if moved or tilled, will send up new shoots from the remaining roots. But goutweed,* RIGHT, *is such a persistent and aggressive plant that it is best grown only in a contained situation—or not at all.*

The common Johnny-jump-up (Viola tricolor), PREVIOUS PAGE, *shines from the shadows.*

manure or sifted compost and a little bone meal, stirred deeply into the planting hole. These same ingredients do wonders if dug into the ground that is to grow any shady herb. See primroses, page 137, for details on preparing the earth.

While perusing an old gardening book, I came across a description of a hardy annual woodruff that was said to seed itself if properly established in a garden. Only once did I see seed for it offered in a catalogue – I hope it will appear again – but each spring, now, little colonies of this delicate 10-inch herb reappear in our garden, where they are prized for their clusters of sky-blue flowers on slender, red-tinted stems. Its Latin name is *Asperula azurea-setosa* (or sometimes *A. orientalis* or *A. coerulea*), but I simply call it blue annual woodruff. Such flowering plants are always the first items to sell at a local herb fair each summer.

LADY'S BEDSTRAW

Galium verum

Lady's bedstraw is a little like the related woodruff in appearance, except that its whorled leaves are smaller and more dense and its flowers are greenish yellow in frothy panicles. This herb does not run but expands outward each year into a widening clump. The name bedstraw derives from the use of the dried plant to stuff the mattresses "even of ladies of rank."

I like to see single bedstraw plants at intervals along the edge of a shaded border. But for those who like balance and formality, such plants are fine focal accents on either side of steps or a path; they will also sprawl decoratively over the top of a retaining wall. Spaced on 12-inch centres, unchecked bedstraw plants soon make a lacy cover; for spring colour, tuck bulbs of snowdrops or dwarf daffodils through it in the fall. More tolerant of sun and

dryness than woodruff, bedstraw still appreciates good ground. Maintenance consists only of clearing away the strawy debris left after the winter and, if necessary, reducing the size of the clumps with a trowel or small spade; a midsummer shearing keeps this lax herb from swamping nearby plants.

Bedstraw was once used as a rennet substitute and called "cheese renning" because its leaves and flowers cause milk to separate into curds and whey and colour the final cheese yellow. The stems and leaves also yield a good yellow fabric dye, while the roots effect a red colouring.

BUGLEWEED

Ajuga reptans

A good neighbour for bedstraw, the common bugleweed is able to hold its own in any company but may be a threat to less ambitious plants. Here is a herb that will cover thickly any expanse of ground with persistent tongue-shaped foliage; the glossy leaves of one variety shine with the verdigris of old copper, another has bluish green foliage, while others are mottled red, white, green and cream. Several sorts planted randomly together weave a colourful tapestry, and in early summer, all hoist decorative short spikes of blue flowers that are lipped, showing their kinship with mints, lemon balm and other labiates. Since ajugas spread quickly and far, it is wise to keep them away from smaller plants and certainly out of a rock garden if one hopes to grow anything else there.

"This herb belongs to Dame Venus," Nicholas Culpeper declared in the 16th century. "If the virtues make you fall in love with it (as they will if you be wise), keep a syrup of it to take inwardly and an ointment and plaister of it to use outwardly always by you." The herb, which he called bugle, sickle-wort or herb-carpenter, "is wonderful in curing all manner of ulcers and sores . . . gangrenes and fistulas also, if the leaves bruised and applied or their juice be used to wash and bathe the place." For anyone who wants to experiment with a simple herbal remedy, this is worth a try.

DEAD NETTLE

Lamium maculatum

A fine aesthetic complement to the preceding three plants and pushy enough to withstand competition is *Lamium maculatum*. This is another labiate that might be more frequently chosen as a ground cover if it were called something other than dead nettle. Far better is its old name – purple archangel. Like the common field yarrow, lamium is said to have haemostatic properties: the bruised leaves applied to bleeding wounds are supposed to stop the flow of blood.

The ordinary lamium is a bit dowdy, with plain green leaves and dull magenta flowers, but several sports are more attractive. My favourite is the white-flowering *Lamium maculatum album*, whose heart-shaped leaves are freshly striped with white. The rare cultivar 'Beacon Silver' also lights up a shady garden. Its foliage is entirely silver-white except for a hairline edge of green, and its flowers are pink.

Rooting as it runs, lamium grows a foot tall and forms a weed-smothering ground cover, but it is easily checked if it covets more than its share of space. There is no trick to growing this mint relative, save finding plants of the better sorts and setting them 16 inches apart in reasonably good ground. Tall daffodils will bloom through lamium for spring colour.

SWEET CICELY

Myrris odorata

At Larkwhistle, one no-care corner is perennially cool green and white. An exuberant mass of white lamium and a few plants of bedstraw form the edging. At the rear are some native cedar trees, in front are clumps of sweet cicely fanning their fernlike foliage and hoisting umbels of white flowers, like giant Queen Anne's lace, on strong 4-foot stems.

It was Gertrude Jekyll, an influential English garden artist of the last century, who first drew our attention (in her book *Wood and Garden*) to sweet cicely, a roadside weed in Britain. "*Myrris odorata*," she says, "for its beauty, deserves to be in every garden; it is charming, with its finely cut, pale green leaves and really handsome flowers." Take her suggestion, and interplant daffodils with sweet cicely; the early fronds create a green setting for the daffodils and then grow up and hide the fading bulb leaves.

Sweet cicely – "sweet, pleasant and spicie hot, delightfull unto many," according to John Parkinson in his 1629 treatise on garden plants – is a favourite herb for our garden visitors to nibble. Neighbouring children

keep coming back for "more licorice"; the stems, leaves and especially the unripe green seeds are intensely flavoured of anise. A friend stews the chopped stalks of cicely with rhubarb or other fruits and reduces the sweetener accordingly; this herb is said to contain as much as 40 percent sugar. I like to mix the leaves with mint and lemon balm for a citrus-sweet herb tea, or mince a bit of leaf with basil, lovage and parsley to scatter over salads. Pieces of the most tender stems and very young green seeds—nibble a few to be sure they are not fibrous—can be baked into cookies, quickbreads and rhubarb or strawberry pies. A single plant is plenty for cooking, but three or more spaced 2 feet apart are more pleasing in the landscape.

Given that small specimens spring up around mature plants and sprout from the compost heap, I do not understand why sweet cicely seed sells for $4 a packet in at least one herb catalogue. True, the seeds germinate only when fresh, and that means a special shipment in July or August for immediate planting, but they are produced in abundance. For neatness' sake and to avoid forever rooting out seedlings, cut back most stalks before the seed ripens. Four dollars a pack? Hmm.

ANGELICA
Angelica archangelica

I am a little in awe of any plant named *Angelica archangelica*. In his 17th-century herbal, John Parkinson put angelica in the forefront of his panoply of medicinals because it was angelically able to ward off evil spirits, spells, witchcraft and enchantments. The whole plant has a scent that cannot be mistaken for that of any other herb, reminiscent of something I have tasted in a monastery liqueur. Its stems and seeds flavour vermouth as well as that strange green firewater, chartreuse, and essence of angelica goes into some perfumes. In herbal medicines, roots are used that, "dried rapidly and placed in air-tight receptacles, retain their virtues for years," says Mrs. Grieve. So-so brandy assumes an exotic taste and, many say, digestion-helping properties, if not only roots but also angelica leaves, stalks and seeds are steeped in it for several weeks. I like a bit of angelica in a herb-tea blend, while others use it in stewed fruits and jams, cooking the slightly sweet whole stalks with the fruit and removing them when cooking has been completed. The plant has proved hardy beyond the Arctic Circle; Finns, Norwegians and Laplanders eat young angelica stalks as vegetables, a dish I intend to try some spring day.

Angelica is a decorative herb at the rear of a bed, especially when its big cartwheels of yellow-green are in flower. Like the related sweet cicely, this 6-foot biennial grows only from fresh seeds—also $4 a pack at my latest appraisal. Rather than cutting down the impressive flower stalk, which is supposed to trick the plant into being perennial, we let angelica flower, ripen and scatter its seeds. So treated, it has stayed in the garden for years.

A shady corner of Larkwhistle, FACING PAGE, *features Lady's bedstraw (lower right), dead nettle (lower left) and sweet cicely (centre). The latter,* RIGHT, *makes a delicious tea when blended with mint and lemon balm.*

Many of the shady herbs were once highly respected for their medicinal properties. Violets, LEFT, were thought to possess a health-giving fragrance; Solomon's seal, ABOVE, was valued for helping bones knit and for bleaching the skin; and the drops of rain or dew on Lady's mantle, TOP LEFT, itself therapeutic, were considered highly potent.

GOUTWEED

Aegopodium podagraria

Warning: if someone gives you goutweed, give it back. Do not plant it in the garden; do not even toss it on the compost heap. Slips of this vegetable strangler are casually passed along as "a pretty green-and-white ground cover that grows itself" — to say the least. Pretty it may be, and, says Nicholas Culpeper, "it heals the gout and sciatica," but I have seen too many small gardens completely swamped by this greedy herb, including one carefully terraced rock garden that cost someone's back several weeks of work and now grows only goutweed. Says Mrs. Grieve in *A Modern Herbal* (1931), "It has a creeping rootstock that spreads rapidly, soon smothering all less rampant vegetation." Once entrenched, especially among rocks, it is next to impossible to get rid of. Recognize the foot-high plant by its pointed, variegated leaves slightly toothed at the edges, with six or eight leaves to a stem; or ask a few questions if presented with an anonymous "pretty green-and-white thing."

LADY'S MANTLE

Alchemilla mollis, syn. *A. vulgaris*

Few gardens grow this plant, perhaps because hot-coloured novelties have blinded us to its subtler beauty. But mediaeval alchemists — from whose science alchemilla derives its name — certainly valued the plant for wounds, for herbal baths and to "promote quiet sleep" if the leaves were placed under the pillow at night. Especially valued were the dewdrops that sat upon the leaves like crystal beads. Nor did Gertrude Jekyll overlook the charms of this quiet plant — an entire page of one of her books is given to a description of a leaf of Lady's mantle.

Indeed, it is mainly for its handsome leaves — broad, pleated blue-green, scalloped along the edges, fresh from spring to fall — that alchemilla is now grown. Like bedstraw, foot-tall Lady's mantle can be a neat specimen plant repeated at intervals along the edge of a shady border or a tallish ground cover, but not in the dry shade directly under trees. For best effect, give each plant an 18-inch diameter to fill without competition. In our coolish northern garden, Lady's mantle grows both in shade and in full sun, but shade is a must in hotter southerly gardens.

Lady's mantle is best started from nursery plants. Seed is slow and uncertain; for me, two plants were all that grew from a packet. Last spring, however, I split one of them into three divisions to extend a planting.

SOLOMON'S SEAL

Polygonatum multiflorum

Our cool corners of cedars and sweet cicely might well include Solomon's seal. Green and white are the colours of this handsome herb (to 4 feet), suitable for the rear of a shaded herb bed or corner of a city garden. I have seen it used to good effect, giving an impression of order and symmetry, in a foundation planting as an alternative to the usual dwarf pines and junipers. Oval ribbed leaves, each tilted forward at a precise angle, are set at regular intervals along gracefully arching stems. Toward the top of the stems, a cluster of wax-white scented bells hangs from each leaf axil. Nor does this tidy plant disappear in midsummer like poppies or delphiniums: its foliage stays fresh until the very last, then colours a warm yellow in keeping with the fall season.

Once valued for helping bones knit, for treating "women's problems" and, says Nicholas Culpeper, for cleansing skin of "freckles, spots or any marks whatever, leaving the place fresh, fair and lovely," Solomon's seal is a close relative of lily-of-the-valley (another favourite for shade) and spreads in much the same way, only slower. Thick white underground stems called rhizomes travel a short way and then emerge as new shoots. A small patch in our garden, crowded by lilacs behind and peonies in front, has not increased much over four years, but there is a corner of a new bed, well enriched with old manure and peat moss, allocated for divisions of this hungry woodlander.

Propagating the plant is an easy matter. Sometime during October or April, divide the rootstock with a sharp knife, allowing each piece of root an eye, which looks like the tip of an asparagus stalk. I cannot recall ever doing anything to or for self-sufficient Solomon's seal after having planted it.

COMFREY

Symphytum officinale

A bold, leafy plant that tends to dominate the spot where it is planted, comfrey is also prominent in its positon in old herbals. Its venerable medicinal reputation probably arises from a mucilaginous substance in its roots, allantoin, which can "promote cell proliferation," noted Dr. Varro E. Tyler of Purdue University in *The Honest Herbal*. Popular old names such as knitbone, bruisewort, boneset and healing herb tell that comfrey once figured in poultices for sprains, swellings, burns and bruises. Taken internally, a decoction of comfrey root was meant to soothe ulcers and respiratory ailments.

Recently, however, the safety of ingesting comfrey, especially large doses over a long duration, has come into question. Some plants contain pyrrolozidine alkaloids, which are carcinogenic—for rats, at any rate. John and Karen Balf of Tansy Farms in British Columbia note that "internal use [is] discouraged at present while research [is] being done into possible harmful effects."

I am not a herbalist, but I would not hesitate to slap a comfrey poultice on any external wound; nor am I concerned about chopping a leaf or two of comfrey into a spring salad, or cooking up an occasional pot of comfrey greens. But whether or not one decides to consider comfrey edible or medicinal, the plant still has a place in the garden. In front of tall shrubs, toward the back of a herb bed or anywhere in the landscape where there is room for its 4-foot bulk, the plant provides an attractive green mound of foliage. Over many weeks in summer, it unfurls coiled spirals of buds and hangs out a succession of small mauve, pink-white or (best of all, if you can find it) bright blue bells.

When this cousin of borage, anchusa, the wild viper's bugloss and the lowly forget-me-not ceases flowering, it begins to look seedy and bedraggled; this is the time to cut stalks and leaves and add them to the compost heap, where they will contribute a store of nutrients mined by deep roots. In fact, comfrey leaves contain such high concentrations of soluble plant foods that the foliage can be brewed—one part leaves in three parts water—and left to steep for a week, to concoct a potash-rich green manure "tea" for watering tomatoes, root crops and cucumber or squash vines. Once cut, comfrey grows a new crop of fresh foliage, so the spot where it grows is always presentable.

At the start, a good gardener is advised to give some thought to the placement of comfrey; not only is it a bulky plant to move, but every root severed in the digging process sprouts into a full-sized plant. Like horseradish and Johnny-jump-ups, comfrey can become one of a gardener's self-inflicted weeds.

VIOLETS

Viola spp

Heartsease and sweet violets are two members of the genus *Viola* that crop up in herbals as medicinal plants. We have had to be strict and plant only one.

Heartsease, better known as Johnny-jump-ups (*Viola tricolor*), are small pert pansies that take to partial shade but will also go to great lengths to look out at the

Dead nettle, or purple archangel, LEFT, *has homeopathic uses only, while the violet,* BELOW, *can flavour teas and salads.*

sun, stretching right through a peony or rosebush to peer blithely over the top. Once, we let them all stay, but soon, colonies of seedlings appeared all through the perennials. Now, a few are left at the bases of rocks that edge the beds; even these manage to jump the curb and take off. If they can have some garden space to themselves, perhaps to carpet a bed of daffodils or lilies, purple-and-gold Johnny-jump-ups are an easy ground cover, as bright as any annual and longer-flowering than most. Often, they are among the first flowers to blossom in spring and are still colourful in a small way in October. No wonder they are such unrestrained seeders.

True sweet violets (*Viola odorata*), most famous of the herbal violets, are not as easy to come by. Several times, I have sent for stock or brought home a tuft of green from a nursery, only to have a crop of nice purple flowers but none of the famous scent described by Francis Bacon in 1625 as "the sweetest smell in the air." Fragrance is what sweet violets are all about. One author states that "white wine vinegar derives not only a brilliant tint but a sweet scent from having violet flowers steeped in it." Violets, with or without fragrance, also make spring salads festive, and young leaves and flowers produce a tea rich in minerals and vitamin C; mint or lemon balm adds flavour.

Perennial relatives of pansies, sweet violets expand from year to year by small creeping rhizomes and, like heartsease, seed a little too generously. They will grow in ordinary ground in sun or shade. "I have an old steamer chair in the tool shed," says Louise Wilder, one of my favourite garden writers (*The Fragrant Path*, 1932), "and when a mild March spell starts the violets to blossoming, I drag it forth and lie by the hour in the sunshine inhaling the delicious fragrance." If I were to drag a steamer chair into the garden in March, chances are I'd be inhaling snowflakes—but the thought is there, and spring always comes.

PRIMROSES

Primula spp

Violets and primroses belong in the same shady garden but not in the same spot. Flowers of spring, both thrive in cool, moist, shadowy places and dwindle if set in dry ground in sun. But primroses are for a special corner away from the rough-and-tumble ajuga, Lady's bedstraw, lamium and such, while violets will fill any vacant nook in the herbal tapestry, even crowding under cedar trees or around the bases of shrubs.

I think all gardeners must have a favourite flower—perhaps a pink poppy they would miss if it did not return faithfully each June, a special rose or some rare alpine they have coaxed from seed to blossom. My favourites are primulas of all sorts. Species of primrose grow all through Europe and Asia. Many are mountain plants that hang from high rock faces in Chinese and Tibetan ranges. Others hide in shaded swamps; Japan is particularly rich in bog primulas. But best-loved in the west are the simple flowers of spring: the cowslips of damp meadows, oxlips of the woodland and the English primroses that follow the courses of streams or sit under hedgerows.

Typical of the genus, all three have crinkled or puckered tongue-shaped leaves, fresh green in colour, with a smooth central rib. But there are distinctions among them. Cowslips (*Primula veris*) grow small, soft yellow or orange concave flowers, each spotted with five tiny red dots and set in a baggy pale green calyx. Oxlips (*P. elatior*) also have many flowers per stem, but this species has smaller calyxes and pale yellow flowers that are wider and flatter. Recognize the true English primrose (*P. vulgaris*) and its derivatives by flat, upfacing flowers so profuse that they all but hide the leaves in well-grown plants. Each blossom sits on its own short stem. Since hybridizers have been mixing primrose genes, colours vary from blue and violet to pink, crimson and orange, but the colour is traditionally—what else?—primrose-yellow. Crosses among the three species have given rise to a race of showy garden primulas—the polyanthus of unnumbered dyes—that flower for more than a month in spring, all through May in our garden, if treated well.

Primroses cannot be plunked willy-nilly into any vacant corner and be expected to thrive. I wonder if I would treasure them as much if they were not a challenge to grow in this mainly sunny, sandy garden. On the shady side of tall white lilacs — a reminder that there was once a farm here — there is a wide border, enriched heavily with old manure, which grows a winding band of primroses. Most were raised from seed; over the years, the best of them have been divided and redivided to carry the spring colour farther.

All primulas have big appetites. Spongy organic matter in all forms keeps them flourishing. Crumbly manure rotted to the black-earth stage and well mixed with half its volume of damp peat moss is excellent, as is leaf mould or screened compost. Add some bone meal too. Since primroses do not root deeply, all of this goodness can be spread over a bed to a depth of 4 inches or more and turned in with a spading fork; then work the upright fork in a side-to-side turning motion to further mix and blend. It does no harm to walk back and forth a few times over a bed so dug — we are not growing carrots here — to consolidate the ground and squeeze out air pockets. But tread lightly if starting with clay soil.

Although primroses may be grown from seed by patient gardeners, an easy way to add to or create a primrose path is to buy potted flowering primroses, usually for sale in midwinter in many city greengroceries or flower shops. Pick favourite colours, enjoy the flowers indoors during the winter, and set them in the garden in spring — the last frost date is about right for these coddled plants. Water well into a shallow earth "saucer" left around each newly set plant. Several gardeners who are unable to water their primroses during the summer tell me that the plants almost disappear during the heat of July and August, only to sprout afresh when fall rains start.

After three or four years,

Primroses, LEFT, and cowslips, RIGHT, seen here in their double form, are relatives that demand good rich soil, shade and sufficient water, especially just after division in June. Their flowers have traditionally been used in salads, conserves, wines and medicinal syrups.

clumps of primroses begin to deteriorate, growing bald in the centre, with a ring of weak leaves. This is the time to split them into separate crowns and replant the divisions in enriched ground. Division is usually done in June, just after the flowers are over. Waterings must be frequent for a month thereafter. But we have divided primroses with good success as late as the first week in September. All this is much less work than it sounds, since primroses are small plants easily pried out of the ground with a hand fork and teased apart with the fingers.

Like violets, the flowers of primulas have traditionally gone into salads, conserves, wines and medicinal syrups. One very old cookbook includes a "primrose pottage," a sort of pudding made with almonds, honey, saffron and ground primrose flowers. Primula flowers were also highly valued in cosmetics, a use that might well be revived today. Nicholas Culpeper declared that "our city dames know well enough the ointment or distilled water of cowslips adds to beauty, or at least restores it when lost." In his 1528 herbal, William Turner had his say on the subject of womanly beauty: "Some, we find, sprinkle ye floures of cowslip with whyte wine and wash their faces with the water to drive wrinkles away and to make them fayre in the eyes of the world, rather than" – I can hear the thunder in his voice – "in the eyes of God, Whom they are not afrayd to offend."

OTHER HERBS

Gardeners wanting to harvest more flavour from a shady site should note that some cooking and tea herbs will do fine in shade. These include lovage, sorrel, parsley, caraway, mint, lemon balm, bergamot and chervil, all of which are discussed in detail in other chapters. None, however, thrives directly under trees or in dry ground matted with the shallow roots of maple trees. But if sun reaches them for part of a day or if they are in the flickering shade cast by high-canopied trees some distance away, certain aromatic plants will grow happily. It is wise to enrich the ground with organic matter and to see that the herbs do not suffer from lack of water.

Among the colourful herbs that will survive in partial shade are foxgloves, aconite, or monkshood, meadowsweet and many beautiful native woodland plants, such as ferns, hepatica, Joe Pye weed, jewel weed, wild clematis, lobelia, fireweed and loosestrife, all used in countless ways by North American native people. For a detailed treatment of the subject of native plants as medicinals, I recommend *Indian Herbalogy of North America* by Alma R. Hutchens (1969) and a good guide to wildflower cultivation such as *Growing Wildflowers* by Maria Sperka (1973). With such plants in it, a shady garden can be deeply satisfying – cool and leafy in the heat of summer, full of subtle variety all season long. Furthermore, most of the shady-side herbs take care of themselves, an important consideration for a busy gardener. Unlike the well-manicured English estate I visited years ago, most shady gardens will not be blessed by the ministrations of several professional groundskeepers, but they can still be as pleasing to the eye as any under the sun.

CHAPTER ELEVEN

UNCOMMON SCENTS

Herbs for fragrance

"Sweet perfumes work immediately upon the spirits," wrote Ralph Austen in his *A Treatise of Fruit Trees* of 1653, "for their refreshing sweet and healthfull ayres are special preservatives to health, and therefore much to be prised."

It is indeed true that perfumes "work immediately upon the spirits." What is it in an invisible fragrance, I wonder, that races to the brain and triggers an instant flood of vivid memories? What makes even the most dour person respond with an involuntary smile – and most kids with a giggle – to a noseful of fresh peppermint? Why do some of us recoil from a whiff of rue, while others take a second hesitant sniff – "Strange, but I think I like that." To describe a

scent, however, is a difficult matter: compared with all the words we have for colours, tastes and textures, the language of smells is lacking – scents are either sweet or not, vaguely pleasant or awful. And yet, for most of us – some unfortunate souls are either partially or totally "smell-blind," or anosmic – there is no getting away from smells. The nose is at work constantly, either seeking information or simply enjoying itself. According to one William Bullein, writing in 1562, this pleasure of the nose (as opposed to its information-seeking function) is a human prerogative: "Humankind only doth smel and take delight in the odours of flowers and sweet things."

Before anyone knew a thing about the chemistry of scents or

the physiology of smelling, those wise in the ways of gardens recognized that fragrances do something remedial and are somehow active. "Physicians," wrote Michel Eyquem Montaigne in the 16th century, "might in mine opinion draw more use and good from odours than they doe." In the first century, botanist Pliny the Elder stated in his *Naturalis Historia*, "As for . . . mint, the very smell alone recovers and refreshes our spirits." The scent of wild thyme was believed to "raise the spirits and strengthen the vital energies"; that of basil, according to 16th-century herbalist John Gerard, "taketh away melancholy and maketh a man merry and glad." And, said Louise Wilder in *The Fragrant Path* of 1934, "To me, the smell

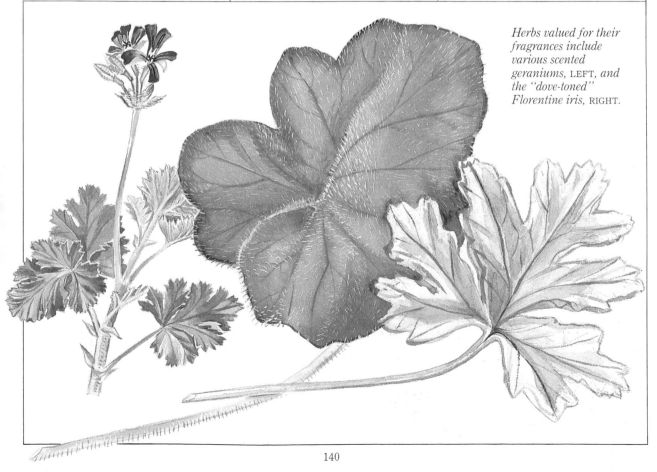

Herbs valued for their fragrances include various scented geraniums, LEFT, *and the "dove-toned" Florentine iris,* RIGHT.

of Clove Pinks is instantly invigorating, while . . . the true old Rose scent is invariably calming." Nowhere is the nose happier than in a garden, and if the garden is filled with herbs, so much the better.

An alternative health practice that supposedly assists recovery through the use of scents—it couldn't hurt, in any case, to have one's forehead and temples massaged with lavender oil—is called "aromatherapy." But therapeutic enough is a stroll around the garden, just after a mild June rain has encouraged roses, pinks and lavender to spill more of their perfume.

OLD ROSES

Rosa spp

Roses once loomed large in every herbal. At one time, fragrant rose petals were so essential an ingredient in plant-based medicines, syrups, scented oils, rose-water, rose vinegar, lozenges and vitamin-rich conserves that botanist John Lindley suggested in 1866 that "the rose could form the sole

basis for the entire pharmacopaeia." Nor was it always thought necessary to brew, stew or otherwise use roses directly; simply to inhale their fragrance deeply was considered curative.

Who can argue? The true old rose scent, always a favourite floral fragrance, is sweet but never cloying, full-bodied but not heavy like that of some lilies or certain night-blooming tropicals. "Pure and transparent" is the apt description given by one old-time garden writer; it is "an odour in which we may . . . burrow deeply without finding anything coarse or bitter, in which we may touch bottom without losing our sense of exquisite pleasure." I remember a visit to Mottisfont Abbey, not far from Winchester, England, a home for a collection of historical roses on the site of a 12th-century monastery. Warm June sun had just broken through the perpetual mist of the past week, and the atmosphere, still laden with moisture, diffused the light into a soft brilliance. The roses—a full half-acre of them—seemed to stir in response to the gentle heat and humidity and exhaled a wave of

sweetness that was the very essence of rose.

Modern roses are to old roses what Vogue models, all bone structure and paint, are to Reuben's female figures—plump, pink and glowing from a bath scented, no doubt, with rose-water. Stop and smell one of the latest coral-coloured creations, and chances are you will detect only a ghost of sweet scent or none at all. But the gardener who wants to grow a rose or two from the past, all of which are full of fragrance, must replace visions of long-stemmed and perfectly spiralled flowers with a picture of roses that are rounder, flatter and more loosely made and coloured crimson, white or, of course, rose-pink.

Reaching back to the dawn of history, the complex genealogy of the rose reads like Leviticus. But to include a few old roses in a corner of a modern herb garden or to fill an island bed edged with lavender, northern gardeners must look for cultivars of the hardier species. *Rosa alba*, the white rose of the House of York, has been in gardens since the 1600s; a cultivar, 'Suaveolens,' is still grown

commercially in Europe as a source of rose oil, while 'Celestial,' 'Königin von Dänemark' and 'Maiden's Blush' are better garden roses. Garden-worthy, too, are varieties of *R. centifolia*, the hundred-leaved, or cabbage, rose, a sort so often depicted in the floral art of the Dutch masters and in the work of rose illustrator Pierre Joseph Redouté that one is called 'Rose des Peintres' and another, 'Prolifera de Redouté.' From *R. gallica*, the French rose, is derived the apothecary rose (*R. gallica officinalis*) of many uses, once in medicine, now in perfumery, as well as 'Rosa Mundi,' my own favourite among old roses. And there are hardy moss roses, old-fashioned favourites for bouquets and nosegays, whose buds bristle with a glandular formation resembling green moss.

Of the dozen old roses growing at Larkwhistle, two stand out for their exceptional beauty, vigour and health. The first, 'Königin von Däncmark' (Queen of Denmark), an *alba* hybrid growing 4 feet tall, blooms through most of July, opening pure pink, highly fragrant flowers that are divided into "quartered" segments, a typical old rose form. The other – and the one I would choose if I could grow only one old rose – is 'Rosa Mundi' (*R. gallica versicolor*). Known before 1580, this beauty is the namesake of "fair Rosamund," one of the unhappy mistresses of Henry II. Its flowers are loosely semidouble, several rows of petals surrounding a central mass of golden stamens; and, unlike any other rose I know, the petals are variously striped crimson, pink and white. The fragrance is heady.

Never have I seen a hint of black spot, fungal bane of roses, on these two, even when the leaves of several moss roses beside them are dark with the disease. 'Rosa Mundi' and 'Königin' are simply immune, a fact that can only endear them to gardeners with neither the time nor the inclination to fuss with chemicals and sprayers.

For three weeks to a month, always in early July (here in central Ontario) after peonies are past, the old roses billow with bloom. Most flower once very generously, but some give a small encore in fall. Like their modern descendants, old roses revel in heavy nourishing ground. Clay is to their liking, as long as it is not brick-dense or soggy; but both clay and sandy soils are best enriched with composted manure, peat moss and bone meal to a depth of 18 inches. An annual mulch of compost or manure maintains fertility. Old roses grow naturally into a lax tangle of upright or arching canes; it is a mistake to think they must be tamed to resemble sparse-stemmed hybrid teas. Spring pruning is necessary, but it consists only of a restrained shortening of the willowy canes by about one-third – cut just above an out-facing bud – and the removal of very weak twiggy growth (especially around the base of the bush); any dead wood is, of course, cut away. After three or four seasons, a few crossed or crowded canes can be cut right to ground level to make room for new growth. Ignore the advice that stems with more than five leaflets per leaf have reverted to wild stock, for many old roses do not fit that pattern.

To protect old roses for winter,

Many of the most venerable herb-garden inhabitants are sweetly scented. Lavender, FACING PAGE, *has a long history of use in sachets, cosmetics and potpourris, and old roses,* LEFT, *have perfumes lost in most newer hybrids.*

we simply bend down the pliable branches carefully until they are lying as close as possible to the ground, then keep them in place weighted down with a large flat rock or two. (This eliminates the messy and time-consuming mounding with earth necessary for delicate modern roses.) After that, snow does the rest, but in snow-sparse areas, give old roses a covering of evergreen boughs or straw after freeze-up to be sure mice have found winter quarters elsewhere.

"One should make a decision," said Ippolito Pizzetti in his comprehensive *Flowers: A Guide for Your Garden*, "to have nothing whatever to do with roses that do not have a roselike fragrance." When the old roses are in full flower above their edging of lavender, I inhale deeply and understand why they have always and everywhere been loved.

LAVENDER

Lavandula spp

I cannot think of better garden company for old roses than lavender. Everyone likes this plant—"best of nose-herbs, cleanest and most invigorating of scents," as one herbalist noted—but many gardeners assume that lavender cannot be grown in a harsh climate. True, this herb does not attain the great size and purple profusion in the north that it does in England or in its Mediterranean homeland. But in one Ontario garden, as cold and clay-bound as any, the hardy dwarf 'Munstead' lavender (*Lavandula spica* 'Munstead'), child of Gertrude Jekyll's Munstead Wood garden, edges a bed of roses and lilies and sends up countless scented spikes—the 40 or 50 plants were all raised from a single packet of seeds. An enormous bush of lavender grows nearby in a small-town nursery; the tireless woman tending to the work of plant propagation there calls it "my mother plant," and every year, she takes hundreds of cuttings that she dips in rooting hormone powder and plants firmly in flats

of sand and peat moss.

All this gives clues to growing lavender in the north. Choose a hardy—that is, dwarf—cultivar, such as 'Munstead' or 'Hidcote,' start from seeds or locally grown (hence acclimatized) plants, and trim plants back by half when flowers have faded or just as spikes are colouring if you want them for drying. Compact plants winter well with a loose covering of straw or evergreen boughs— under snow, lavender is safe. Sun and good drainage are other essentials for this modest grey-leaved herb.

The old herbals speak enthusiastically of lavender's use in all sorts of remedial syrups, sweet waters, potions and pills. It was "especially good," said 17th-century gardener and writer John Parkinson, "for all griefes and paines of the head and brain." A lavender-scented oil, pleasant for general massage or kneading sore muscles and joints, is easy to make: dry a quantity of lavender flowers and buds by stripping them from the spikes cut just as the first flowers open, and place them in a single layer on a screen in an airy, shaded place—do not let them become damp with rain or dew as they dry. Fill a clear glass container loosely with dried lavender, top with olive oil, cap the container, and leave it in a sunny place for a few weeks, shaking every few days. Finally, strain the oil into another container through a funnel lined with a square of cotton, pressing and squeezing the flowers to extract more scent. For a more potent oil, repeat the process once or twice more. Lavender oil rubbed into the temples is said to alleviate nervous headaches and depression, and a few drops will scent a bath. I find it refreshing just to bury my nose in a bush of flowering lavender and inhale deeply.

A lavender-scented cosmetic vinegar, used as an astringent wash or a simple homemade perfume, is concocted in exactly the same way as the oil, except that the process must be repeated three times, with a new batch of flowers each time. White wine vinegar takes on a lavender tint, but apple cider vinegar does not.

I like to mark the pages of favourite reference books with spikes of lavender—a neighbour braids them with ribbon—and in winter I am surprised by a sudden sweet scent of summer. Lavender sachets are for linen closets or drawers; and last summer, I filled a small square of cloth with lavender and tucked it between pillowcase and pillow— sweet dreams.

FLORENTINE IRIS

Iris florentina

About a month before roses and lavenders appear, the Florentine iris, one of the faithful "flags" of older gardens, scents a corner of my herb garden. This iris species is so old and out of fashion that it rarely turns up in catalogues. We found a clump lingering by the lilacs in a chaos of quack grass, costmary, meadowsweet and burnished day lilies that often marks the site of a long-abandoned farm garden. Recognize this sun-loving fleur-de-lis by fragrant flowers that are not grey or lavender but a kind of blurred opalescent colour—"dove-toned," says one old book. It blooms in late May and June in this Ontario garden, just in time to make a picture with the last pink and crimson tulips and a clump of bleeding hearts—a crab apple tree could add its rosy glow to the scene.

Old roses and lavender make a classic potpourri. When dried, the roots of this iris are scented of violets; pulverized, they become orrisroot powder, a herbal fixative that enhances and holds the fragrance of other ingredients in potpourris and perfumes. In this age of chemically concocted scents, it is surprising to learn that as recently as the mid-1800s, the cultivation and processing of orrisroot was a major industry in Italy. Thousands of tons of the fragrant powder went to perfume distilleries in Florence

Both pinks, ABOVE, *and lavender,* FACING PAGE, *are traditional edging plants, although lavender is taller and woodier than the softly mounding species of* Dianthus.

(namesake of the flower that is the city's emblem) and throughout Europe. One record shows that in 1876, 10,000 tons of orrisroot were exported to the United States alone.

CARNATIONS, PINKS

Dianthus spp

As the Florentine iris fades, the first of the "gillyflowers," beloved in the Middle Ages, appears. Clove-gillyflower is the old name of the frilled and spice-scented florist's carnation (*Dianthus caryophyllus*) that, like the old roses, once flavoured a variety of syrups, vinegars, candies and conserves for both medicinal and table use. One name for the plant, sops-in-wine, indicates its role in home wine making; an old recipe begins by calling for a "bushel of carnation petals clipped and beat with leaves of lemon balm." "As they are in beauty and sweetness, so are they in virtue and wholesomeness," says the author of *The Country Housewife's Garden*.

Carnations and all members of the *Dianthus* genus revel in light limy soil in full sun. Drought seldom damages them, but standing water can be fatal. Wet heavy ground increases the chances of winterkill. In the north, where carnation survival is dubious at the best of times, buy seeds of the hardiest strains, or look for plants of "sub-zero" carnations. Or simply grow dwarf dianthus, also called pinks, hardy mountain plants whose low mounds of foliage are hidden for weeks in June and July under pink or white flowers as sweet as any carnations. The sandy ground at Larkwhistle grows pinks to perfection. In keeping with a resolve to fill the garden with plants suited to site (and reserve a few specially prepared corners for fussier things), there are pinks tumbling over border edges and filling the June air with a sweet fragrance detectable from yards away. In

older days, pinks were popular in "nosegays and to deck up houses." And, said John Rea in his 1665 *Flora*, "They . . . serve to set the sides of borders . . . mixed with buds of Damask Roses." In today's gardens, they do the same.

Among the best species of dianthus are Cheddar pinks (*Dianthus caesius*), native to Britain, with round, flat flowers in shades of – what else? – pink, and the sand pink (*D. arenarius*), which produces a short, dense turf of green covered in June by fringed flowers like scented snowflakes. Mats of this white pink (listed in some catalogues as 'White Princess') were among the first flowers to go into a perennial bed at Larkwhistle eight years ago – they are still in place and flourishing. *D. × allwoodii* has double or semidouble pink, white or crimson flowers, some zoned like the variegated flowers in Renaissance paintings. A single packet of seed grew enough plants to edge a 60-foot border, and no two were alike.

Gardeners wanting "real" carnations the first season from seed (and willing to start them annually) might grow the fast and fragrant 'Juliette' or 'Scarlet Luminette.' Start seed carefully indoors – at 10 seeds for about $2, care is called for – six weeks before the last frost date, planting a seed or two to a 3-inch peat pot or equivalent. Set the seedlings in a sunny, fertile spot after the last frost.

Perennial dianthus, however, are less expensive and more durable, and their small, dull black seeds sprout as swiftly as lettuce. Sow these in a flat or outdoor seed bed in early May, then transplant from flats, or thin them to 8 to 10 inches apart as they grow. The grey or green mounds are ready to set in place the following spring for summer flowering. Any especially fine specimens can be propagated by taking cuttings in midsummer.

Dianthus are in their element clinging to the south face of a dry-built stone wall or in edging beds, where they like to hug a warm rock and bask in the sun. They also make a sweet ground

cover for a dry bank difficult to mow; just be sure that all perennial weeds have been thoroughly evicted – few garden jobs are as tedious as extracting choking bindweed or, worse, sow thistle. Maintaining these amiable plants in the garden means a close shearing (think brush cut) after flowering is over; a pair of large, sharp scissors works better for me than often dull and awkward garden shears. Plants look a little "strawy" and forlorn at first but soon bristle with new growth. Tight, compact mounds winter better than stragglers. Any bits that do suffer winterkill need spring snipping to prepare pinks for a new season of bloom.

SCENTED GERANIUMS

Pelargonium spp

All of the plants I have so far described are winter-hardy perennials in most gardens, but one group of tender herbs is also grown just for fragrance. They are among those baffling plants that accurately copy the scent of the fruit, flowers, leaves and seeds of unrelated species. There are any number of leafy lemons, for instance – thyme, balm, verbena, even lemon catnip – but the herbal masters of mimicry are the scented geraniums (*Pelargonium* spp), visually unassuming southern African relatives of the bright, summer bedding geraniums. The varied foliage of the scented sorts may be redolent of apples, almonds or anise, cinnamon, nutmeg or *Old Spice*, roses, lavender, strawberry, lime, mint, musk, camphor, coconut, violets, even pines and, of course, lemons. How they manage the trick, and why, will probably remain a mystery.

Scented geraniums are among the best container herbs for high-rise gardens or ground-level porches or patios in summer, provided they can sit indoors in a sunny place for the other seven months of the year. If they were

Now almost unknown, the Florentine iris, RIGHT, was a valuable trade commodity only a century ago. Not only is it fragrant in its own right, but the root, BELOW, which is planted just under the soil surface like that of any other iris, may be powdered and used as a herbal fixative.

hardy, I would not hesitate to fill a garden bed with different types as much for curiosity as for nose treats. As it is, I am content to grow three sorts chosen from the bewildering array that lines benches of Mrs. Richter's scent-filled greenhouse in Goodwood, Ontario. One species, *Pelargonium tomentosa*, is a furry-leaved sprawler strongly reminiscent of peppermint; this variety makes "an unusual hanging basket," says the Tansy Farms catalogue. Another, *P. graveolens*, is a dead ringer for rose, while *P. crispum minor*, the "finger-bowl" geranium, smells of lemons.

Although they are easy to grow, the scented geraniums do need specific attention – pruning and relocating – twice a year. A plant that arrives from a nursery in a 4-inch pot in spring should be set directly into an 8-inch container – unless you are keen on shifting plants into progressively larger flowerpots. A recommended soil mix is three parts garden loam to one part each of coarse sand and peat moss, well flecked with bone meal (bagged potting soil is fine). One grower suggests planting scented geraniums in the ground for summer, then redigging in September, pruning roots and tops before repotting and leaving plants outside for several weeks to "lessen the shock" of a move indoors. This is altogether more work than I am willing to give to these fragrant but otherwise unspectacular novelties – let them live in pots all year. Come June, a scented geranium can grow anywhere outdoors in the sun where, like all container herbs, it will need frequent watering. Alternatively, sink plant, pot and all into a garden bed or oversized window box where rain showers will probably suffice. Feed it several times from June to September with a liquid plant food high in phosphorus – indicated by a high middle number of the fertilizer analysis.

Because scented geraniums wither at the slightest frost, they must be brought into a bright window, sunroom or greenhouse from mid-September until early

POTPOURRI

Gather ye roses – sweet-scented only – while they are half to almost fully open; pull the petals away from the calyx and lay them in a single layer on an elevated window screen. Harvest lavender when, as Jekyll said, "a good portion of the lower flowers in the spike are out" and screen dry in the same fashion; when the spikes are dry, strip off the flowers and buds. Dry leaves of scented geraniums, lemon verbena, lemon basil, rosemary, anise-hyssop, bergamot and/or eau de cologne mint either on a screen or by hanging bundles of several stalks in an airy, shaded place.

If all the potpourri ingredients are collected for drying one fragrant July morning after the dew has dried, everything will be ready for blending three or four days later. In the meantime, prepare or purchase, from a health food store or herbal supply shop, some fixative, a powder or gum of animal or vegetable origin that absorbs and retains the volatile scented oils of a potpourri; most common are the dried and powdered roots of *Iris florentina* – orrisroot powder – or sweet flag or calamus root (*Acorus calamus*), alone or in combination.

To assemble the potpourri, allow one heaping tablespoon of fixative for every quart (approximately 2 double handfuls) of dried petals and leaves. Mix the fixative with an equal amount of ground spices, which may include freshly grated nutmeg, ground whole cloves, bits of crushed cinnamon stick or ground anise or fennel seeds. Moisten the fixative/spice mixture with 2 drops of an essential oil.

Mix and blend the dried ingredients well in a large bowl, add 2 tablespoons of blended fixatives/spices to each quart of herbs, and toss "until all is duly mixed," as Jekyll wrote. Store the potpourri in a covered, opaque container for six weeks to allow scents to mingle and mellow, then divide the finished product among corked glass or other jars.

June, rather longer than just "over winter," as one catalogue states. If a plant has shot up during the summer, then moderate pruning and pinching is in order before it comes indoors. This counts as harvesting, for potpourris or sachets. Indoors, water thoroughly but only when the soil is fairly dry. Do not feed a scented geranium in winter until lengthening February days spur the plant into active growth again. Late spring is the time to prune or pinch away at least half of the winter-spindly growth to prepare the plant for another summer outdoors.

When a plant grows too large for the space I have for it, I root a few cuttings in late summer and compost the original. I always root a few spares for city friends who I think would appreciate a little summery scent in winter, especially after seeing a scrawny specimen of "finger-bowl" geranium in a fancy food-shop window priced at a shocking $17. The very best scented geraniums seem to grow for decades in the large, bright windows of old-fashioned barbershops.

The oils expressed from the leaves of these herbs now flavour chewing gum, candy and ice cream. The home gardener is more apt to use a leaf or two in jam and jelly making, herb teas hot or cold, fresh fruit desserts and baked goods. Dried leaves are also perfect for a potpourri, alone or with any other fragrant flowers, seeds or leaves, a few drops of essential oil and a herbal fixative such as orrisroot.

In her *Home and Garden*, English garden designer Gertrude Jekyll described the making of a potpourri, literally "rotten pot," which included primarily rose petals and sweet geranium leaves, with lesser amounts of lavender, "sweet verbena" (lemon verbena?), bay leaves and rosemary, all mixed with strips of dried orange peel stuck with cloves, orrisroot powder and "various sweet gums and spices." Jekyll made this mixture in such quantity that she graduated from mixing it in a large pan to preparing it in "a hip bath, in later years in a roomy wooden tub; but now the bulk is so considerable, it can only be dealt with on a clear floor space."

The "moist" method Jekyll described involved layering semidry rose petals and herb leaves with salt in separate stoneware crocks, their lids weighted down. The ingredients were left to cure until fall, when "the pressed stuff . . . is so tightly compacted that it has to be loosened by vigorous stabs and forkings with an iron prong," after which the ripened ingredients were tossed together with the powders and gums in a heap that "grows like one of the big anthills in the wood until, at last, all the jars are empty and everyone's hands are either sticky with salt or powdery with sweet spices. Now the head Potpourri maker takes a shovel and turns the heap over . . . until all is duly mixed."

Some fun, but who has the bushels of rose petals and geranium petals required, not to mention the floor space and the extra hands? While Jekyll admits that dry potpourri is "neither so sweet, nor so enduring," it is nevertheless "much the easier and quicker to make." (See the recipe on the facing page.)

Potpourri is one way to use plants that otherwise seem unlikely garden candidates. If they were not fragrant, scented geraniums, for instance, would have disappeared from windowsills and flowerbeds long ago. In truth, they are not very pretty plants—many have dull, coarse-textured leaves, and only a few have fine flowers. Come to think of it, who would grow lavender if it were not so sweet? I suspect that the old roses, too, have survived in gardens for centuries chiefly due to the charm of their fragrance. And rightly so—there is more in a garden than meets the eye. The last word must go to John Gerard, from his *Grete Herball* of 1597: "If odours may work satisfaction, they are so soveraigne in plants and so comfortable that no confection of apothecaries can equal their excellent Vertue."

A sweetly scented mixture whose perfume lasts long after its ingredients have been harvested, a potpourri may contain flowers, such as carnations, ABOVE, and leaves, perhaps those of scented geraniums, BELOW.

CHAPTER TWELVE

WINTER SEASONINGS

Herbs indoors

No matter how long they spend outdoors, almost all herbs eventually end up in the house, either in their entirety or, more likely, as bits and pieces. For instance, every few days, summer through fall, I prepare some variation on the theme of deluxe sauté. This dish is a changing mix of vegetables and herbs that always begins with onions, garlic and ginger stirred in oil; then come vegetables: snow peas, broccoli, Chinese cabbage, red peppers, cauliflower pieces, carrot slivers, sticks of turnip or kohlrabi, Swiss chard stems—the list is as long as the garden is productive. The final additions are minced lovage, basil, summer savory, celery leaf, tarragon, lemon thyme, fennel leaves and a splash of soya sauce. Served over rice or pasta, this simple meal provides a colourful treat for the eyes and a sudden burst of flavour for the taste buds. The sauté supplies the best of nourishment and is a fine reminder of garden providence.

I am also more than happy to sit down to a supper consisting only of some good bread or homemade crackers spread with herbed cream cheese, perhaps smoked fish, a helping of chilled dilled green beans and a large garden salad. By salad, I mean rather more than a few shreds of head lettuce swimming in a syrupy dressing. Besides lettuce—all shades of red and green, all textures from crisp to buttery—and the requisite cucumber and tomatoes, I like to include grated cabbage, carrots, beets (raw or cooked), slivers of small turnips or kohlrabi, radishes, green onions, peas (snow, sugar-snap or shelled), snippets of sorrel and nasturtium leaves, sprigs of watercress or roquette, tiny florets of broccoli or cauliflower (raw or lightly cooked), all tossed with an impromptu blend of minced fresh herbs and dressed simply with olive oil, lemon juice, salt and pepper. A German visitor once showed me how to blend all of the minced herbs thoroughly with the dressing ingredients—sometimes including a dollop of yogurt or a little herbed mustard—in the bottom of a large salad bowl: simply add the well-dried "saladings" (to use a descriptive old word), and then toss at the table just before serving.

INDOOR CONTAINERS

Fresh is how many of us like culinary herbs best, in salads, sautés or whatever, but in winter, fresh herbs are not to be had so easily. It would be nice to simply move everything indoors, but a thriving indoor herb garden depends, first of all, on good sunlight, such as that provided by a large, south-facing window, sunroom or greenhouse—

In winter, homegrown herbs may be available fresh, as is the case with easily potted plants like rosemary, LEFT, or they may be preserved in any of a variety of colourful ways, RIGHT.

anything less limits the range of herbs that will survive and flourish.

A herb that has been dug from the garden in September and squeezed into a small flowerpot cannot be expected to yield a crop worth bothering about, but given sun and root room, some herbs do grow indoors, albeit at a reduced rate in the darkest months. There are three ways of growing culinary herbs indoors, and the method of choice depends on the herb in question. Annual herbs do better if they are reseeded directly into containers in late summer for winter use; perennials and the biennial parsley should be pot-grown all summer long and then shifted indoors in fall; bulbs like the culinary alliums respond to forcing indoors like any tulip after a dormant spell of cold.

The following are some of the most successful herbs for fresh winter use:

¶Basil: rather than digging up seedy and often insect-damaged basil plants in fall, consider a second seeding in mid-August. Sow about a dozen evenly spaced basil seeds around the edge of an 8-to-10-inch pot filled with a nourishing potting mix. As seedlings develop and touch, thin them to five well-spaced plants, and bring them into the sunniest indoor window before the first frost. Young plants will provide a modest harvest well into fall and may come through the winter if light conditions are ideal. A late-summer reseeding is also appropriate for other annuals such as chervil, dill, coriander and summer savory.

¶Parsley: this useful herb has long-ranging roots that cannot be restricted to a small container; it requires a pot at least 12 inches wide. If parsley is to be brought in from the garden in fall, it must be dug up carefully to keep as much of the root intact as possible. Even so, some of the foliage will die, but more will continue to sprout throughout the winter, especially if the plant is fertilized once a month. A better way to pot-grow parsley is to sow it in a container from the start. I use a tough plastic pot, 8 inches across and a full 8 inches deep, filled with garden loam enriched with old manure, perlite and a little bone meal. Sometime in May, I tuck three small plants around the edges of the pot and then sink it up to its rim in the garden; the parsley is fed and watered but not picked. By October I have a lush ball of greenery that comes into the house with no shock at all.

¶For fresh winter use, small divisions of tarragon, any of the thymes, oregano, mints or the hardy savories can be set in large pots in spring and tended outdoors during the summer as one does parsley. All of these herbs respond to moderate pinching and pruning by becoming bushy and compact. A sage seedling (rather than a

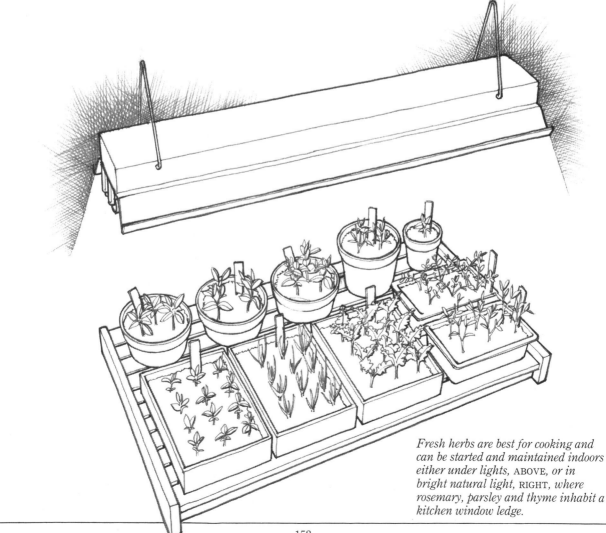

Fresh herbs are best for cooking and can be started and maintained indoors either under lights, ABOVE, *or in bright natural light,* RIGHT, *where rosemary, parsley and thyme inhabit a kitchen window ledge.*

division) can be treated in the same manner. To simulate a brief spell of winter, I leave perennial herbs outdoors until early December. This gives them a bit of rest before they carry on growing indoors, long past the usual season.

¶Chives and other alliums: like the tulip, a related member of the family Liliaceae, alliums grow from bulbs; again like tulips, several edible alliums can be forced for lively greens in the dead of winter. Sometime in September or October, fill several 8-inch-diameter bulb pots (shorter by half than ordinary flowerpots) with potting or garden soil. Into this growing medium, close enough so that they all but rub shoulders, push single shallot bulbs, cloves of garlic, individual sets of multiplier onions, top bulblets of Egyptian onions, even cloves of wild leeks dug from the fall woods. Different sorts planted in a single pot make for a varied

harvest. Set the containers anywhere that is uniformly cold (35 to 40 degrees F), such as the refrigerator, garage or cold cellar; an occasional dip below freezing does no harm. Early in the new year, bring the containers into a warm, bright place in succession – try to duplicate the gentle warmth of April, not torrid July heat – and watch them sprout. Snip the fresh foliage for salads, omelettes, sauces, herbed butters, cottage or cream cheese.

¶Tender herbs: rosemary, several tropical sages, bay, ginger, lemon verbena and all of the scented geraniums must winter indoors if they are to survive. These tender sorts are easier to manage if they are pot-grown year-round and shifted from indoors to out as the seasons change. Rosemary is a particularly amenable house herb, adapting better to lower light than some. Provided the room is not overly hot or dry,

a biweekly misting keeps the foliage fresh. Scented geraniums and tender sages appreciate more sun. The pretty sweet marjoram, a small, tender sprawler that I have dug from the fall garden and planted in a flowerpot slightly larger than its root ball thrived all winter in a coolish, sunny place indoors.

PRESERVING HERBS

Although fresh herbs are best for cooking, they are not always on hand in winter. Besides, for all their flavour and texture, fresh herbs are bulky, need tending and, once harvested, must be used quickly. Drying is a time-honoured and exceedingly easy way to ensure that there will be garden sage for the festive bird, savory and lovage to

flavour cold-weather soups, oregano to top a pizza, tarragon to crumble into a special salad dressing or sauce, and balm, mint and bergamot to blend and brew for tea. One's own carefully dried herbs are superior to overpriced supermarket alternatives, are free of the chemicals that routinely contaminate commercial herbs and are easy to store in relatively little space.

In general, the more pungent herbs such as oregano, lovage and savory turn out the most useful dried product, especially if they have been harvested just before the plants begin to flower, when the aromatic oils that give herbs scent are most concentrated. If possible, avoid a day that may be the start of a very humid or rainy spell. Cut branches as soon as the morning dew is off the plants, and pick off insect-nibbled or yellowing leaves. Then spread the leaves on screens or tie the branches into loose bundles of three or four stems (larger bunches dry unevenly).

We hang herb bundles from a dowel that is suspended over the wood stove – several days of gentle heat will crisp them perfectly. A neighbour suspends herbs from the rafters of her unfinished attic. A garden shed or shady screened porch is also a good drying space, but a greenhouse is not, nor is any place that is at all wet or even humid. The enemies of drying herbs are, of course, moisture and, less obviously, sunlight. Damp air slows drying and encourages mould, while the sun leaches both colour and flavour. Drying herbs outdoors, then, is not the way to obtain the best finished product.

Leafy herbs are dry when they flake into small bits when rubbed. At this point, as decorative as the plants may look hanging by the wood stove, there is no point in leaving them there to gather dust. Spread out a clean sheet of newspaper, strip the leaves from the stalks by hand, and roll the stalks between the palms to get the last crumbs. Funnel the herbs into clean, dry jars or canisters for storage. Glass jars must be kept in a dark cupboard, while opaque containers, whether ceramic, tin or wood, can sit anywhere away from excessive heat.

Screen-drying, an alternative method, is the most efficient way to handle a quantity of lavender spikes and the only way to dry calendula or other flower petals

Herbs dried indoors, LEFT, can be both decorative and useful. Those with edible seeds are best suspended in a paper bag that will collect the seeds as they fall. However, thyme, ABOVE, can be had fresh and free for the picking from a sunny, warm spot.

for flavourings or potpourris. For this, any fine mesh screen will do. I use a 2-by-3-foot aluminum window screen propped on four flowerpots, again set in an airy dry place. A smaller screen can be set on the stove during a baking session to take advantage of the rising heat. Pluck leaves from their stems and flower petals from their calyxes, and spread them in a single layer over the screen, as it is important that air circulate all around. From time to time, jiggle the screen to turn the herbs.

There are other ways to dry herbs too. Oven-drying has its proponents. I have never tried it, but a friend says that even the lowest setting on her oven is too hot for the best drying. No doubt, success depends upon the oven in question; a temperature of about 100 degrees F—usually possible only with the door left open—is best. Zapping herbs to a crisp in a microwave oven just does not seem fitting to me, but David Schmierbach of the Dacha Barinka seed company in British Columbia has found that by wrapping herbs in paper towels or a clean dish cloth and leaving them in the microwave for just a few minutes, depending on the thickness of the stems, acceptably dry herbs can be produced quickly.

Some herbs yield flowers or leaves that are as easily dried as ornamentals, without special sand or silica gel. The flat heads of all species of yarrow dry perfectly if hung upside down, as do the decorative globes of flowering onions, poppy seed heads, the seed heads of Umbelliferae, such as dill and lovage, and the wands of several artemisias. Monarda retains little of its bright colour after drying but is still attractive and pleasantly fragrant, as is dried lavender. Costmary, rue, mints and catnip can also be added to dried bouquets or wreaths to add scent. These stems may be everlasting, but I lose all interest in dried flowers the moment the first spring snowdrop hangs out a bell. Dried arrangements in this house are winter expedients that hit the compost heap come spring.

FREEZING

Since parsley, sage and savory will thaw out after months in the winter garden's deep freeze and still be perfectly edible, it is no surprise that many herbs can be squirreled away in the freezer for winter seasoning. Pick herbs in their prime, shake off any grit or, if necessary, wash them and let them air-dry, then pop them into small plastic bags and put them straight into the freezer. Individual leaves or stems can be pulled out as needed. Alternatively, bunches of dill, chervil, fennel, parsley, summer savory, sweet cicely, tarragon, comfrey, sage and sorrel can be pressed together as tightly as possible into a sort of thick herbal cigar enclosed in aluminum foil or plastic freezer film; the wrapper is peeled back and the frozen herb shaved with a sharp knife, as needed. I use frozen herbs in roughly twice the quantity of dried, mincing them very finely to add to any dish—soups, sauces, dressings, marinades, stuffings, stir-fries and stews—except salads, where only the crunch of a fresh summer leaf seems right to me.

VINEGARS

Herbs may be kept in vinegar, oil or spirits for the winter. The liquids add flavours of their own, of course, but this is part of the attraction of these condiments or beverages. I have flavoured vinegar with a single herb or as many as six; one particularly toothsome salad vinegar combines tarragon, lovage, basil and lemon thyme with a crushed shallot bulb. It is virtually a salad dressing in itself—just add oil at the table. Although I prefer apple cider vinegar for both taste and economy, white wine vinegar assumes the delicate green tints of herbs or turns the colour of lilacs if chive blossoms are steeped in it. Standard white vinegar makes an acceptable, if less sophisticated, herbal condiment.

There is no trick to making herbed vinegars. Select whole, well-coloured leaves, harvesting them in the morning after all dew has dried. Push the leaves into glass bottles, jars or a crock, fill the containers with vinegar, cap or cork them, then leave them to stand in a warm place (in the sun is very good) for a week or two, or until the flavour is to your liking. For best appearance, strain out the herbs while pouring the vinegar into decanters or other bottles—well-washed, clear or pale green wine bottles are fine—and add a sprig or two of the herbs (and perhaps a label) for identification. Store the vinegars in a cool place out of direct sunlight, which may bleach the colour. The best herbs for vinegar include: ¶Basil—the opal variety tints white vinegar deep pink; add green basil for better flavour. Garlic and tarragon combine well with basil.

¶Borage – flowers tint white vinegar lavender-blue.

¶Burnet – a traditional vinegar herb with a light taste of cucumber.

¶Cayenne – 5 to 10 chili peppers make a fiery vinegar.

¶Chives – blossoms give white vinegar a mild taste of onions and turn it a pretty mauvish pink.

¶Dill – leaves and seed heads make a pickle-flavoured vinegar.

¶Lemon thyme, lemon balm and/or lemon verbena – singly or in combination with other herbs – produce a lemon-flavoured vinegar.

¶Lovage – a leaf or two with other herbs adds a taste of celery.

¶Tarragon – the classic vinegar herb, wonderful in salads.

¶Violet flowers – tint white vinegar lavender while adding a hint of sweetness.

¶Any and all mild herbs, including chervil and fennel leaves and seeds, are suitable for vinegars, but such herbs as sage, savory and oregano are not.

ALCOHOL, OIL AND SUGAR

Like vinegar, alcohol extracts the flavours of herbs. Herbal practitioners claim that spirits also assume a plant's medicinal properties; hence the proliferation of herb-based liqueurs and aperitifs said to aid digestion or stimulate the appetite. With a few leaves, seeds and roots, it is possible to concoct a unique, homemade potion with the ambience of a costly imported monastery liqueur. Last fall, I decided to experiment: into a quart bottle of brandy, I dropped 8 or 10 half-inch slices of angelica stem, several small chunks of washed angelica root, two tiny leaves of rue, a palmful of anise seeds, three 1-inch sprigs of hyssop,

several yarrow (the common milfoil) leaves and flower clusters and six small pieces of well-scrubbed valerian root. The brandy and herbs were left to marry in a sunny window for a few weeks. The result, dubbed brandy bitters, was a tongue-tingling drink with a complex herbal bouquet and flavour – the angelica and anise predominated – and a decidedly soothing effect because of the valerian. As the months passed, the brew grew more potent. Friends have been unanimously enthusiastic, and a few have put in orders for some of the next batch.

Herbs in alcohol make what is known as a medicinal tincture. Brandy bitters are meant to be taken as a tonic in small doses. For use as a liqueur, leave out the mildly sedative valerian root and the controversial rue.

Salad oils, too, can be flavoured with herbs, with one caveat – oil does not have the preservative properties of alcohol or vinegar, so herbed oils must be refrigerated lest they spoil. I routinely make three herbal oils: garlic and cayenne peppers season two culinary oils, while calendula petals and lavender flowers turn olive oil into a scented, golden salve for dry skin, massages and, according to one mother, diaper rash. I like to use the fragrant green oil that flows from the first (or virgin) pressing of olives, but it is very expensive and not really necessary – any vegetable oil will do.

September is the month to make oils for winter from fiery cayenne peppers and crisp cloves of freshly dug garlic. Steep 5 to 10 cloves, crushed with the broad side of a stainless steel knife, or as many halved chili peppers, in a litre (or quart) of vegetable oil for a week at room temperature; shake occasionally. Once the oils are seasoned, refrigerate them. There is no need to remove the garlic or peppers. Combined with herbed vinegar and mustard, garlic oil is the basis of a delicious dressing for green salads, cold bean or lentil salads or steamed vegetables that are marinated

Garlic, ABOVE, *is one herb that needs little preparation in order to store well. Ensure that the bulbs are clean and dry, and keep them in bulk or braided in strings. Many other herbs,* RIGHT, *are best dried and stored in labelled, tightly closed jars.*

HERBED MAYONNAISE

¾ cup vegetable oil
1 egg
2 Tbsp. herb vinegar
1 tsp. salt
½ tsp. mustard powder
1 clove garlic, minced

Place ¼ cup of the oil and all other ingredients in a blender or food processor. On low speed, allow all ingredients to mix for about five seconds, then add the remaining oil slowly in a thin stream. Although preparation on a humid day may result in a thinner mayonnaise, this recipe will always yield a tasty salad dressing.

and chilled. Chili oil kindles any of the recently popular Latin American, Chinese or Indonesian dishes to a slow burn; use it with restraint as a seasoning rather than as a sautéing oil.

Oils will preserve the qualities of some herbs, such as basil and tarragon, whose flavours change or almost disappear with drying. Using a blender, food processor or sharp knife and breadboard, chop or blend about 2 cups of herb foliage, and mix with ¼ cup of oil. Refrigerate or freeze in small batches. Chervil, dill, fennel, coriander, garlic, parsley, horseradish, sage and sorrel also preserve well in oil. Pesto is, of course, an elaborate herb-flavoured oil that keeps well over winter if frozen in single-meal portions.

Like vinegar, sugar is a fine preserving agent. Candied herbs, especially flowers, have been used as garnishes for centuries. Dip the flowers of violets, roses, borage or scented geraniums or leaves of mint, lemon balm, lemon verbena or scented geraniums in one egg white lightly beaten with a tablespoon of cold water. Set the dipped plants on a tray, and sprinkle with finely granulated sugar to cover all surfaces. Allow to dry, and store in single layers in airtight tins in a cool place. A neighbour flavours her own maple syrup with the leaves or flowering sprigs of thyme, rosemary, sage, lemon verbena and any of the sweet-leaved geraniums or tender tropical sages, one herb at a time or several in combination. Warmed maple syrup is poured over the bruised herbs in a suitable sterilized container. The jars are capped and left at room temperature for a week to allow the aromatics to permeate the syrup, after which time the herbs are strained out and the syrup is refrigerated, to sweeten tea or glaze crêpes, pancakes, toast or biscuits.

Herbs in the house over winter recall the green and golden days of summer and keep a cook in seasonings until the first fresh blades of chives or the new shoots of lovage, sorrel and tarragon sprout again in spring.

CHAPTER THIRTEEN

ON THE INCREASE

Starting and propagating herbs

"How I got my herbs," wrote Louise Beebe Wilder in *My Garden* in 1916, "would make a chapter in itself." At Larkwhistle, too, and I suspect in every garden, different herbs have arrived by different routes. Visitors bring assorted treasures: among them, a special peony (later identified as *Paeonia tenuifolium*) with fennel-like foliage and satiny crimson single flowers a month before any others; a piece of grey-leaved "mousy thyme" (*Thymus serpyllum lanuginosus*) that, three years later, cascades, in a small way, over a shoulder of stone edging a flowerbed; a wedge of red bergamot that we have split and resplit to create some of July's most colourful pictures. Trips to other gardens usually yield some new plants—backroad wanderings can lead to the unexpected. In an old farm garden, we discovered clumps of Florentine iris, meadowsweet and costmary that had held out against quack grass and twining nightshade for half a century. Seeds and plants arrive in the mail too, and established plants we further increase by dividing, cutting and layering.

HERBS FROM SEED

Those who find themselves shying away from starting plants from seed should take heart. Even experienced gardeners are often intimidated by seeds. "I never quite get over the wonder of my early gardening years," wrote Wilder, "that seeds come up at all." It takes an imaginative leap to convince oneself that locked inside those inert-looking specks rolling out of a seed packet are, indeed, several hundred basil bushes. Faith falters when an envelope labelled "sweet marjoram" seems to contain a few shakes of pepper, despite the catalogue's assurance that "a packet contains 300 seeds." Some herbs produce almost unimaginably tiny seeds, as fine as dust.

Seeds in hand, otherwise sensible gardeners turn into doubters and are moved to pour the entire contents of a packet over a flat or flowerpot in the vague hope that a few seeds will prove lively. The seeds, of course, do what fresh seed cannot help doing, given warmth and water; 86 percent of them sprout "as thick as the hair on a dog's back," as an old neighbour says when his carrots come up on top of each other. The

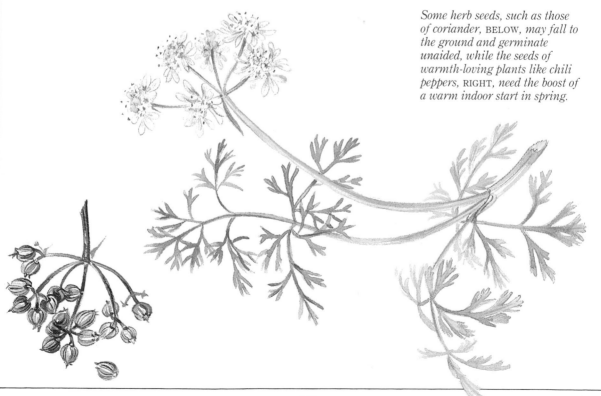

Some herb seeds, such as those of coriander, BELOW, *may fall to the ground and germinate unaided, while the seeds of warmth-loving plants like chili peppers,* RIGHT, *need the boost of a warm indoor start in spring.*

astonished gardener is left wondering what to do with hundreds of basil babies or a flowerpot covered with a little turf of marjoram. Rare is the gardener strong-willed enough to thin 200 to the needed 12. One neighbour routinely calls on my partner to thin assorted seedlings for her because "he's so ruthless." ("Just realistic," says he.) Nor is any plant off to a good start if it is first crammed and then uprooted. One must have faith and give tiny seeds space to grow; once sprouted, they should be thinned before their roots intertwine.

But why grow plants from seeds at all when you can find them in nurseries, where they are already past their tricky infancy? For one thing, seeds are the very least expensive way to come by plants of any species in quantities greater than one or two. And seeds open the door to variety; nurseries may have basil, period, but one catalogue lists seeds of 16 variations on that theme; wouldn't it be nice to try lemon basil or spicy globe basil or holy basil along with the regular kind? Finally, sowing seeds connects a gardener with the whole cycle of plant life. One learns much about plants by seeing them through the early stages, and this gardener always has a special feeling for any plant nurtured from seed to flowering.

At Larkwhistle, early April is the time to begin indoor seeding; the seeds have arrived, and the last spring frost date is about six weeks away. In other areas, judge accordingly – discover the estimated date of the last spring frost, and subtract six or seven weeks. Then, one must decide how many plants are needed. For most gardens or kitchens, three to five of any one species will usually suffice. Ornamental herbs are more effective in groups of three to seven, and a dozen basil plants are enough for even a large family of pesto fans.

Having decided on numbers, a gardener must assemble suitable containers. Seedlings are grown in all sorts of quirky things from egg cartons to half eggshells, provided water can drain through holes punched in the bottom. But to grow as many as 12 plants of any perennial herb, I like 6-to-8-inch-diameter bulb pots. Meant for forcing spring bulbs, these are shallower than regular flowerpots and have less tapered sides, giving seedlings more root room. To start annual herbs – some of the best culinary sorts among them – 2¼-inch-square peat pots snugged into a wooden flat are useful. Just as good are the little sectioned plastic six-packs that fit into plastic trays. One such 10-by-20-inch tray holds 12 six-packs and every spring grows for us a dozen each of sweet basil, bush basil, summer savory, sweet marjoram, sometimes dill or some of the unusual basils – all seeded at once toward the end of April and set out in late May.

The growing medium is the next consideration. Doug Green, a commercial grower of flowers and herbs, recommends a mixture of one-half bagged potting soil and one-half perlite, a medium that has several advantages. The ingredients are readily available in March when the ground may still be winter-crusty. The mix is lightweight, porous to air and water but water-retentive. Such a store-bought blend is also weed-free. Whatever sprouts is what you planted, so you are not left wondering what is basil and what is not. Finally, potting soil and perlite are free of fungus spores and plant diseases – one avoids the messy business of sterilizing soil in the oven or the disheartening prospect of watching seedlings keel over from "damping off," a fungus disease often carried in unsterilized soil.

That said, however, we have grown many herbs, vegetables and flowers from seed for years in ordinary (but quite sandy) garden soil well flecked with bone meal and mixed with one-third its volume in humus – sifted compost, very old cow manure and/or peat moss. Nevertheless, I would recommend Green's mix for the reasons given.

All is ready. Fill the containers with the growing medium, tamp the soil down to firm it lightly, and make it level. Add more soil, filling shallow flats or six-packs right to the top for extra root room. Water the containers well before seeding; moisture and warmth move dormant seeds to sprout. Clear plastic draped over a container retains the moisture in previously well-watered and seeded ground, while warmth can come from soil-heating cables, a radiator, baseboard heater, wood stove or simply the sun. One gardener I know sets seed pots on saucers on an electric heating pad. Such warmth – 80 or 90 degrees F is about right – speeds germination remarkably, but even at lower temperatures, seeds will sprout, although they may take a week or two. In general, seeds of hardy perennials germinate at lower temperatures than seeds of the heat-loving annuals.

Some instructions call for thick sowing initially, followed in several weeks by "pricking out," transplanting seedlings into other containers at their proper spacing. I prefer to leave out this step. Instead, I make shallow saucer-shaped indentations in the soil at 2- or 3-inch intervals in a grid across the flat or around a bulb pot. Into each indentation, I drop three to six seeds, press them gently into the earth and cover very lightly. As the seedlings develop, I thin first to the best two and then to the sturdiest one in each spot.

Only a jaded gardener (if such a species exists) is not a little entranced by the slow dance of seed sprouting that Nathaniel Hawthorne called "one of the most bewitching sights in the world." Once the seeds have sprouted, the greatest necessity is sunlight, at least five hours a day, or an artificial substitute such as fluorescent grow lights suspended several inches over the emerging seedlings. Never allow the soil to become completely dry, and when the young plants have developed their true leaves – that is, the second set of leaves – begin fertilizing them with a dilute fish or seaweed mix or with manure tea, a liquid made by diluting about a quart of manure in a gallon of tepid water.

As the spring weather begins

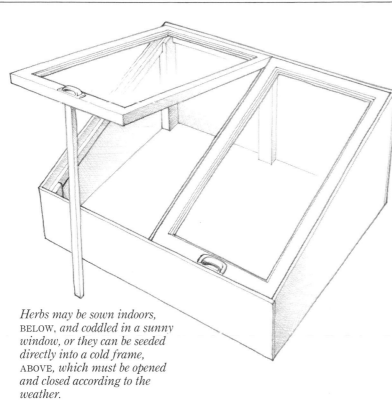

Herbs may be sown indoors,
BELOW, *and coddled in a sunny window, or they can be seeded directly into a cold frame,* ABOVE, *which must be opened and closed according to the weather.*

to warm up, the seedlings should spend fine days in a cold frame and chilly nights indoors; by mid-May at Larkwhistle, they are in the frame full-time except during very cold nights. On sunny days, wedge the frame sash open for ventilation, but as the temperature rises above 65 degrees F, remove the sash altogether to accustom the seedlings to the open air and direct sunlight—a process called hardening off. Gardeners who do not have a cold frame can simply leave the young plants outdoors in a sheltered place for increasingly long durations to harden them off until planting time.

But gardeners without much indoor exposure to sun or plant lights will have better success using a cold frame from the start. Set it in a sheltered, sunny place outdoors. If you want to seed directly into the ground, see that the soil in the frame is light and porous. As with pots, make little indentations in the soil, sow two or three seeds in each hole, and label each short row.

Alternatively, put the seeded flats and pots in the cold frame. Frame sowing should be put off until about a month before the last frost date; germination may take longer than indoors, but you will raise a batch of little toughies. A bevy of old blankets ought to be on hand to cover a frame of tender annuals on cold nights; perennials can take it, however. Indoors or out, once seedlings show several true leaves, thin them to stand a few inches apart. Given plenty of space from the start, seedlings fill out, becoming bushy and sturdy, rather than stretching upwards.

For most herbs, transplanting time comes around the date of the last spring frost. Tender annuals can be kept under cover for another week or two. Some gardeners become terribly timid at transplanting time, digging a small hole, squeezing in the seedling and pushing a few crumbs of soil over the roots. But after raising young plants for a month, it is a shame to lose some because of sloppy transplanting. My advice is: be generous, be firm. Choose an overcast day if there is a chance that roots will be disturbed; full sun is stressful to plants lacking a fully operational root system. Trowel out an oversized transplanting hole; scoop in a double handful of a prepared mix of sifted compost, old manure and/or damp peat moss whitened with bone meal; stir this blend into the hole and the surrounding earth. Firm the earth with a gloved fist. Set in a young plant at the depth it was growing, backfill with earth or that nourishing mix, and firm the soil with fingers or a blunt stick—I use the end of the trowel handle—to ensure close contact between roots and soil. Fill the hole about three-quarters full, then water generously with half-strength liquid fish emulsion, or the equivalent, before topping up with earth. When an area has been planted, fluff and level the soil around the young plants with a hand cultivator.

At transplanting time, annual herbs (and biennials used as annuals) go directly into their summer spots—basil in a wooden half-barrel, neat bush basil along the front of a flowerbed, parsley in the vegetable garden, and so on. Perennials can either go into a permanent bed or border, if the earth is cleared and ready, or else into a vegetable garden bed to size up until the following spring. The latter plan is useful if a gardener is raising a crop of perennials while working at the same time on a new garden area.

Annual or biennial herbs such as anise, ABOVE, *often develop long taproots that make them difficult to transplant successfully. Bulbous perennials such as chives, however, usually survive lifting,* RIGHT, *and being separated into individual plants.*

ROOTSTOCK DIVISION

Some herbs cannot be grown from seed. French tarragon, for one, sets no seed; and seeds of hybrid plants, whether spontaneous "sports" or the deliberate offspring of gene-jugglers, usually do not come true—that is, they do not duplicate the parent plant. Other herbs such as sweet woodruff or Lady's mantle take so long to germinate that one loses patience, especially when a starter plant or two can, by division, be conjured into six or ten after a season. Division of the rootstock—one method of vegetative or asexual propagation—is the obvious way of increasing many perennials, most of which proliferate underground from year to year. Division is done not only to increase a plant one wants in greater numbers but also to rejuvenate a deteriorating older clump by allowing the gardener to start over with lively side shoots. Cutting away great chunks of a mat of mint is a kind of rough-and-ready division meant to check the spread of a fast-moving herb. There are, however, gardeners who want mint and will appreciate some of these excess pieces.

sharp knife, or sever the necessary ties with pruning shears before prying sections apart with a hand fork.

¶Pieces from the outer edges of a clump are always livelier and reestablish themselves more quickly in a new locale. Discard the woody middle.

¶Two to five shoots with roots make a good new division, but rare plants can be split into as many single-crowned bits as they will yield. Just be sure the plant is, in fact, divisible – I once carefully dissected a favourite gentian raised from seed into six new bits and lost the lot. A large clump may yield 20 or 30 divisions, some clearly better than others, as well as a mound of broken roots, severed shoots and other debris; select as many divisions as you need from among the best – resisting the impulse to keep every last shoot – and compost the rest.

¶Replant the divisions firmly in ground enriched with humus. The fine-textured organic matter hastens the formation of new roots.

HERBS FROM CUTTINGS

A cutting is any plant part, whether stem, root, leaf or even a piece of a leaf, that under certain conditions will regenerate into an entirely new plant identical to the parent. African violet fans are used to rooting leaf cuttings, while a gardener who takes a tiller through a swath of horseradish knows that every severed root will give rise to yet more horseradish. But for the herb grower, stem cuttings are an especially practical method of increasing certain herbs, particularly rosemary and the tender tropical sages so good for tea. Stem cuttings are also the quickest method of obtaining new plants of hardy cooking sage, winter savory, lavender and the like. Seed-grown lavender plants, for instance, often vary in habit and flower

Throughout most areas, mid-April to mid-May and mid-September to mid-October are the ideal times to divide most perennials. The exceptions are primroses and irises, which are best split just after they have bloomed – primroses in mid-June, irises in mid-July. Root division proceeds as follows:

¶Pry and lift a clump out of the ground with a spading fork.

¶Shake, brush or wash away some of the earth from a clump to expose more shoots and roots, the better to see where the plant splits naturally into separate crowns. Plants that tend to untangle themselves are easily pried and pulled apart by hand into separate pieces. To split more tightly woven species, slice down between the shoots and right through the roots with a

colour, but it is possible to perpetuate the best of the lot with cuttings:

¶Young spring stems – technically known as softwood cuttings – are the easiest to root. Select side shoots about 3 inches long and, being careful not to crush their stems, detach them from the main stem. Alternatively, snip the top 3 inches from any vigorously growing branch, cutting just below a leaf. Morning is the recommended time, since a plant is then at its maximum turgidity;

that is, it is as full of water as it will ever be.

¶Pick the leaves from the bottom one-third of the cutting, and dip the stem end in a rooting hormone powder formulated for softwood cuttings.

¶Have ready a clean 4-inch-diameter flowerpot – one for each three to five cuttings of the same species – filled with a mix of one-half sand and one-half damp peat moss.

¶Poke a small hole in the rooting medium with a pencil point, and insert the leafless third of the cut

stem into the medium. Firm gently around each cutting, and water.

¶Slip a roomy plastic bag over each pot, and slit a few air holes in the bag with scissors. Be sure that the bag does not touch the cuttings.

¶Keep pots of cuttings in a moderately warm place – 70 to 75 degrees F – out of direct sun but in the light.

¶Softwood cuttings usually take 10 to 20 days to put out roots, at which time tender herbs are potted individually, while hardy

sorts are set outdoors in a shaded cold frame. In either case, water thoroughly.

The advantages of cuttings are several. In as little as three weeks, a small plant will attain a size that could have taken three months if grown from seed – if it could be grown from seed at all. Also, cuttings allow one to propagate shrubby herbs that cannot be divided and to obtain fresh starts of certain tender herbs such as scented geraniums that have grown over-large for the available indoor space.

LAYERING HERBS

In the process of layering, shoots root while they are still attached to the parent plant. Examine a tuft of lemon thyme or winter savory or a large clump of cooking sage or wormwood, and chances are you will find that the lax outer branches lying on the ground have put down a

few roots where their stems touch the earth. This natural tendency to layer can be encouraged.

¶Select an outer branch that already tends to bend toward the ground; press it against the soil, and then pick the leaves from the section of stem touching the ground. Scrape the underside of this section with a knife.

¶Loosen the ground around the plant, and press the stem into the earth. If the garden soil is heavy clay, lay down an area of sandy soil under the contact spot, and push the stem into this. Press earth firmly over the stem to a depth of at least an inch.

¶Layered branches have a tendency to spring back up. Peg them down with a small stone, forked stick, bent bit of wire or sturdy hairpin.

Because layers do not have the benefit of controlled heat and humidity, as do cuttings, they often take as long as two months to root. But since they are supplied with nutrients as long as they are attached to the mother plant, there is no rush for them to establish an independent root system. Early summer layers can stay in place until September, when they are snipped from the parent plant and transplanted to a life of their own.

By taking a hand in the various processes of plant procreation, a gardener ensures a steady supply of plants at little or no cost. Perennials are renewed occasionally by division; annuals and biennials, like dill or parsley, become full-time garden residents if one gathers seed for another season. Bare corners of the garden are quickly filled with a few slips of something from across the path; one clump of thyme becomes five or six and intriguing herbs, rarely found in nurseries, can be raised from seed. Any gardener who grows a flat of lemon basil or splits a favourite clump of red bergamot always has extras to hand along to appreciative friends. In the endless, lively circle of plant growth and exchange, each of us has a tale to tell of "how I got my herbs."

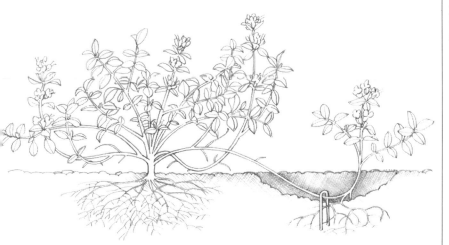

Propagation without seeds can be accomplished by division, as with a clump of catnip, LEFT; by layering, as with thyme, ABOVE; and by cuttings, as with pineapple sage, BELOW.

SOURCES

The following mail-order source list includes the price of the 1986 catalogue, which may change in subsequent years. A self-addressed stamped envelope or, if appropriate, an International Postal Reply coupon (available at any post office) sent to the company will encourage it to advise the customer about the current catalogue price.

HERB SEEDS AND PLANTS—CANADA

U.S. customers will have no difficulty in importing seeds from Canadian sources, but other plant materials must be shipped with a Phyto-Sanitary Certificate supplied to the nursery by Agriculture Canada.

Butchart Gardens
Box 4010, Station A
Victoria, British Columbia
V8X 3X4
Seeds for old-fashioned flowers.
Catalogue $1, refundable.

C.A. Cruickshank Ltd.
1015 Mt. Pleasant Road
Toronto, Ontario
M4P 2M1
Flower bulbs, seeds and plants.
Catalogue $2, refundable.

Dacha Barinka
46232 Strathcona Road
Chilliwack, British Columbia
V2P 3T2
Seeds for garlic, herbs, oddities.

Send a self-addressed stamped envelope for price list.

Dominion Seed House
Georgetown, Ontario
L7G 4A2
Vegetable and flower seeds; some herbs, to Canada only.
Catalogue free.

Ferncliff Gardens
SS 1
Mission, British Columbia
V2V 5V6
Irises, peonies. Catalogue free.

Fish Lake Garlic Man
RR 2
Demorestville, Ontario
K0K 1W0
Organically grown garlic seeds.
$2 plus self-addressed stamped envelope.

Folklore Herbs
2388 West 4th Street
Vancouver, British Columbia
V6K 1P1
Herbal products, books.
Catalogue free to Canada, $1 (Can.) to U.S.

Gardenimport, Inc.
Box 760
Thornhill, Ontario
L3T 4A5
Bulbs, seeds of flowers, vegetables, herbs. Catalogue $2 for two years.

Gilbert's Peony Gardens
Elora, Ontario
N0B 1S0
Peony plants. Catalogue $1.

The Herb Farm
RR 4
Norton, New Brunswick
E0G 2N0
Herb plants and seeds. Price list $1, refundable.

The Herbal Touch
30 Dover Street
Otterville, Ontario
N0J 1R0
Herb workshops. Send self-addressed stamped envelope for information.

Les Herbes Fines De Saint-Antoine
480 Chemin l'Acadie
Saint-Antoine-sur-Richelieu,

Quebec
J0L 1R0
Herb plants and seeds.
Catalogue $1, refundable.

Hopestead Gardens
6605 Hopedale Road
RR 4
Sardis, British Columbia
V0X 1Y0
Perennial plants. Price list free.

Hortico
RR 1
Waterdown, Ontario
L0R 2H0
Roses. Catalogue free.

Carl Pallek & Son
Box 137
Virgil, Ontario
L0S 1T0
Roses to Canada only.
Catalogue free.

Pickering Nurseries Inc.
670 Kingston Road
Pickering, Ontario
L1V 1A6
Roses. Catalogue free.

Richters
Box 26
Goodwood, Ontario
L0C 1A0
Herb seeds and plants, unusual plants. Catalogue $2.

Sears-McConnell Nurseries
Port Burwell, Ontario
N0J 1T0
Perennial flowers, food plants.
Catalogue free.

Stirling Perennials
RR 1
Morpeth, Ontario
N0P 1X0
Perennial, ground-cover plants.
Catalogue $1, refundable.

Stokes Seeds Ltd.
1436 Stokes Building
St. Catharines, Ontario
L2R 6R6
Seeds of herbs, vegetables, flowers. Catalogue free.

Tansy Farms
RR 1—5888 Else Road
Agassiz, British Columbia
V0M 1A0
Herb plants, scented geraniums.
Catalogue $1.50.

West Kootenay Herb Nursery
RR 2
Bedford Road
Nelson, British Columbia
V1L 5P5
Herb plants catalogue free.

HERB SEEDS AND PLANTS—INTERNATIONAL

John Chambers
15 Westleigh Road
Barton Seagrave
Kettering, Northants NN15 5AJ
England
Unusual herb seeds. Catalogue two International Postal Reply coupons.

Chiltern Seeds
Bortree Stile, Ulverston
Cumbria LA12 7PB, England
Seeds of unusual herbs, flowers, shrubs, trees. Catalogue $2 (U.S.).

Culpeper, Ltd.
Hadstock Road
Linton, Cambridge CBJ 6NJ
England
Herb seeds and products. Price list free.

HERB SEEDS AND PLANTS—U.S.

Unless indicated, the following companies will accept Canadian orders. When ordering plant materials—that is, anything other than seeds, which can be imported without difficulty—from the United States, request an "Application Form for Permission to Import" from the Permit Office, Plant Health Division, Agriculture Canada, Ottawa, Ontario K1A 0C6. Obtain one application form for each foreign company. When paying for imported goods, use a money order in the appropriate currency. These can be purchased at any bank or post office.

Abundant Life Seed Foundation
Box 772
Port Townsend, Washington 98368
Nonprofit organization specializing in seeds of the Pacific Northwest; also herbs, flowers, vegetables, trees. Annual membership $5 (U.S.) to Canada; $4 to U.S.

Blackthorne Gardens
48 Quincy Street
Holbrook, Massachusetts 02343-1989
Plants of perennial flowers, including alliums. Catalogue $2 (U.S.), refundable.

Borchelt Herb Gardens
474 Carriage Shop Road
East Falmouth, Massachusetts 02536
Herb seeds. For price list, send a self-addressed stamped envelope from the U.S. or an International Postal Reply coupon from Canada.

W. Atlee Burpee Co.
300 Park Avenue
Warminster, Pennsylvania 18974
Seeds of vegetables, flowers, herbs to U.S. only. Catalgue free to U.S.

Casa Yerba
Star Route 2, Box 21
Days Creek, Oregon 97429
Seeds and plants of rare and common herbs. Catalogue $1.50 (U.S.) to Canada; $1 to U.S.

Catnip Acres Farm
Christian Street
Oxford, Connecticut 06483
Herb seeds, plants, scented geraniums. Seeds only to Canada. Catalogue $1 (U.S.), refundable.

Companion Plants
Route 6
Box 88
Athens, Ohio 45701
Common and rare herb plants and seeds; scented geraniums. Catalogue $1.50 (U.S.), refundable.

The Cook's Garden
Box 65050
Londonderry, Vermont 05148
Exotic salad greens. Catalogue $1 (U.S.), refundable.

Cook's Geranium Nursery
712 North Grand
Lyons, Kansas 67554
Geranium plants, including scented species. Catalogue $1 (U.S.), refundable.

The Country Garden
Route 2H, Box 445A
Crivitz, Wisconsin 54114
Cut-flower seeds, bulbs and plants to U.S only. Catalogue $2.

Cricket Hill Farm, Ltd.
Glen Street
Rowley, Massachusetts 01969
Common and uncommon herb seeds and plants, herbal gifts. Plants to U.S. only. Catalogue $1 (U.S.).

Far North Gardens
16785 Harrison
Livonia, Michigan 48154
Seeds and plants of herbs, flowers, primroses. Catalogue $2 (U.S).

Fox Hill Farm
440A W. Michigan Avenue
Box 7
Parma, Michigan 49269
Herbs, especially basil; herbal products, books. Catalogue $1 (U.S.).

The Fragrant Path
Box 328
Fort Calhoun, Nebraska 68023
Seeds for fragrant, rare and old-fashioned plants. Catalogue $1 (U.S.).

Gladside Gardens
61 Main Street
Northfield, Massachusetts 01360
Flowers, rare bulbs. Catalogue $1 (U.S.).

Halcyon Gardens Herbs
Box 124
Gibsonia, Pennsylvania 15044
Herb seeds. Catalogue $1 (U.S.), refundable.

Heirloom Gardens
Box 138
Guerneville, California 95446
Seeds of herbs, unusual vegetables. Catalogue $2 (U.S.).

Herb Gathering, Inc.
5742 Kenwood Avenue
Kansas City, Missouri 64110
Seeds of herbs, gourmet
vegetables. Catalogue $1.25
(U.S.) to Canada; $1 to U.S.

Herbiforous
Route 1
Elkhart Lake, Wisconsin 53020
Herb seeds, plants and products.
Catalogue $1 (U.S.) or $1.30
(Canadian).

The Herb Market
Jail Street
Washington, Kentucky 41096
Herb seeds, plants and products.
Catalogue $3 (U.S.).

Heritage Rose Garden
16831 Mitchell Creek Road
Fort Bragg, California 95437
Roses. Catalogue $1 (U.S.).

High Country Rosarium
1717 Downing at Park Avenue
Denver, Colorado 80218
Roses to U.S. only.
Catalogue $1.

Horticultural Enterprises
Box 810082
Dallas, Texas 75381-0082
Mexican seeds, including chili
peppers, cilantro. Price list free.

J.L. Hudson, Seedsman
A World Seed Service
Box 1058
Redwood City, California 94064
Seeds of herbs, flowers, unusual
plants. Catalogue $1 (U.S.).

Izard Ozark Native Seeds
Box 454
Mountain View, Arkansas 72560
Herbs of Ozark bioregion. Price
list free.

Jackson & Perkins Co.
Box 1028
Medford, Oregon 97501
Roses, ornamentals. Catalogue
$2 (U.S.).

Johnny's Selected Seeds
Foss Hill Road
Albion, Maine 04910
Seeds of vegetables, herbs.
Catalogue free.

Larner Seeds
Box 60143
Palo Alto, California 94306

Native seeds of California and
New England. Catalogue 50
cents (U.S.).

Logee's Greenhouses
55 North Street
Danielson, Connecticut 06239
Herbs, geraniums, rare
ornamentals. Catalogue $3
(U.S.), refundable.

Lost Prairie Herb Farm
805 Kienas Road
Kalispell, Montana 59901
Herbs, ground-cover plants to
U.S. only. Catalogue $1.

**Lowe's Own Root Rose
Nursery**
6 Sheffield Road
Nashua, New Hampshire 03062
Ungrafted roses shipped in fall
'only. Catalogue $1 (U.S.).

**Le Marché Seeds
International**
Box 566 Dixon, California 95620
Gourmet Seeds. Catalogue $2.50
(U.S.) to Canada; $2 to U.S.

McLaughlin's Seeds
Buttercup's Acre
Box 550
Mead, Washington 99021-0550
Three catalogues, one for herbs.
Catalogue $1 (U.S.).

Meadowbrook Herb Garden
Route 138
Wyoming, Rhode Island 02898
Herb plants and seeds to the
U.S.; seeds only to Canada.
Catalogue $1 (U.S.).

Merry Gardens
Box 595
Camden, Maine 04843
Herbs, scented geraniums.
Catalogue and newsletters $2
(U.S.).

Milaeger's Gardens
4838 Douglas Avenue
Racine, Wisconsin 53402
Herb and perennial plants to
U.S. only. Catalogue $1.

Nichol's Garden Nursery
1190 North Pacific Highway
Albany, Oregon 97321
Herb seeds and plants.
Catalogue free.

George W. Park Seed Co.
Box 31

Greenwood, South Carolina
29647
Herb, vegetable, flower seeds.
Catalogue free.

The Pepper Gal
10536 119th Avenue North
Largo, Florida 33543
Chili pepper seeds. Price list
free.

Prairie Nursery
Box 365-A
Westfield, Wisconsin 53964
Seeds of wildflowers, native
perennials. Catalogue $1 (U.S.),
refundable.

Raleigh Gardens
24236 Evergreen Road
Philomath, Oregon 97370
Garlic and shallots, several
kinds.

Rasland Farm
Goodwin, North Carolina 28344
Herb plants, scented geraniums,
herbal products. Herbal products
only to Canada. Catalogue $1.50
(U.S.).

Redwood City Seed Co.
Box 361
Redwood City, California 94064
Seeds of herbs, flowers,
vegetables. Catalogue $1 (U.S.).

Robert's Herb Farm
Route 1, Box 259
Greenfield, Indiana 46140
Herb plants and herbal products
to U.S. only. Catalogue $1.

**Roses of Yesterday and
Today**
Brown's Valley Road
Watsonville, California 95076
Roses. Catalogue $2 (U.S.).

Sandy Mush Herb Nursery
Route 2, Surrett Cover Road
Leicester, North Carolina 28748
Herb plants and seeds.
Catalogue $2 (U.S.), refundable.

Shady Hill Gardens
765 Walnut Street
Batavia, Illinois 60510
Geranium plants and seeds.
Seeds only to Canada. Catalogue
$1 (U.S.), refundable.

Stokes Seeds Ltd.
1436 Stokes Building
Buffalo, New York 14240

Seeds of vegetables, flowers, herbs. Catalogue free.

Sunnybrook Farms Nursery
9448 Mayfield Road
Box 6
Chesterland, Ohio 44026
Perennials, herbs, houseplants. Also holds workshops. Catalogue $1 (U.S.), refundable.

Taylor's Herb Gardens, Inc.
1535 Lone Oak Road
Vista, California 92083
Herb plants and seeds to U.S. only. Catalogue $1.

Thompson & Morgan, Inc.
Box 1308
Jackson, New Jersey 08527
Seeds of herbs, flowers, vegetables, unusual plants. Catalogue free.

MISCELLANEOUS

American Herb Association
Box 353
Rescue, California 95672
Both professional and regular memberships, quarterly newsletter, book service.

The Botanic Medicine Society
Box 103
Norval, Ontario
L0P 1K0
Newly formed. Write for information.

The Bu$iness of Herbs
Box 559
Madison, Virginia 22727
Newsletter for herb businesses. One year (six issues) $18 to the U.S.; $20 (U.S.) to Canada.

Dominion Herbal College
7527 Kingsway
Burnaby, British Columbia
V3N 3C1
Correspondence courses in herbalogy since 1926. Brochure and application forms free.

The Herb Gardener's Resource Guide
Northwind Farm
Route 2, Box 246
Shevlin, Minnesota 56676
Guide to sources of herb seeds,

products, botanical gardens, courses. $8.95 (U.S.) to Canada; $7.95 to U.S.

Herb News
Box 12602
Austin, Texas 78711
Quarterly magazine for herb businesses and individuals, published in conjunction with the Herb Research Foundation and the American Herbal Products Association. Contact for subscription information.

The Herb Quarterly
Box 275
Newfane, Vermont 05345
Elegant magazine for herb fanciers. Contact for subscription information.

Herb Research Foundation
Box 2602
Longmont, Colorado 80501
Promotes research into the medicinal uses of herbs. Membership $25 annually, includes the quarterly magazine *Herbalgram*.

The Herb Society of America, Inc.
2 Independence Court
Concord, Massachusetts 01742
Membership by invitation only; provides scholarships, develops herb gardens. Contact for information.

The Ontario Herbalists Association
Box 253 Station J
Toronto, Ontario
M4T 4Y1
Annual membership $20; includes the quarterly *Ontario Herbalists Association Newsletter*.

The School of Herbal Medicine
Box 2446
San Rafael, California 94912
One-year correspondence course offered by the U.S. branch of the National Institute of Medical Herbalists of Great Britain. Contact for information.

INDEX